BUILD THE PERFECT
BUG OUT BAG

Creek Stewart

BUILD THE PERFECT
BUG OUT BAG
YOUR 72-HOUR DISASTER SURVIVAL KIT

Creek Stewart

BETTERWAY HOME
CINCINNATI, OHIO
WWW.BETTERWAYBOOKS.COM

CONTENTS

INTRODUCTION

YOU CAN HEAR THE SIRENS in the distance. Your electricity is out, and your home phone has no dial tone. When you try to use your cell phone, you get the same message over and over: "All circuits are busy." You know a disaster is quickly approaching. And you know that waiting this one out is not an option. In the breathtaking stillness, you can hear the clock on the wall. Tick-tock, tick-tock. The eleventh hour is here. You have to leave your home immediately or you and your family will die.

Like it or not, disasters happen. And they do not discriminate. It does not matter what you look like, where you live, what you drive, or how much money you have—no one is exempt from the threat of disaster. Disasters strike suddenly and give little, if any, warning. There are few moments in one's life when every second and every action count. It is in these critical moments that nothing else matters except life itself. In the few moments you have just before a disaster strikes, your preparedness level will define the rest of your life.

Disaster preparedness is no longer a mentality reserved for the subculture survivalist. This awareness is quickly becoming a mainstream phenomenon as people from all walks of life begin to embrace the reality of the following statement: It's not *if* a disaster will strike, but *when*.

Highly visible media coverage of countless natural and man-made disasters in recent years has heightened the senses of the inner survivalist in all of us. History repeatedly confirms that city, state, and federal emergency systems, however well intended, are not able to adequately cope with large-scale disasters. Normal public safety and operating procedures crumble under the overwhelming chaos that follows a disaster. This awareness has led many very normal people on a journey of self-sufficiency and preparedness. They, like yourself, are realizing the need to proactively prepare in advance for sudden and unexpected disasters.

Oftentimes, a disaster will threaten the safety of you and your family in your own home. Suddenly, staying at home and "hunkering down" is no longer the safest decision. To stay alive, the best decision may be to leave. The buzz term for this decision is *bugging out*.

BUGGING OUT: DEFINED

The term *bugging out* refers to the decision to abandon your home due to an unexpected emergency situation —whether a natural disaster or one caused by man. The thought of having to evacuate your home due to a sudden and imminent threat is not at all unrealistic. The reality is that sudden and uncontrollable events of

7

nature and man do happen. Natural disasters such as hurricanes, storms, earthquakes, floods, wildfires, heat waves, and volcanic explosions can strike fast and hard—wreaking havoc on homes, vehicles, roads, medical facilities, and resource supply chains, such as food, water, fuel, and electricity. Time and time again, we have seen disasters strike the United States and abroad forcing tens of thousands of people from their homes with little warning. Unprepared and with no emergency plan, many of these people are left completely dependent on scavenging and hand-outs while living in make-shift shelters—fending for themselves in a time of complete chaos and disorder. Given the world's unstable and unpredictable political and economic climates, we would be foolish to completely rule out the chance of a terrorist or military attack from forces domestic or foreign that could possibly force us to evacuate our own homes. An act of war is not the only threat from man. Dams burst, power plants go down, pipelines explode, oil spills occur, and other man-made structures and facilities can fail, resulting in disaster. Outbreaks of sickness and disease could also warrant an evacuation.

We cannot control when, where, or how disasters strike. But we can control how prepared we are to deal with a disaster. There is a fine line between order and chaos and sometimes that line can be measured in seconds. When every second counts, having a plan and the tools to see that plan through are crucial to survival. A 72-Hour Emergency Kit packed with survival essentials is a priceless resource in any Bug Out scenario. This kit, called a Bug Out Bag, is an important resource in your overall Bug Out Plan and may very well be your key to survival one day.

BUG OUT BAG: DEFINED

A Bug Out Bag (BOB) is a self-contained kit designed to get you through at least 72 hours of independent survival while on the journey to your destination, often called a Bug Out Location (BOL). This kit is also referred to as a 72-Hour Bag, a Get Out Of Dodge Bag (GOOD Bag), an EVAC Bag, a GO Bag and a Battle Box. Regardless of the name, a BOB is a well-thought-out 72-hour survival kit tailored specifically to meet the needs of you and your family. Bug Out Bags are prepared in advance of a disaster and are typically stored in your home ready for deployment at a moment's notice.

YOUR BUG OUT BAG GUIDEBOOK

Many fine books have been written about Bugging Out. This is not a book

The Bug Out Bag, a 72-Hour Disaster Survival Kit

about Bugging Out. This book is your complete guide from start to finish and everything in between about how to build your own Bug Out Bag capable of assisting you and your family through 72 hours of independent survival in the event that you choose to Bug Out. In this book, I cover much more than just building a BOB for a fit, single young adult. You'll find specific instructions for preparing BOBs for families, children, the elderly, the physically disabled, and even pets.

The specific category checklists included make it simple and easy to ensure all of your bases are covered. The function and importance of each pack item is thoroughly explained and I also provide instructions on how to use most items.

The book takes into account all of the most common disasters and makes special notations of things to consider or add to your pack should you live in an area prone to specific disasters. I will guide you through the "build" every step of the way, helping you create a complete Bug Out Bag tailored specifically to your comfort level and environment. You will not find a more thorough and well-thought-out guide anywhere about how to build your own Bug Out Bag.

You've heard the phrase "If you build it, they will come." When discussing Bug Out Bags and disasters, my survivalist motto is "Build it, they are coming."

Let's get started.

1 MEET BOB— THE BUG OUT BAG

DISASTERS CAN DELIVER some of the harshest survival scenarios on the planet. They are sudden and chaotic. They make otherwise very normal tasks incredibly complicated and dangerous. Disasters are life–and-death situations.

Assembling a Bug Out Bag (BOB) capable of contending with these unpredictable and unforgiving survival environments can be an overwhelming task—especially if you have no formal survival or preparedness training. Before you start to build your own kit, let me outline some important basic concepts you need to understand about a BOB to give you a clear understanding of exactly what to expect in this process and dispel any misguided expectations you might already have. In my training courses at Willow Haven Outdoor, I call this part "Getting to know BOB the Bug Out Bag."

GETTING TO KNOW BOB
BOB is simple, yet deep.

The purpose of a Bug Out Bag is very simple—to provide you with basic survival needs. In reality, however, this is easier said than done. Just building or buying a BOB will not save your life. You have to understand how to use the contents of your BOB to maximize its true life-saving potential. Disasters do not create ideal survival environments. If survival were easy and fun, it would be called camping. Providing yourself with basic survival needs in perfect conditions can be challenging. Add a horrific, chaotic disaster to the mix and there is no doubt you will need to intimately understand how to use your BOB as a tool and resource. This comes *only* from experience and practice. The bottom line about your relationship with BOB: You will get out of it what you put into it.

Often, the Bug Out Bag is over simplified by people I call "sofa survivalists." These are people who dole out survival advice and instruction but have little to no hands-on field experience. The closest they come to fire by friction is the heat generated in the wheel of their computer mouse. *Beware* of over simplified Bug Out survival advice.

BOB and Its Many Facets

BOB is an investment.

Like any worthwhile relationship, BOB will require a certain degree of commitment in order for things to work out. He is not a one-night stand. Plan on spending some time building your Bug Out Bag. It will take time to source and assemble the contents of your kit. Learning how to use the survival tools will also require an investment of time and energy. BOB wants and needs quality time.

Also, don't plan on taking BOB to a cheap burger joint and expect him to save your life for the unforgettable experience.

Building a proper BOB that you can depend on in an emergency is going to cost some money. Many of the individual components are economical, but combined, it all adds up. Plan to spend a few hundred bucks. This, of course, will vary depending on how many items you already have on hand. I don't suggest cutting corners when it comes to procuring supplies that you will use to save the lives of you and your family. In my experience you get what you pay for. Your BOB is an investment in your future.

Your relationship with BOB changes as you do.

All long-term relationships evolve as your life circumstances change, and this evolution can take effort. Your relationship with BOB needs to evolve as well. Expect to update your Bug Out Bag when you update your life. For example, if you are now single and get married, then you will need to update your 72-hour kit accordingly or add a second kit. Or, if you have a new addition to the family, such as a child, there will be new considerations for your Bug Out Bag.

BOB Requires Some Time

BOB Costs Some Money

If your job relocates you from Northern Maine to Southern California, the clothing in your BOB will change. You get the point.

Your Bug Out Bag will also require a little maintenance. I recommend a biannual review, which I will discuss later.

BOB is an insurance policy.

I carry the following insurance policies:

- Car insurance
- Home insurance
- Life insurance
- Health insurance
- SHTF insurance

The last policy listed, my S#!t Hits The Fan Policy, is my trusted buddy BOB. It's easy *not* to prepare for the "what-ifs" in life. You aren't required to buy a SHTF Policy, and your employer probably isn't going to help with your premium. Regardless, you should have a Bug Out Bag in place. Life insurance is paid *when you die*. Look at BOB as a "don't die" policy for you and your family. What could be more important than this insurance? You really can't put a price on peace of mind.

BOB can be a fun and rewarding friend.

Spending time with BOB can be fun and rewarding for the whole family.

Building a Bug Out Bag is so much more than just filling a backpack with supplies and tossing it on a shelf. Knowing how to use the tools and kits in your Bug Out Bag effectively takes practice. "Practicing" is the best part of the build.

BOB presents so many learning opportunities for adults and children. Learning how to use tools to provide yourself and others with basic survival needs is challenging and encourages creativity, problem solving, teamwork, patience, self-sufficiency, and determination. Everyone can benefit from the lifelong character-building lessons that can come from assembling your own Bug Out Bag. Think of the sense of accomplishment and peace of mind you'll find as you learn new skills.

FOUR KEY ATTRIBUTES OF A BUG OUT BAG

Now that you have a broader mental scope of the project, let's look at the four key physical attributes to a well-contrived Bug Out Bag.

A 72-Hour Kit

Your BOB should be designed to sustain you and your family for 72 hours. You should be able to reach a safe destination with access to supplies within a 72-hour time frame. In the right hands, a BOB as described

Bugging Out on Foot

Urban Camouflaged BOB

in this book will provide the necessary resources to survive much longer than 72 hours.

Manageable and Comfortable

In an ideal situation, if Bugging Out is your only option, you will want the luxury of traveling by vehicle. We have to assume, though, that this is not a guarantee. Some events that might render vehicle travel impossible are:

- no fuel or access to fuel
- road closures or roads destroyed
- traffic jams
- vehicle break-down

Consequently, you (and your family) need to be prepared to travel by foot. For this reason, your BOB needs to be manageable and comfortable. It needs to be sized appropriately for your build. Its total weight needs to fall within a range that allows you

to carry it for extended periods of time—hours and even days. The style, size, and weight of a BOB will vary from person to person depending on personal preferences, build, and fitness level.

Ready, Set, GO!

Your BOB needs to be prepared in advance and stored for swift deployment at a moment's notice. Disasters are merciless, and your ability to react and evacuate in an instant is critical. With that said, do not advertise your BOB to visitors in your home. As I said, your BOB is an investment. You likely keep your valuables in a safe in your home to protect them from burglars. Take the same precautions to protect your BOB from theft.

A BOB should be stored in a place that is out-of-sight, but not out-of-mind. It needs to be hidden but easily accessible. I camouflage my BOB on a shelf leading out my back door. To the average person it looks like a pile of towels and some cleaning supplies. In reality, it is one of the most critical resources in my entire home. I call this urban camouflage.

Custom and Tailored

Every Bug Out Bag should be different because they are designed for and by unique individuals. Your Bug Out Bag should be a reflection of your particular tastes, needs, and requirements. Do *not* buy a premade BOB. Premade kits are designed to provide the most "stuff" for the least "cost" to make the highest profit margin for the company selling it. This is not an equation on which I'd like to stake my life. Premade kits are also generic and lack many elements that should be tailored to you and your environment. A premade kit is better than no kit at all, but you are truly robbing yourself of the knowledge gained from designing and building your own custom kit.

SUMMARY

Building a Bug Out Bag is not a "matter-of-fact" process. It is subjective and allows for a certain amount of creative freedom and personal ex-

pression. There are no definitively right or wrong answers. This book defines how I build my kit. You may have different solutions to solve similar problems. And there are other tools and gear that I have not listed that you may prefer to use. This is completely acceptable and expected. As my mom always says, "There's more than one way to skin a cat." Every time I teach a Bug Out Workshop, I learn from my students, and I love that. I will present the facts about basic survival needs as well as my ideas about solutions to provide those basic needs. If you build your kit exactly as I do, then you are missing a key point of this project. This is *your* kit.

Building a BOB is not a one-day project. It's not even a weekend project. Preparing for a Bug Out is a mindset and a way of life. In life, nothing worth having comes easy, and the same is true for a top-notch Bug Out Bag. When your kit is finished, you should feel confident in the items you have chosen and in your ability to use those items to save the lives of you and your loved ones in the event of an emergency disaster evacuation—a real life Bug Out.

2 ▶ THE BUG OUT BAG: CHOOSING YOUR PACK

YOU HAVE NUMEROUS STYLE OPTIONS available when you select your pack. I have experimented with, used, and tested countless pack styles in environments all over the world—from single-sling backpacks to duffle bags and everything in between. In my opinion, *every* Bug Out Bag (BOB) *must* be a backpack with two shoulder straps. Here's why:

- A backpack is designed to distribute weight evenly—thus reducing fatigue from extended use.
- Backpacks allow your hands to be free for other tasks. Limiting the use of your hands is a huge compromise you make when carrying a hand-held-style kit such as a duffle bag.
- Backpacks offer a more streamlined contour, which allows for less restricted travel.
- A backpack is strapped and attached to you, which reduces incidence of loss.

BACKPACK STYLES

There are literally thousands of backpacks available from hundreds of different manufacturers and retailers. Choosing only one can be a daunting task, but it's your first very important decision in building your BOB. Function and comfort are your two top priorities. The guidelines on the following pages will help you wade through the sea of choices. Almost all backpacks fall into one of three main categories.

Frameless

These packs are typically the smallest and offer the least support. They are also the cheapest both to manufacture and to buy. I don't recommend using a frameless pack as a primary BOB. Save these for going on a picnic or to the beach, not for hauling life-sustaining survival supplies.

External Frame

I own many external-frame backpacks, and I like this style very much. External-frame packs are known for their performance with heavy loads. They do a great job of distributing weight to your hips, which helps to reduce fatigue in your shoulders, upper body, and back. Because the pack is mounted to a frame and not directly

Frameless Backpacks

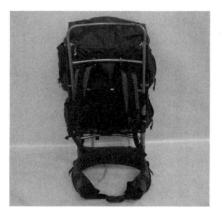

External Frame Backpack

External Frame Pack Against Back

against your back, this style also offers excellent air circulation, which you will appreciate in hot weather.

External-frame packs can feel "shifty" and top heavy because the weight is mounted slightly away from your back. They also tend to feel slightly bulky as compared to other styles. My personal BOB was an external frame pack for a very long time. This style works well as a BOB.

Internal Frame

Most of the backpacks you will find for sale are internal-frame style packs. The rigid support system that gives the backpack structure and shape is built into the pack body. These supports can be plastic, metal, or even foam. Internal-frame packs are very popular with adventure sports enthusiasts because of their sleek, agile appearance. They are close-fitting and hug very snuggly to the body,

which causes poor air circulation—the number one frustration with this style of backpack. This can be annoying in warmer climates.

The form-fitting nature also reduces load shifting, which helps with balance—especially on rough, uneven terrain. These packs are very maneuverable and also are easier to store in your home because they typically have a smaller overall footprint. Internal-frame packs make excellent BOBs. My current BOB is an internal-frame pack.

SIZE DOES MATTER
Balancing Act

Choosing your BOB pack size is a balancing act between comfort and necessity. It needs to be large enough to contain a certain amount of necessary gear while still remaining comfortable and manageable during extended periods of use.

Internal Frame Backpack

Internal Frame Backpack Side View

Too Big and Too Small BOBs

Follow Your Gut

Choosing the right pack is a gut feeling. There are no right or wrong answers, only shades of gray. Your pack shouldn't be too small, and it shouldn't be too large.

Some of my students collect all of their Bug Out gear first and save the pack decision for last. This is certainly an option. Choose a medium-size pack that feels right and looks appropriate on your body frame.

Seeking Help

Don't order your pack online! Many specialty outdoor and camping stores (especially independently owned stores) will help you find backpacks tailored to your size and weight. Some packs can even be heat molded to your specific form, which is a pricey but cool feature.

Retailers can add weight bags to the pack while you are in the store to give you an idea of how the pack wears and feels when loaded. When asking for help, a good rule of thumb is to tell the store associate that you are taking a three- to five-day backpacking trip. This will help narrow the field into the size category that is appropriate.

Making the Wrong Decision

Choosing the wrong pack can have painful consequences. There is

What Not To Do

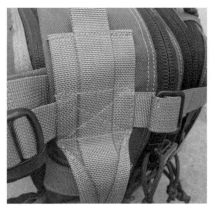

Reinforced Corner With Double Stitching

nothing more miserable than hiking all day with an uncomfortable and ill-fitting backpack. And, packs are expensive. When buying a backpack, make sure there is a satisfaction guarantee and warranty. If you use it and don't like it, *return* it!

Hey! They've Got Stuff!

Building a "tricked out" looking Bug Out Bag is a bad idea. You might as well put a bull's-eye on your back.

It's human nature to show off our cool stuff. Resist the urge and be humble when it comes to your BOB. It's good practice to ask yourself, "What can I do to look *less* prepared?" Supplies of all kinds will be at a premium in any disaster scenario, and you will be carrying an incredibly valuable assortment of merchandise on your back. If you choose to share, that's great, but being forced to share is something totally different.

Desperation can bring out the worst in people, and you will have enough problems without sending signals to "scavenging opportunists" that you and your family are stocked with survival rations.

Rioting, looting, mugging, and pillaging are all very common (guaranteed) in disaster emergencies. Do yourself a favor and keep your BOB low-key.

KEY FEATURES OF A BOB
Durable Construction

Not to state the obvious, but the pack you choose needs to be built and designed to take abuse. Some telltale signs of a well-constructed backpack are reinforced seams and double stitching.

No cheap zippers are allowed! If it has zippers, make sure they are good ones. Some packs have watertight zippers. This is a great feature.

Compartmentalized

Choosing a BOB that has defined compartments helps to organize gear and facilitates quick access to important items. Sifting through a pack with one cavernous compartment is not only frustrating, but also inefficient.

Being organized is extremely important. In time-sensitive situations, such as signaling for rescue, your level of organization can change the course of your entire experience.

Water Sealed Zipper

Water Resistant

Wet gear, clothing, and bedding can be deadly in certain conditions and down right miserable in *all* conditions. Choose a pack constructed from waterproof or water-resistant material. Some packs have built-in rain covers.

I've learned from outdoor experience to line my BOB with a construction-grade trash bag as an added layer of water-proof security. I suggest you do the same.

The Black Hole BOB

Pack Support

Choose a BOB with padded shoulder straps. Thin shoulder support straps can cause blisters and sores over long distances.

Many medium- to large-sized backpacks have built-in hip belts that help distribute the pack load to your

A Compartmentalized BOB

Snug Pack With Rain Cover Extended

Trash Bag BOB Liner

hips rather than on your shoulders and upper body. A hip belt can drastically reduce shoulder and neck fatigue by supporting up to 90 percent of a pack's weight and centering that weight nearer the center of mass. For extended carry, I wouldn't even consider a pack without a hip belt unless I had no choice.

FOR FAMILIES, DOES EVERYONE NEED A BOB?

All family members need to be considered in a Bug Out disaster evacuation. There are certain considerations that must be addressed when it comes to Bugging Out with children, the elderly and even pets (discussed in chapter fifteen).

The Primary Bug Out Bag

If you're single, this is the only pack that concerns you. Families will also have only one primary BOB. This pack contains all of the essential survival tools for the family along with the user's personal items. This is the one pack you *don't* want to leave home without in the event of a disaster Bug Out. This pack is carried by the group's strongest and most able-bodied adult.

Additional Adult Packs

Additional adults include all able persons eleven years of age and older. These packs should contain only personal survival items such as water, food, clothing, hygiene items, and bedding. Anything else is optional. All of the group's survival gear, such as shelter, fire building tools, etc., will be carried in the Primary BOB. The style of this pack does not need to be as functional or elaborate of the Primary BOB because it will weigh significantly less. A basic, frameless school-style backpack will work just fine.

MULTI-USE ITEM: CONSTRUCTION-GRADE TRASH BAG

★★★★★ FIVE-STAR RATING

Besides serving as a BOB pack liner, a quality trash bag has many multi-functional survival uses. Among those are:

- water-collection device
- ground tarp
- make-shift shelter
- poncho
- flotation device (filled with air and tied securely)
- comforter (filled with dried leaves or grasses)
- rescue signal

Hole Lined with a Trash Bag to Collect Water

Ground Tarp

Sun Shade Shelter

Poncho

Flotation Device

Rescue Signal

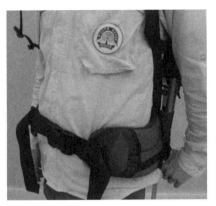
Hip Belt in Action

Kelty Brand Baby Backpack

Youth Packs

The general age range for a youth pack is six to ten years old. These should contain only light-weight items such as clothing, hygiene items, bedding, and maybe a small toy. All other survival essentials, such as food and water, will need to be split among adult packs or carried in the primary BOB.

Children Under Six Years Old

It's unrealistic to expect to bug out on foot while carrying not only the necessary survival gear but also a small child or children. This situation exceeds most adult's physical limitations and just isn't practical. If you have small children who are unable to travel independently, purchase a wagon or stroller to use specifically in the even of a Bug Out.

Not only can a pull-behind wagon transport small children, but it can also help carry other gear as well.

From the traditional Radio Flyer to more rugged off-road models, many different wagon styles are available. Your local lawn and garden center will offer several options. Wagons can be stowed in the trunk or mounted to a car roof rack in the event of Bugging Out in a vehicle.

A rugged, three-wheeled, collapsible stroller is also a great "infant-toting" alternative. These are light-weight and very quick to deploy. The three-wheeled models are better suited for rough terrain and faster travel. Many styles also have storage areas as well. Don't even consider the four-wheeled options with the cheap plastic wheels.

For even greater mobility, consider a baby backpack. This pack style integrates a seat and harness for toting small children and many also have sizable compartments and extra lashing points for gear. A pack like

Additional Adult Pack

Youth Pack

Radio Flyer Wagon

this could serve as both an additional adult pack and a baby hauler.

Disasters often disrupt transportation systems such as roads, trains, buses, and subways. Road closures, traffic jams, and fuel shortages can force you to travel by foot. Having a Bug Out wagon or stroller at the ready can make this possibility much more practical.

Elderly and Disabled

When Hurricane Katrina struck the United States in 2005, hundreds of elderly and disabled people were left behind and consequently died in the disaster's aftermath. To a certain extent, the elderly and disabled must be treated in the same way as small children. You need to be prepared to transport them *and* their personal survival supplies.

Never bug out with a battery-powered wheelchair or mobility device. Insufficient resources to recharge batteries can leave you stuck with few options. Without a charge, these modern contraptions are bulky and virtually impossible to move. A traditional push-powered wheelchair should be on hand and ready to use in the event of a Bug Out. Bug Out Bags can be mounted to the wheelchair for assisted travel.

In the event that vehicle travel is not possible, a manual push

Beefy Off-Road Wagon

Wheeled Stroller

Wheelchair With Bug Out Bag

wheelchair might be the only solution that allows an elderly or disabled person to continue on a Bug Out journey with you. Please give yourself this option. You cannot carry them.

STOCKING YOUR PACK

Up to this point, building your own BOB has been fairly conceptual—mainly defining expectations about the build. From here on out, this is a *hands-on* project. It's time to start collecting gear to stock your Bug Out Bag. And, it's time to begin understanding this gear and start learning how to use it. This is the *fun* part. There are twelve supply categories that need to be considered when stocking your Bug Out Bag. They are:

- Water and hydration
- Food and food preparation
- Clothing
- Shelter and bedding
- Fire
- First aid
- Hygiene
- Tools
- Lighting
- Communications
- Protection and self-defense
- Miscellaneous supplies

CHAPTER ORGANIZATION

I have devoted the following twelve chapters to each of the supply categories. I will list exactly what needs to be included in your pack (or packs) and explain why those items need to be there. At the end of the book, there are supply checklists divided into the following three levels.

Level P1

This level is for the Minimalist Packer. It is designed for someone with outdoor knowledge and survival experience. A level P1 packer is comfortable in the outdoors with minimal gear. In the world of survival, there are many instances when knowledge can replace gear. And knowledge is very lightweight. Simply put, more experience and more knowledge allows for less gear in a Bug Out Bag. Areas of redundancy are kept to an absolute minimum with P1 checklists as a user depends more on skill than gear. Consequently, a P1 pack will be smaller and will weigh less.

Level P2

This is the supply checklist level for the Average Packer. P2 packs will include gear designed for someone with an average level of survival skills and knowledge. The majority of the population will fall into the P2 pack category. Redundancy will exist in critical survival areas, such as fire tools and water purification.

Level P3

Level P3 supply lists are designed for individuals or families who are completely at the mercy of the gear on their back and have very little confidence in their outdoor survival skills. A P3 pack will be the heaviest of the grouping and may be limited by one's ability to handle the increased weight and bulk that comes with additional resources. P3 pack lists will include the most instances of redundancy in critical survival categories.

A Note About Customizing

These three pack levels are recommended guidelines. You will need to further personalize and customize your BOB supply list depending on your very specific needs or wants. You might decide to pick and choose between the lists in certain supply categories. This is absolutely expected and recommended.

DISASTER PRONE CONSIDERATIONS

Each chapter includes special notations for specific disaster scenarios. Take note of the suggestions for disasters common to your region.

3 WATER & HYDRATION

IN THE WORLD OF SURVIVAL, remember the rules of three.

Rule 1: You can live for three hours without shelter (in extreme conditions).

Rule 2: You can live for three days without water.

Rule 3: You can live for three weeks without food.

The average adult needs at least one liter of water per day for proper hydration. This amount is slightly reduced by size and age. Thirst is the first symptom of dehydration. Others include dizziness, headache, dry mouth, dark urine, and light-headedness. Dehydration can set in very quickly and the effects often lead to poor decision making and/or injury. Proper hydration is absolutely critical in *every* Bug Out scenario.

Because a Bug Out Bag (BOB) is a 72-hour kit, I suggest you pack a minimum of approximately three liters of fresh drinking water per person. Even with three full liters, there is little margin for error. Certain weather climates increase the amount of water a person needs to survive. You'll consume more water if your journey is especially rigorous. Personal hygiene can also tap into your water supply. The water you carry will constitute a large percentage of the overall weight of your BOB. The good news is that the weight will decrease as you hydrate. In a survival situation, a good water container can be invaluable. Your choice in water containers is very important.

CONTAINERS

Divide your water supply up among different containers. I never suggest carrying all three liters of water in a single container for two reasons.

1. If you have only one container and you lose or break it, you no longer have a viable way to carry and store water. This can present a very serious threat. Natural water-tight containers are not easy to find or make.
2. It's easier to distribute the weight of the water in your BOB when it is divided into two or three smaller containers.

I suggest dividing your water into the following three different containers.

32-oz. Wide-Mouth Nalgene Hard Bottle

These bottles are durable and crush resistant. I have used them in countless adventures and never has one failed me. I've even dropped one from fifty feet while rock climbing and it came out unscathed. Get the wide mouth version. They are easier to fill and they can double as a dish to eat from if necessary. On their sides are printed measuring units, which is convenient for preparing dehydrated

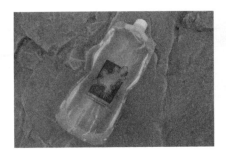

Platypus Soft Bottle Full

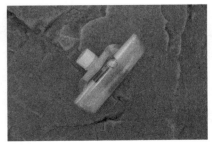

Platypus Soft Bottle Empty

meals. I've also never had one leak. You can trust it in your pack.

Metal Water Bottle

These canteens weigh about the same as any Nalgene bottle. Rather than just carrying two Nalgene bottles, I suggest opting for a metal alternative. A metal container can be used to boil and purify drinking water collected "in the field" should your immediate supply run dry.

Collapsible Soft Bottle

Packing a collapsible soft container allows you to reduce bulk as water is used. Consume the water in this container first. When empty, they take up virtually no space and weigh just a few ounces. They are not as durable, but with the two other containers listed above, you can afford to sacrifice durability for weight and space with this option. There are many different styles of these available at most outdoor retailers. The brand I use is Platypus.

WATER PURIFICATION ON THE GO

There are many factors that can impact how long three liters of water will last. If the weather is hot and arid, you will naturally consume more water. Traveling by foot through rough terrain can require more water as well. Personal hygiene will also deplete water rations. Because water is so critical to survival, I highly recommend packing two water purification options to safely replenish supplies when given the opportunity. While your BOB is planned for 72 hours, there is no guaranteed timeline. You need to be prepared to collect water from resources in route to your Bug Out Location.

Boiling Water

Bringing water to a rolling boil is one purification option, but it's certainly not always the most convenient when headed out of or through a disaster zone. Boiling water takes valuable time and fuel resources. Building a fire may also draw unwanted attention. It is a good idea to have at least one additional (if not two) method of purifying water.

Advantages:
- no need for fancy equipment
- 100 percent effective in killing harmful bacteria, viruses, and cysts

Disadvantages:
- requires fuel source
- weather can interfere
- takes time

Hand Pump Filter System

Manufacturers have created an assortment of amazing backpack-friendly filter systems to meet outdoor enthusiasts' increased demand for smaller and lighter water filter options. The most popular of these systems is a hand pump water filter. They are incredibly effective and robust. However, for a Bug Out Bag, they can be a little pricey—ranging from eighty

SURVIVAL QUICK TIP

Wrap your Nalgene Bottle with ten to fifteen feet of duct tape! Not only does it help protect your bottle, but duct tape is an excellent multi-use survival resource. It has hundreds of uses. Some of these include: first aid bandage, cordage and tarp/tent/gear repairs. Wrapping your water bottle instead of packing an entire role of tape saves you space and weight.

Emergency Bandage

Repair Tear in Tarp

Nalgene with Duct Tape

Shelter Building Cordage

Pump Filter System

Katadyn MyBottle Purifier

to three hundred dollars depending on the features. In my BOB, I carry the Katadyn Hiker Pro, which costs around eighty dollars.

This pump filter is about the size of a pop can and weighs in at 11 oz. It can filter up to one liter of water per minute, which is almost as fast as any

water faucet. It's durable, easy-to-use and perfect for a BOB. Similar models are made by other manufacturers, as well.

Advantages:

- speed of delivery—up to one liter per minute
- no skill or experience required

SURVIVAL QUICK TIP

There are several fresh water sources that do not need to be purified.

1. Snow: Pack snow into a container and melt with body heat or next to a fire.
2. Rain: Harvest rainwater by funneling into a container using a tarp, poncho, or garbage bag.
3. Dew: Soak up morning dew with clothing or bandana and suck it out or ring it into a container.
4. Vines: Large vines can store water. Cut at a diagonal toward the bottom and let water drip into a container. In the US, grapevines are perfect for this. Avoid vines that seep milky, discolored or strong-smelling liquid.
5. Trees: In the spring, trees such as maple and birch can be tapped for drinkable sap. Cut a V-notch in the tree and use a small stick or leaf to drip sap into a container below.

- effective in removing Cryptosporidium and Giardia
- includes multi-use tubing

Disadvantages:
- takes up valuable BOB space
- pricey: $80+
- useless if broken
- most do not remove viruses

Integrated Bottle Filters

Several manufacturers have also introduced an integrated bottle and filtering system. This combo unit allows you to scoop up questionable water and then drink out purified water through a built in filter and chemical treatment system inside the bottle it-self. These are very good water purification solutions for Bug Out Bags.

Advantages:
- no skill or experience required
- effective in removing Cryptosporidium and Giardia
- can be used as one of your three water containers

Disadvantages:
- Pricey: $45+

Straw Filters

Often called Survival Straws, these are exactly what they sound like—a straw with a filter attached. They are very inexpensive (around fifteen dollars), lightweight, effective, and compact.

MULTI-USE ITEM: RUBBER TUBING

★★★ THREE-STAR RATING

The rubber tubing that comes with a hand pump filter kit can also be used as a fuel siphon, an emergency tourniquet, or a long straw for inaccessible water sources.

Tubing as Fuel Siphon

Straw to Reach Water in Hollow Tree

Emergency Tourniquet

Aquamira Frontier Filter in Action

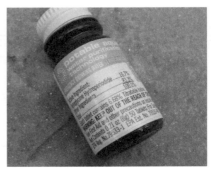
Bottle of Tetraglycine Hydroperiodide Purification Tablets

These are excellent BOB filtering systems. For the price, performance, and size, you just can't beat a straw-style filter. I keep one as a backup should anything happen to my pump system.

Advantages:

- no skill or experience required
- effective in removing Cryptosporidium and Giardia
- lightweight and compact
- inexpensive

Disadvantages:

- filters up to twenty gallons
- most do not remove viruses

Chemical Treatment Tablets

Chemical treatment tablets are extremely lightweight and take up almost zero space in a BOB. They are also pretty cheap and readily available at most any outdoor retailer. When it comes to these, I ask, "Why wouldn't you include them in your BOB?"

SURVIVAL QUICK TIP

Water with floating particles and debris should be pre-filtered before running through one of the above-listed purification methods. Several items in your BOB can serve as a Multi-Use Crude Water Filter. Three of these options are:

1. Bandana
2. Socks
3. Dust mask

Using a Bandana as Crude Pre-Filter

Depending on the brand, one tablet usually treats one liter of water. The purification wait time can be anywhere from thirty minutes to four hours. You can fill up a bottle, toss in a tablet and let it work while you continue to hike. For minimalist packers, these are a perfect purification back-up option. And, if stored properly, they have a very long shelf life.

Advantages:

- no skill or experience required
- very effective when used properly according to instructions
- lightweight and compact
- inexpensive

Disadvantages:

- water must be clear—cloudy or dirty water drastically impacts results
- have an expiration date

WATER FILTER VERSES WATER PURIFIER

Many people use these terms interchangeably when in fact, they are very different. A water filter does just what you would think—it filters debris from water. Most do an excellent job of filtering out threats such as bacteria and protozoan cysts. However, many filters don't remove viruses. Viruses are best killed using some sort of chemical or UV treatment. Water purifiers combine both a filter and a chemical treatment for an all-in-one system. The threat of water-borne viruses is very low in the US and Canada and a .2–3 micron filter is considered sufficient. In third world countries, though, a combination purifier is recommended.

SUMMARY

When it comes to water, I have some redundancy in my personal BOB. In addition to three fresh liters, I also pack a Pump Filter, a Survival Straw, and Purification Tablets. I could also boil water with my metal canteen or cooking pot if necessary. I've been sick from drinking bad water in the field and it was one of the worst situations of my life. I recommend you have at least two water purification methods in your BOB. Find the Water and Hydration Organizational Supply Checklist in the appendix.

COMMON DISASTER CONSIDERATIONS

If you live in an area prone to heat waves or drought, consider packing more than three liters of fresh drinking water, and also pack a local map that indicates waterways and bodies of water.

4 FOOD & FOOD PREPARATION

WHEN PREPARING for a 72-hour survival Bug Out, food doesn't top your list of priorities. You can survive three weeks with no food at all. However, when you use up more calories than you consume, there are undesirable consequences, including light-headedness, lack of energy, weakness, and poor thought-processes. All of these effects can be dangerous. In a survival situation, it's important to be clear-minded, strong, and confident of your decisions and capabilities. Your body is an engine that runs on calories. Refueling your body with calories is critical to maintaining your physical and mental endurance. With that said, however, don't worry about planning well-balanced three-course meals. This is three days of survival—not three days of vacation or car camping.

BUG OUT SURVIVAL FOOD
Open and Eat
The best types of BOB foods are what I call "open-and-eat" meals. The foods you pack need to be easy to prepare. Therefore, the best solutions are packaged meals that can simply be opened and consumed with little to no preparation. Little prep work saves time and fuel resources.

Long Shelf Life
Save your organic fresh-foods diet for normal and peaceful conditions, not disaster emergencies. Bugging out is the one instance when I promote the consumption of foods with a long shelf life. Remember, your BOB is prepared in advance and all of these items need to be packed and at the ready for months at a time. Choose foods that can be safely stored in your BOB for up to six months. Otherwise, you will need to review and replace your BOB food rations more frequently.

Lightweight
Your food choices need to be lightweight and packable. You might have to travel by foot, so keep it simple. As I tell my students, follow the KISS rule: *Keep It Simple, Stupid*. All foods should be sealed in durable, waterproof packages or resealable bags to prevent contamination and/or spills in your pack. Weight should take priority over taste.

Carbs + Calories
Your strict diet is not a priority during a Bug Out so forget about counting calories. Choose foods that are high in both carbohydrates and calories. Our cells and muscles are fueled by carbohydrate-rich foods. Carbohydrates are converted into sugars, which our bodies burn as energy. This "fuel" is critical in keeping us mentally and physically energized. Dried cereals, grains, pasta, and rice are all very rich in carbohydrates.

Meals Ready to Eat (MRE)

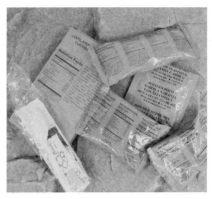

MRE Package Contents From MRESTAR

High-calorie foods are also important. Calories = energy. Your body needs calories (energy) to maintain vital functions. Two great high-calorie BOB food sources are dried meat and nuts.

SPECIFIC SUGGESTED BOB FOODS
Meals Ready to Eat (MRE)

Soldiers are issued MREs while serving in the field. Essentially, these are completely self-contained meal kits. They typically contain an entrée, a condiment pack, a large cracker, a small dessert, and a water-activated chemical heat source. Often, the outer package serves as the heating container. These meal kits are time-tested in the field and are very reliable and nutritious BOB food rations. They contain the most calories of any food item listed in this chapter—typically 1000+ calories per meal. The government restricts the commercial sale of official military MREs. You can still find them in Army/Navy surplus stores and at gun shows. However, these are typically overpriced. The better option is to buy what are called "commercial" or "civilian" MREs, which are very similar to the military version and often produced by the same manufacturers that sell direct to the military. I don't recommend buying MREs on eBay—there are just too many imposters and it can be difficult to tell the difference. Below is a list of reputable companies from which to purchase commercial MREs. You can compare the prices and kits and make your own choice. I have purchased from each of them with no issues.

- MREdepot.com (sells MREs from a variety of manufacturers)

Dehydrated Camping Meals

Ramen Noodle and Beef Jerky Meal Cooking Over Fire

- MRESTAR
- AmeriQual (US Military MRE Contractor)

The MRESTAR MRE in the photo includes:

- 8 oz. entrée (e.g., Lentil Stew with Potatoes and Ham)
- 2 oz. dry fruit (e.g., banana, pineapple, papaya)
- 2 oz. raisin mix (e.g., raisins, peanuts, almonds, sunflower seeds)
- 2 oz. sugar cookies
- Drink mix (e.g., Orange Flavor with Vitamin C)
- Accessory pack (spoon, coffee, sugar, creamer, salt, pepper, napkin, moist towel)

Advantages:

- very high in carbohydrates and calories
- durable, water-tight packaging

- easy to prepare
- complete meal in a bag
- does not require additional heat source
- can be eaten cold if necessary

Disadvantages:

- pricey: $8+ per meal kit
- a little extravagant for a 72-hour BOB
- bulky and heavy (1–1.5 pounds)
- better-suited for longer-term survival than a 72-hour Bug Out

Dehydrated Camping Meals/Noodle Meals

Most, if not all, outdoor retailers sell dehydrated camping meals designed for backpacking enthusiasts. These meals are also readily available online. They come in a variety of entrée choices and are surprisingly tasty. Dehydrated meals are excellent lightweight BOB meal options and have very long shelf lives. They are a no-frills meal and typically just contain one main entrée, unlike MREs, which contain several food items.

I would also add ramen noodles and similar just-add-water noodle meals to this category. While not specifically designed for backpackers, noodle meals are very similar in nature to dehydrated camping meals. They are lightweight, portable, and easy to prepare. And, for the price (around fifty cents each), it's hard to beat ramen-style noodle meals. Add in a little beef jerky and you've got a very practical and nutritious Bug Out meal.

Because these meal options are dehydrated, they need to be reconstituted with water. You will need a heat source, such as a fire or small pack stove, to prepare these meals. Depending on the circumstances, bringing water to a boil is not always the most convenient option. However, in a worst-case scenario, these meals are palatable if soaked in room-temperature water for a while.

Advantages:

- adequate in carbohydrates and calories—200–400 calories
- nice-quality meals
- light-weight and functional

Disadvantages:

- require boiling water (or time) to reconstitute
- not an open-and-eat meal

Bars

Energy bars, candy bars, and granola bars are the most practical eat-on-the-go mini-meals available. There are hundreds of different brands and varieties from which to choose. A handful of these would be more than sufficient to satisfy the basic energy needs of an average adult for three days. They wouldn't be a suitable long-term solution, but they are perfect for a short-term Bug Out. Bars are packed with carbohydrates and sugars, and they are compact and lightweight. These single-serving bars are easy to tuck into small spaces within a BOB, so they don't add bulk to the bag the way other food options can.

They are very affordable. But, most importantly, they require no preparation; just open and eat.

Advantages:

- no preparation
- adequate in carbohydrates and calories—200–400 calories
- lightweight and very packable
- huge variety to choose from
- prepackaged in single servings

There are no disadvantages to using energy bars and candy bars for 72-hour Bug Out purposes.

Other Great BOB Food Items: Rice, Instant Oatmeal, Beef Jerky, Tuna Packs, and Nuts

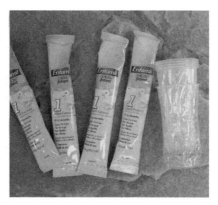

Powdered Baby Formula and Disposable Bottle Inserts

Honorable Mentions

There are five other items that are not necessarily category-specific but make good BOB food ration additions. These are:

- whole-grain rice
- instant oatmeal
- beef jerky
- soft tuna packets
- nuts

In addition to being lightweight and pack friendly, each of these items has an amazing shelf life if stored properly. Each has its own individual nutritional and functional benefits.

Whole grain rice needs to be prepared with water, but is high in carbohydrates and is also very filling, which will satisfy hunger pains.

Instant oatmeal is a very healthy stick-to-your-bones meal and can be quickly prepared with boiling water or soaked longer with room temperature water. For more food energy, select oatmeal with added raisins, nuts, and sugars.

Beef jerky can be eaten on the trail or can be reconstituted with other ingredients in water, such as ramen noodles. Tuna packs require no preparation and are very nutritious. Tuna also mixes very well with other ingredients; such as pastas. Don't get cans, choose the soft-foil packs, which are lighter and easier to pack.

Nuts are another high-carbohydrate, no-prep snack that be eaten on the go. You can repackage canned nuts in resealable bags to save weight and space.

BABY/INFANT FOOD ITEMS
Breastfeeding

For infants still on a liquid diet, breastfeeding is the obvious best option. It provides milk at the perfect

Soft Packaged Baby Food

Dehydrator

temperature with no food preparation, heat source, or equipment. If breastfeeding is not an option, powdered formula is the next best thing.

Powdered Formula

Several manufacturers package powdered baby formula in watertight, easy-pour, single-serve packets that makes preparing formula very simple. Consider packing these packets with disposable bottle liners and nipples to eliminate the need for bulky containers and messy clean-up. Everything is light-weight, very packable, and easy to prepare. Your metal cup (mentioned later) can be used to heat water for mixing. Be sure to pack a bottle and collar.

Solid Foods

For infants on semi-solid baby food, you have three good options:

- Mash up your own food into the consistency of baby food.
- Pack baby food. Soft-foil packaged baby foods work great and have a long shelf life (a year or more).
- You can make your own dehydrated powder baby food mix by dehydrating vegetables and blending them into a powder consistency using a food processor or blender. Then, mix this powder with water for rehydrated soft baby food.

SPECIAL DIETARY NEEDS

While not detailed earlier in this chapter, food adjustments and substitutions must be considered for people with special dietary needs. These may include individuals with certain allergies, diabetic concerns, or cardiovascular conditions. The same dietary guidelines that you or your family follows due to certain medical conditions must be reflected in your BOB food supply.

BIANNUAL REVIEW

I recommend a biannual review of your BOB food items. Regardless of the expiration date, I replace all of the food items in my BOB twice each year. I do this at the same time I change out my winter and summer clothing items—November and May. This schedule ensures that the food in my BOB is always safe to eat. If you wait for the food items in your BOB to expire, then you are wasting them. Exchanging them before they expire allows you the opportunity to cook the older food items and practice your Bug Out food preparation methods. Coordinate your food review with your clothing review to save time.

FOOD PREPARATION

Regardless of how easy the food you pack is to prepare, it's a good idea to include a simple cooking kit in your BOB. Having this kit on hand gives you the option to prepare more complicated meals if necessary. Even if you are just boiling water to reconstitute dehydrated meals, having the necessary tools on hand is critical. It's better to have it and not need it than to need it and not have it.

BOB COOK KIT CONTENTS
Metal Cooking Pots

A metal pot can be a life-saving survival tool. There are virtually no viable natural substitutes for a simple, everyday metal cooking pot. We take them for granted in our daily lives. Without one, however, it can be extremely difficult to perform very simple cooking tasks such as boiling water. The ability to boil water is an absolute Bug Out necessity. Although not totally necessary, it's best to purchase a metal pot designed for camping. These pots usually have a folding or collapsible handle and can be found at any camping or backpacking retailer. Pots designed specifically for camping and backpacking can be very expensive. You can use a generic metal pot. Below are some guidelines:

- Size: one liter minimum. (Larger families should consider a two-liter pot or bigger to reduce multiple meal preparation sessions and conserve fuel.)
- A handle: this allows you to maneuver the pot while hot. You can use the pliers in your multi-tool (see chapter ten) as a makeshift handle.
- Non-stick finish: reduces messy clean-up.

If you do not have the means to boil water in your BOB, then you are *not prepared*.

Metal Pot Options

Meal Heating Over Esbit Cook Stove

Cooking Items Packed Inside of Metal Pot

Boiling is one way to purify water and it's the cooking method for most of your Bug Out meals that are not open-and-eat.

Even the vast majority of wild edible plants are best (and easiest) prepared in a pot. It is also most advantageous to prepare wild caught meat and fish as a stew. This allows you to consume every last bit of nutrition—all the oils, fats, and juices, which are lost when meat is cooked over an open flame. A small metal pot takes up very little room in a BOB because other items can be packed inside of it to maximize space.

I personally pack my meals and other cooking items inside and use the pot as my "cooking kit" container. When I'm ready to eat, I know exactly where to go!

Metal Cup

I use my small metal cup more than almost any other piece of gear while on extended stays in the wilderness. They have all the advantages of a metal pot and are perfect for smaller, individual servings. These cups are also very easy to clean. There are several styles of metal cups on the market. Instant oatmeal is a perfect metal-cup meal. Just boil your water in the cup and pour in the oats. Metal cups are also ideal for making hot cups of tea or coffee, which can help warm you

Metal Cup Options

Nalgene Bottle with Glacier Bottle Cup From gsioutdoors.com

Canteen With Canteen Cup by Canteenshop.com

up if you are bugging out in cooler climates. A metal cup with measuring units can help eliminate guess work when preparing camp meals. Many of the inexpensive metal cups (like the one I use) do not have this feature. Luckily, most Bug Out meals are not an exact science.

Choose a metal cup that fits snuggly on the bottom of one of your water containers, as shown in the photo. This keeps your cup and water together and conserves valuable pack real estate. Based on my experience, I recommend either of the metal cup options in the photograph.

Utensils

When it comes to utensils, you can't go wrong with a combination spoon and fork, or spork. Don't grab a handful of cheap plastic sporks from your local fastfood restaurant. They won't hold up to the rigors of cooking in the field. Get one made from a heat-resistant material such as metal or polycarbonate. These are available at most outdoor retailers or online. To conserve weight and pack space, I recommend sharing utensils with small children and infants rather than packing extra sets. Your survival knife (discussed in detail in chapter ten) can double as your kitchen knife. The knife you pack will prove to be an invaluable food preparation tool.

Polycarbonate Spork, Titanium Spork

CONVENIENCE ITEMS
Can Opener
Even if you don't pack canned food items, I suggest including a small, lightweight, manual can opener. Having this tool on hand gives you a quick and easy way of opening canned food should the need arise. I suggest purchasing a military P-38 can opener from any Army/Navy surplus in your area. It will cost around fifty cents and is smaller than a normal house key. I keep one of these on my key ring as Every Day Carry (EDC).

Pot Scrubber
Keeping your cooking items clean is important for food safety and hygiene. Dirty cooking utensils in your BOB will contaminate the entire contents with food particles and food odor that may attract insects. The smell of food will also attract animals, especially at night, and these animals could damage your BOB trying to get to the food. Purchase a small, inexpensive scrubbing sponge from a grocery store for your BOB cook kit. Cut it in half to reduce weight and size (every ounce counts when you are carrying weight for extended periods). A general all-purpose soap can be used for washing (detailed in

SURVIVAL QUICK TIP
If you are on a budget, a great substitute for a BOB metal cooking pot is a coffee can with a metal coat hanger handle.

Makeshift Coffee Can Cooking Pot

P-38 Military Can Opener

Pine Cone Pot Scrubber

chapter nine). A pinecone is an excellent natural scrubber alternative.

HEAT SOURCES

In order to boil water or prepare hot meals (with the exception of MREs that include water-activated chemical heating systems), you will need a heat source. Ultimately, you need a heating solution that is:

- lightweight
- easy to use
- compact
- efficient

When it comes to heat sources, you have several great lightweight options that are well suited for a BOB. I have listed the best three below.

Fire

Fire is one of your most important Bug Out survival resources. There is an entire chapter dedicated to fire later in the book. Fire is the oldest heat source known to man and is an excellent way to cook or heat foods and boil water. Fire is also very lightweight—weighing only as much as your ignition device (also discussed later). However, fire is not a turn-key cooking solution. You can't just pull it out of your pack and turn it on like other heating options. It takes practice and skill to build a fire. And building a fire isn't always the most convenient cooking heat source for a Bug Out. In damp conditions or in environments where there is very little fuel to burn, starting and maintaining a fire can be nearly impossible. Even in perfect conditions, starting and building a fire sufficient for boiling and cooking can be a challenge. Fire may also draw unwanted attention to your location. Sometimes, a less noticeable heat source is advantageous. Even still, the means to create fire should be at the top of your BOB heat source options.

Esbit Stove Opened

Esbit Stove Closed

Advantages:

- lightweight (mostly skill)
- very effective
- huge variety of fuel sources— from furniture to pinecones
- most affordable option

Disadvantages:

- requires practice and skill
- requires sufficient fuel that you must find on-location
- affected by environment and conditions

Because of the challenges and drawbacks that fire presents, you should also include one of the other heating sources from this list in your BOB.

Solid-Fuel-Tablet Stoves

The most popular solid-fuel-tablet stove is the Esbit stove. This compact folding-style stove is a German design that has been issued to military troops around the globe for decades. The Esbit-style stove folds down to about the size of a deck of cards and weighs only a few ounces. Several fuel tablets can be stored in the folded stove.

It uses Esbit (or similar) solid fuel tablets that burn for eight to twenty minutes. The burning tablets can be blown out and relit for future use, and they are very easy to ignite. Solid-fuel-tablet stoves are perfect for small cook pots and one-cup meals. Depending on the conditions, these stoves can bring one pint of water to a boil in just a few minutes. Though not as efficient as solid fuel tablets, you can also burn small twigs and pinecones as fuel in this style stove.

I recently went on a four-day backpacking trip and used natural-found fuel such as twigs and pinecones in an Esbit stove frame to boil water and prepare eight full meals.

Canteen Cook Set Assembled Together

Canteen Cook System Set Up to Cook With Solid Fuel Tablet

Natural fuel isn't as convenient, but it is an excellent alternative should you run out of tablets.

Similar style stoves can be purchased in outdoor retail stores and Army/Navy surplus stores, and online. They all burn a version of solid fuel tablets with varying chemical compositions. All solid fuel tablets can pretty much be used interchangeably.

An Esbit stove with six fuel tablets costs around ten dollars. A package of twelve fuel tabs can be purchased from Campmor.com for only $5.99. In a recent effort to reduce weight in my own BOB, I substituted an Esbit stove for the canister stove (discussed next) that I had been using. If you decide to use a solid-fuel-tablet system, I recommend packing six fuel tablets per two adults. These small-scale systems are not the best solutions for large groups or families unless you pack multiple stoves and pots.

The Canteen Cook System by CanteenShop.com is another great option. Their uniquely designed metal stove fits directly over a standard-issue military canteen cup, which then slides over a standard-issue military canteen. This makes an excellent compact cooking set for any BOB.

It's a water container, a metal cook cup, and a multi-fuel stove all in one package.

Advantages:

- lightweight and compact
- easy to use and ignite
- eight-minutes (or more) burn time per tablet
- stoves can use solid fuel tablets and natural-found fuel
- affordable

Disadvantages:

- not a great solution for large families

MSR Superfly Mounted on Pressurized Fuel Canister

MSR WhisperLite Stove From ForgeSurvivalSupply.com

PRESSURIZED GAS STOVES
Pre-Pressurized Canister Stoves

Pre-pressurized canister stoves are available from several manufactures and are sold at a variety of price points. They are also easy-to-use and work well in almost any environment, except extreme cold. They do tend to depressurize in low temperatures, but a few minutes under your shirt will bring the pressure back up to a suitable performance level.

The fuel comes in small, self-sealing pressurized canisters that simply screw onto a stovetop. Screw on the stove, turn the knob to "on," light it, and you are ready to cook or boil water. Look at this stove as a miniature BBQ gas grill.

Depending on the size, some canisters can burn upwards of thirty minutes or more. Thus, a couple of canisters would be sufficient for a 72-hour Bug Out Bag. While these are very popular, very efficient and very easy to use, the canister stove is actually my last choice as a Bug Out heat source solution because it is so dependent on store-bought pressurized canisters. If you run out, game over.

Multi-Fuel Liquid Gas Stove

With a multi-fuel liquid gas stove, a manual pump pressurizes liquid fuel inside the fuel bottle. The liquid fuel is then vaporized and burned from an external burner attached with a flexible pipe. The benefit of this stove is it can burn several different liquid fuels including white gas, gasoline, kerosene, and jet fuel. This makes it a more flexible heating option than the pre-pressurized canisters because you can fill up the fuel bottle on your own if you have access to liquid fuels. This versatility makes this style stove a very practical BOB heating solution. Multi-fuel liquid gas stoves also work very well in all temperatures because you manually pump the pressure.

Advantages:

- easy to use
- effective for boiling water (1 liter boils in under 4 minutes)
- manual pump models can use a variety of liquid gas fuels
- better-suited for larger multi-person meals

Disadvantages:

- pricey: $40+ (without fuel)
- completely dependent on liquid fuel and/or fuel canisters
- fuel is heavy and bulky
- stove top can get damaged

SUMMARY

If you are packing dehydrated meals, also pack one additional heating option besides the ability to make fire. Don't pack any food that requires more than hot water for preparation. Anything more complicated is a waste of time, resources, and energy.

COMMON DISASTER CONSIDERATIONS

If you live in an area prone to heat waves, droughts, or wild fires, prepare your fire/cooking area accordingly. Keep at least a 36" diameter of bare earth or noncombustible material around any open flames.

SURVIVAL QUICK TIP

On a tight budget? You can use a coffee can to make your own Bug Out hobo-style stove that works excellently with natural-gathered fuel, such as small sticks and pinecones. Simply remove one end of the can and make a 4"×4" cut out along the bottom edge. Then, drill five 1" holes around the bottom and five 1" holes around the top and five to ten 1" holes in the top to make a grilling/cooking area. Build the fire in the stove and feed it through the 4"×4" fuel cut out. You will be surprised at how well a simple stove like this works!

Bug Out Hobo-Style Stove

5 CLOTHING

HYPOTHERMIA is the number one killer in outdoors settings. By definition, hypothermia is when a person's core body temperature drops dangerously low. Hypothermia sets in with exposure to cold weather and is intensified by wind and water. Hypothermia leads to heart and respiratory failure and eventually death. Low temperatures, wind, and moisture make a lethal combination for the ill-prepared.

The exact opposite, hyperthermia also ranks high as an outdoor killer. Hyperthermia occurs when someone's core body temperature rises dangerously high. When left untreated for even a short period of time, hyperthermia is debilitating and lethal.

Proper clothing is your first line of defense against overexposure to the elements—hot or cold. You're especially at risk of exposure when traveling by foot in the aftermath of a disaster. Consequently, clothing is a very important Bug Out supply category. It's not very exciting but it's important. Children and the elderly are even more susceptible to exposure, so pay special attention to ensure their clothing needs are met. This chapter includes several considerations and guidelines for Bug Out clothing.

WEATHER APPROPRIATE

If you live in northern Minnesota, your clothing needs are going to be vastly different from someone who lives in southern Florida. Because there are so many different weather regions all over the world, clothing is a somewhat personalized supply category. Common sense is required. I conduct a biannual review of my Bug Out Bag and change out my clothing items every November for the onset of winter and every May for the onset of spring and summer. If you live in an area with distinct seasons, I suggest you follow a similar clothing review/replacement schedule. You will not have time to think about what clothing items to take when a disaster strikes.

CLOTHING SPECIFICATIONS

When selecting Bug Out clothing, remember rule number one: Stay away from cotton. On the scale of available fabrics, cotton is probably the worst for survival. Cotton is like a sponge—it retains moisture and is slow to dry. It's also bulky.

In survival situations, you need fabrics that wick moisture away and that are fast drying. In cold temperatures, these are especially important qualities. The best survival fabrics are wool and wool blends, fleeces, nylons, and polyesters.

Following is a quick list of attributes your Bug Out wardrobe should possess:

- quick-drying
- moisture-wicking
- durable
- nonrestrictive
- loose-fitting
- muted colors (just in case you need to hide)

BUG OUT CLOTHING GUIDELINES

You should have two sets of clothing during a Bug Out—one on your body and one in your BOB. This includes a shirt, pants, socks (three extra) and underwear.

You should have only one each of any accessories, such as a jacket, gloves, and hat. An extra set of clothing is important because as clothing becomes soiled with body oils, grime, and dirt, the clothing loses its core insulation properties and also becomes less breathable. Both of these consequences drastically reduce fabric performance.

Excellent All-Season BOB Clothing Options

Light-Weight Long-Sleeve Shirt: Regardless of the season, full coverage protects from weather exposure and insects.

Mid-Weight Fleece: Fleece is lightweight and very packable and its good practice to carry one in any weather condition. Even in warm climates, a mid-weight fleece can be useful on chilly nights.

Moisture-Wicking Short Sleeve Undershirt: The word "wicking" refers to a fabric's ability to draw moisture away from your body to evaporate more quickly. Wicking fabrics are

WOOL FABRIC PROS & CONS

Wool is a natural fiber fabric made primarily from sheep fur. It performs best in cold weather environments due to it's insulation properties.

Pros:
- maintains insulation properties even when damp or wet
- extremely durable and rugged
- non-flammable
- breathable
- naturally wicking material—absorbs moisture from skin

Cons:
- heavy
- bulky—does not compress well
- holds moisture
- takes a long time to dry

Extra Set: Shirt, Pants, Socks, Underwear

Boonie Style Jungle Hat

Wool Socks

light-weight and fast drying. They help regulate your body temperature more efficiently.

Nonrestrictive Long Pants: No jeans allowed! Cotton-denim jeans are your worst enemy when wet. When selecting a fabric for pants, my favorites are light-weight wool blends or polyester-nylon blends.

Light-weight Crushable Brimmed Hat: This style hat can be a lifesaver in protecting your head and face from elements, such as sun, wind, and rain. A severe sunburn can turn into a serious medical crisis without proper care. I recently planned a 120-mile canoe trip through the state of Indiana. One of the guys had to cut the trip short because of an extreme blistering sunburn on his face. A "Boonie" style hat could have prevented this.

PROTECTING YOUR FEET

I can't stress enough how important it is to have proper foot protection. If you are Bugging Out on foot, your feet are your only means of transportation. If your feet give out and you can't walk, your bug out is over. You're stuck where you are. Take care of your feet and they will take care of you.

Wool Socks

To ensure my feet are properly taken care of, I pack three extra pairs of wool hiking socks. Don't pack socks

Wool Socks Hanging From Carabiner

Ankle High Hiking Boots

made from any other material! Wool is naturally breathable. This allows for better airflow, which helps to prevent blisters. Prolonged hiking can really give your socks a workout. Wool excels in hard-use environments because of it's durability and resiliency. I prefer the brand Smart-Wool. They are a little expensive but worth every penny. Below are some specific features/benefits of Smart-Wool socks:

- made from top quality no-itch Merino wool
- blended with elastic and nylon which helps to hold shape even with extended wear and washings
- Merino wool properties regulate temperature and moisture, which helps to reduce foot odor

When you have extra socks, you can switch them out regularly if your feet are damp or wet (whether it's sweat or outside moisture). You can dry used socks by keeping them close to your body or by hanging them off your pack. I keep an extra carabiner clipped to the outside of my BOB for just this purpose.

Hiking Boots

Get a pair of durable, waterproof, ankle-high hiking boots. There are many different styles and brands that will work just fine. These don't need to be packed inside your BOB but should be kept very close to it as you will be wearing these boots in the event of a Bug Out. Break them in! Don't plan on wearing a new pair of hiking boots in a disaster Bug Out. You could potentially be walking for several days with a twenty- to thirty-pound backpack. Your BOB boots need to be broken in, tested, proven, and comfortable.

Outer Shell

Heavy Fleece: Rated 300-Weight Fleece

COLD WEATHER ESSENTIALS

Bugging out in cold weather adds to the severity of any disaster. The 2011 Tohoku earthquake and tsunami in Japan forced thousands of people to Bug Out in freezing conditions. Many of these people fled into the mountains with only what they could carry.

Ideally, you will be wearing most of the items listed below in a cold weather Bug Out.

These are items that don't necessarily need to be kept in your BOB year-round.

The key to warmth is layering, not one bulky parka or snowsuit. Layering is incredibly effective because it creates dead air space between the layers of clothing. Heat stays trapped within that air space. Layering also lets you to control your body temperature by adding and shedding clothing items as necessary. I've spent days at a time in temperatures below 10°F with the following layering system.

Outer Shell

Your outermost layer is the outer shell. An outer shell is critical to any cold weather layering system. It has two primary functions:

- wind break
- rain protection

Wind and rain can turn even moderately cold weather into a hypothermic situation. Protecting your core from these elements is critical and that's what your outer shell will do. It is a protection layer, not an insulating layer, so your shell should not be big and bulky. This shell could be a waterproof rain jacket. Be sure it has a hood. In most conditions, you will only need a shell for your upper body. In extreme conditions, outer shell pants would be a great idea. This depends on where you live.

Balaclava Face Mask

Rain Poncho

Heavy Fleece (Rated 300-Weight Fleece) or Wool Sweater

Beneath the outer shell is a rated 300-weight fleece. This is an upper-body warmth layer that is especially important in low temperatures. The structure of fleece fabric allows for trapped air within the fibers. It has excellent insulation properties. A heavy wool sweater is also an excellent choice. Wool is hands down the best survival fabric on the planet. Wool's biggest drawback is that it can be bulky.

Mid-weight Fleece (Rated 200-Weight Fleece)

Beneath the rated 300-weight fleece is a rated 200-weight fleece. This, too, is an upper-body warmth layer. A mid-weight fleece is the most popular weight. It can easily be used as an outer layer in moderate temperatures, but is very well suited for layering. This is the layer I shed most often while adventuring in cold weather environments. If you are starting to sweat, then you need to shed layers or reduce your physical exertion. Sweating moisture into your clothing can kill you. Cold temperatures and damp clothing is the perfect recipe for hypothermia.

Light-Weight Wicking Base Layer

The base layer is the layer of clothing against your skin. In cold temperatures, I wear both upper- and lower-body base layers. The function is to hold and trap warmth. Choose a base layer made from a wicking fabric designed to draw moisture away from your body. It should be breathable, stretchy, and very comfortable. *No itchy base layers allowed.* For this reason, wool is a not a recommended base layer fabric. These garments should also be form fitting—not loose and baggy.

COLD WEATHER ACCESSORIES
Wool or Fleece Hat

Up to 30 percent of your body heat can be lost through your head. Warm head protection is critical. In extreme conditions, a balaclava is an excellent alternative that provides face and neck protection.

Cold Weather Gloves

Don't risk frostbite to your extremities. A pair of cold-weather gloves should be in your pack or on your person if bugging out during the winter season. In a survival situation, the ability to use your fingers and hands is imperative. Almost every survival function requires good hand dexterity—using a knife, lighting a fire, tying knots, preparing food, administering first aid, etc. Nothing will cripple your hands like cold weather—*pack gloves!* The pair I pack is a very simple set of 100 percent wool gloves I bought at an Army/Navy surplus store for $5.99.

MULTI-USE ITEM: RAIN PONCHO

★★★★★ FIVE-STAR RATING

The military-style rain poncho can also be used as an emergency survival shelter. Here are three different configurations that I've used:

Poncho Ridge Line Lean-To

Poncho Tent

Poncho Diagonal Lean-To

RAIN PONCHO

A light-weight military-style poncho will prove to be one of your most valuable Bug Out items. I would probably put this on my top ten list of Bug Out items. While there are many different makes and models of ponchos, the most popular are constructed from sealed rip-stop nylon. This makes them very light-weight and crushable—perfect for a BOB. They come with a drawstring hood and also with metal grommets in key points around the edge. The grommets add versatility and multifunctional uses. Using these grommets, some cordage, and a little creativity, you can use the military poncho as a quick and effective survival shelter.

DURABLE WORK GLOVES

From shelter building to collecting firewood, there will never be a shortage of manual chores to complete when the grid goes down. Your hands are one of your most valuable tools in disaster survival scenarios—protect them. Include a durable pair of leather work gloves in your BOB. You can pick up a pair at any hardware store for just a few bucks. You will not be able to purchase a new pair of hands after yours are blistered and shredded from hard labor.

MULTI-USE ITEM: SHEMAGH

★★★★★ FIVE-STAR RATING

This large square scarf is similar to a bandana but much larger—typically around 40"×40". It can be used for hundreds of different survival applications. A few are listed below:

Cordage for Tripod

Face and Head Protection

First Aid Arm Sling

SHEMAGH

Pronounced *schmahhg*, the shemagh is a large square scarf worn primarily in the desert regions of the world to protect one's face from sun, wind, and sand. It's an item widely used by American and British troops serving in the Middle East. The shemagh is much more than just a head and face wrap. It's probably the most multifunctional survival item I have ever owned with literally hundreds of uses. It makes an excellent BOB addition. It can be purchased at many Army/Navy surplus stores and we also carry several different colorways at www.willowhavenoutdoor.com.

SUMMARY

Thoughtful preparation and planning is absolutely necessary if you expect to survive the extreme elements. Use common sense when choosing clothing for your immediate environment. If you have distinct seasons where you live, be sure to change out the clothing in your BOB at least once a year.

COMMON DISASTER CONSIDERATIONS

If you live in an area prone to winter blizzards or snow storms consider packing snow shoes. Heavy snowfall can be nearly impossible to travel in by foot.

SHEMAGH SLING PACK

Through a series of folds and rolls, a shemagh can also function as a makeshift sling- pack to tote additional supplies.

Makeshift Sling Pack: Step 2

Makeshift Sling Pack: Step 1

Makeshift Sling Pack: Step 3

6 ▶ SHELTER & BEDDING

THE BEST SHELTER SYSTEM for a Bug Out Bag is a subject heavily debated within the survival community. Everyone has his or her own opinion and favorite pick. There are many different options ranging from makeshift tarp tents to hammocks.

A Bug Out shelter needs to be light-weight and packable. These are your two primary concerns. It also needs to be tested and proven in extreme conditions. Protection from rain, wind, sun, and snow is essential. The shelter also needs to be easy and quick to set up—even in low-light conditions. And the shelter should not be dependent on certain environmental crutches. Hammocks, for example, are dependent on an environmental crutch. They requires two solid anchor points—either trees or other fixed objects. For this reason, hammocks don't pass my BOB shelter criteria even though a hammock is my preferred way to sleep when I venture into the woods.

As I said, shelter is a heavily debated topic. This chapter will cover what I believe are the two best options for BOB shelters based on my field experiences.

BOB SHELTER OPTION 1: TARP SHELTER

Tarps are incredible survival resources that can be deployed and set in a variety of shelter configurations. Several manufacturers offer tarps in many different sizes and materials. Some tarps are better suited for a BOB than others.

Don't buy the thick, blue polypropylene woven tarps that you see at hardware stores and big-box retailers. Though they are inexpensive, price is about the only advantage these have over other options. This type of tarp is heavy, bulky, and loud.

If you choose a tarp shelter, you need to purchase a light-weight nylon tarp specifically designed for camping and backpacking. These are much better suited for a BOB. They are thin, water repellent, durable and quiet to use. An 8"×10" tarp is sufficient to build a one- or two-man shelter. For two to four people, select a larger size, 10"×12".

Many experienced survivalists and outdoor enthusiasts prefer a

Hammock

tarp shelter because of its simplicity. Though simple, a tarp shelter can be configured in a variety of sets. And, with practice and experience, tarp shelters can offer just as much protection as any store-bought tent. Following are four very popular tarp shelter configurations. They are anchored using an adequate supply of cordage (discussed later in chapter fourteen).

Lean-To Tarp Set

The lean-to tarp shelter configuration is the most basic of all shelter designs. This would be considered a three-season design and would not be ideal in extreme cold environments. It simply puts a roof over your head to protect against rain, dew, snow, and wind. This tarp shelter works best when set so that the slanted roof *faces* the wind. If you can determine a primary wind direction, setting the shelter in this way drastically reduces exposure

and also helps prevent the wind from catching your shelter like a sail. It also prevents the wind from blowing rain or snow in through the open faces. From an efficiency perspective, this design works as a very effective heat shield. The heat from a fire built in front of the shelter will be reflected down on the sleeping area, maximizing warmth. To further reduce exposure, this configuration can also be set against a large object such as a rock, earth mound, or fallen tree.

Ridge-Line Lean-To Tarp Set

This set is very similar to the basic lean-to but with the addition of a ridge-line, which allows you to angle the front face and further reduce exposure. This ridge-line can be a pole lashed between two anchor points or a piece of cordage pulled taught. The same considerations apply to this configuration as with the basic lean-to.

Basic Tarp Lean-To

Ridge Line Tarp Lean-To

You can also configure a center ridge-line for an overhead canopy design. This set is best in warmer climates because it lacks protection from any of the sides. This is also a great way to shelter a hammock.

Tarp Tent Set

This set is best suited for windy and rainy conditions. It is very similar to the overhead center ridge-line tarp canopy except it's directly on the ground. Because of the design it has limited "inside" space. It's typically pretty tight sleeping quarters, which can be an advantage in cold weather environments when retaining body heat is critical to warmth.

Diagonal Tarp Set

Anchoring the corner of a tarp to a tree or pole allows you to stake the other three corners to the ground and create a diagonal tarp set. This creates a very well protected shelter area. A guy-line pulling on the center back of the tarp helps create more inside head room. Anchoring to a large tree can also help reduce exposure on the front open side.

TARP SHELTER INSIGHTS
Drawbacks

The drawbacks of choosing a tarp as your BOB shelter are threefold:

Overhead Center Ridge-Line Tarp Canopy

Tarp Tent With Center Ridge-Line

Diagonal Tarp Set

1. Constructing an effective tarp shelter requires experience and skill. If poorly constructed, a tarp shelter can be a disaster in and of itself. To properly execute a tarp shelter, you must have knot-tying skills and practice setting up the shelter.

2. Many tarp tent configurations have at least one open wall, which can allow mosquitoes and other biting insects inside to feast while you sleep. To counteract this, see *insect repellent* in chapter eight.

3. Because tarp shelters are single-walled shelters and have at least one exposed face, they are best for three-season Bug Outs. Using this style of shelter in extreme cold can present a serious risk without a nice big fire or sufficient bedding.

Grommeted Corner

Reinforced Tie-Downs

50' Paracord

Tie-Downs and Cordage

If you like the idea of a tarp shelter, make sure the tarp you purchase has either metal grommets around the edges or reinforced tie-downs.

Having adequate attachment points is critical in using a tarp as a shelter. Even more important is cordage. I suggest keep a minimum of fifty feet in your BOB. The best cordage for the job is 550 Parachute cord. I detail why in chapter fourteen.

Tarp Shelter Summary

Regardless of whether or not you feel a tarp is the right shelter match for your BOB, you should consider packing a backpacking tarp anyway. They are very light-weight and fold up very small. The weight-risk versus the survival-reward makes the tarp an excellent BOB pack item.

THE MANY USES OF A TARP

When you are limited in the amount of resources you can pack, the ability to use an item for multiple functions is a value-add to any piece of gear. A light-weight, waterproof tarp is a multifunctional survival item that can be used in a variety of ways in addition to shelter. A tarp can be a very valuable piece in your BOB. Following are just a few ways a tarp can be used to provide survival needs in a Bug Out crisis.

Rain Catch

The great advantage of rainwater is that it doesn't need to be purified. It can be collected and consumed with no processing. Rainwater can also be used for hygiene needs. A tarp can be used to funnel rainwater into a hole in the ground that is lined with the bottom of the tarp. The tarp is the funnel as well as the container. Or, it can direct water into another container, as shown.

Ground Cover

Protecting your body from the cold or wet earth is equally important as protection from the elements. You can have the best shelter in the world, but the shelter won't matter if you are sleeping on wet ground. Tarps make excellent waterproof ground covers. They don't offer insulation, but they are a moisture barrier.

Emergency Stretcher

In the event of a demobilizing condition or injury, a tarp and two sturdy poles can make a functional emergency stretcher. Simply roll the poles up three or four times from the edge of the tarp on each side and it will not come loose when someone is being carried.

Tarp Configured as a Rain Catch

Tarp Ground Cover

Sleeping Hammock

In extremely damp, flooded, or swampy conditions, it might not be possible to sleep on the ground. In this situation, you would typically construct a platform off the ground to elevate sleeping quarters away from the water. Another option is to use a tarp as a makeshift sleeping hammock. Roll a golf-ball-sized rock or stick in opposite corners for a tie-down anchor point and secure the tarp between two trees. I've slept in a makeshift hammock this way before in pouring rain. I was able to throw the other corners over me for protection. It was like a tarp hammock cocoon. Some water did get in at my head and feet, but it was better than any of my alternative options at the time.

BOB SHELTER OPTION 2: TENT SHELTER

Almost every modern tent manufacturer has models designed specifically for light-weight backpacking. These

SURVIVAL QUICK TIP

Through a series of folds and rolls, a tarp can also function as a makeshift sling-pack to tote additional supplies.

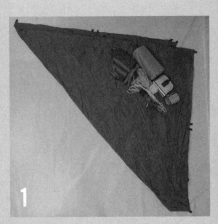

Makeshift Sling Pack Using a Tarp: Step 2

Makeshift Sling Pack Using a Tarp: Step 1

Makeshift Sling Pack Using a Tarp: Step 3

Makeshift Tarp Hammock

Emergency First Aid Stretcher

Light-weight Backpacking Two-Person Tent

ed from light-weight, waterproof fabrics and poles. A tent can feel like a home away from home. When the zipper closes you are in your own private space and feel less vulnerable and more protected than in a tarp shelter. Tent shelters have many advantages:

- require little skill to set up
- easy to set up even in the dark
- very practical four-season shelter
- more privacy
- keeps out insects and critters
- built in ground cover
- more practical for families

Choosing a BOB tent shelter will ultimately come down to decisions that involve what I call the *backpacker's trilogy*:

- price
- weight
- footprint (space that it takes up in your pack)

Your trilogy equation and final valuation will be different from mine and any other BOB prepper out there. I can only offer guidelines to choosing a BOB tent shelter. It's up to you to

tents are the perfect shelter solution for any BOB. Backpacking tents range in size from single-person to multi-person for families and are construct-

determine how much you are willing to spend, how much weight you want to carry and how much pack space you want to devote to your tent.

Tent Shelter Guidelines

- Total tent weight should not exceed two pounds for each adult in your Bug Out team. If you have two adults, you can have a four-pound tent and evenly split up the tent equipment between your two BOBs.
- Choose a three-season tent. This is the most versatile tent option.
- No bells and whistles. Don't get sucked in by fancy (and heavy) add-ons, such as vestibules, pockets, multiple entrances, gear lofts, etc. You just need a shelter. This is not for a family vacation and you aren't competing with your neighbors.
- If your tent comes with steel stakes, replace them with lighter-weight aluminum alternatives.
- If the tent canopy (the top) has mesh panels, make sure a *rain fly* is also included.
- Bathtub bottom tents are better. The bottoms of tents are made of thicker waterproof material. In a bathtub bottom tent, the bottom material extends three to five inches up the tent walls, an added protection against groundwater and rain.
- The lightest tent poles are aluminum.
- Choose a free-standing tent. This style is not dependant on trees or anchor points. They're also very easy to move.

Mesh Panels

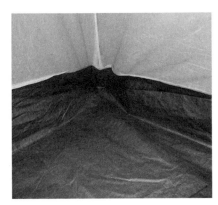

Bathtub Bottom

PONCHO SHELTER

As mentioned and illustrated in chapter five, a military-style poncho with grommets can be used as a makeshift survival shelter. It can also be used as a ground cover coupled with a tarp shelter design. Ponchos make excellent waterproof moisture barriers. Again, 550 paracord is my cordage of choice for erecting poncho shelters.

BUG OUT BEDDING

The final layer of defense in the shelter category is bedding. There are two components to an effective multi-season Bug Out bedding system: a sleeping bag and a ground pad.

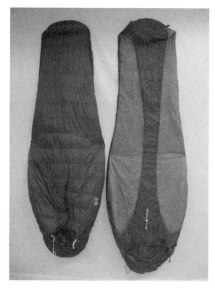

Two Sleeping Bags

BUG OUT SLEEPING BAG

A Bug Out sleeping bag is no different from sleeping bags designed for light-weight backpackers. Choosing a sleeping bag is a numbers game. You are trying to find the best offering in all of the following categories:

Degree Rating

A sleeping bag's degree rating denotes the lowest temperature at which the bag is generally comfortable. For example, a 30-degree rated bag should be comfortable for most people down to around 30°F. You need to choose a degree rating that makes sense in your environment. A practical year-round rating is 30–40

Mummy Hood

degrees. While not totally necessary in warm climates, it still gives you security in cold weather. Even in 10-degree temperatures, a 30-degree bag will keep you alive. It won't be fun, but you'll live. Remember, this isn't car camping—it's disaster survival. Choose a mummy-style bag with a built-in hood. This will help to trap and retain body heat.

Sleeping bags are filled with one of two insulation materials: down feathers or synthetic fibers. Natural down is lighter-weight and more compressible but is more expensive. Synthetic insulation is not as compressible but it isn't so hard on the wallet either. Their performance is very similar. Neither perform too well when wet. I prefer down-filled sleeping bags.

Weight

Every ounce counts when trying to keep the overall weight of your BOB manageable. You want the lightest-weight sleeping bag at the lowest degree rating. Try to keep your sleeping bag weight in the 2–3 pound range. Any heavier and your sleeping bag will be too bulky.

Size

If your sleeping bag does not come in a compression sack, buy one. Compression sacks are designed to crush and compress bags into small packages. Size is critical. Ideally, your sleeping bag will be about the size of a cantaloupe.

Price

Not only do you want the best bag but you want it at the best price pos-sible. Your sleeping bag will be one of the most expensive items in your BOB if purchased new. Don't sacrifice quality and performance for price. A good sleeping bag is an investment that should last a lifetime. You can and will use this for years to come. Try eBay or craigslist for used BOB sleeping bags. I have purchased many slightly used camping and backpacking items on these sites for a fraction of their original cost.

GROUND SLEEPING PAD

Sleeping on the ground can compromise the performance of even the best sleeping bag and shelter system. A ground pad reduces conductive heat loss between you and the earth. Besides insulation, a sleeping pad provides cushion for added comfort. Sufficient rest is critical in any survival situation. For many, lack of rest can have dangerous mental and physical consequences. For example, if I am sleep deprived, I get nauseous. Clouded mental processing can lead to poor decisions. Sleeping pads work by trapping dead air space between your body and the ground. This dead air space acts as an insulation barrier. If you do not have a ground cover such as a tarp, a sleeping pad can also function as a moisture barrier. Ground pads come in two main styles.

Sleeping Bag in Compression Sack

Therm-a-Rest Sleeping Pad in Stuff Sack

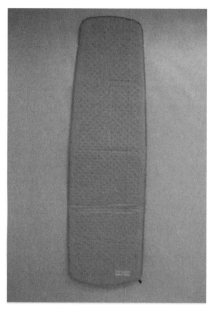
Therm-a-Rest Sleeping Pad Inflated

Air-Filled Ground Pad

Air-filled grounds pads are basically blown up before use and deflated when ready to pack. An air-filled pad provides a very soft sleeping surface and works as an excellent cold and moisture barrier. Many air-filled ground pads are extremely compact when deflated, as can be seen in the photo on this page. However, you pay for the benefits of being light-weight and compact—they aren't cheap. If punctured, these pads loose almost 100 percent of their insulation properties. Each brand of these ground pads also has a small repair kit available for purchase. If the possibility of puncturing concerns you, one of these small and light-weight kits can easily be tucked into your BOB.

Advantages:
- very comfortable
- very compact

Disadvantages:
- expensive for a BOB
- no insulation value if punctured

Foam Pads Rolled

Foam Pad Packed and Ready to Go

Foam Pads

Foam pads are very light-weight but bulky in size. They are inexpensive and durable. In addition, these ground pads are molded from solid closed-cell waterproof foam—making them an ideal moisture barrier from the wet or damp ground. I use one of these as my BOB sleeping pad. There are many models available from different manufacturers but each design is very similar.

Puncture holes will not affect their performance. Because of its size, this style pad is best mounted to the outside of a BOB.

MULTI-USE ITEM: FOAM SLEEPING PAD

★★★ THREE-STAR RATING

Foam pads are wonderful multi-use products. In addition to being a sleeping pad, they can be used for a number of survival functions.

Foam Pad Life Preserver

Foam Pad Camp Chair/Recliner

Advantages:

- very durable—almost inde-structible
- affordable

Disadvantages:

- bulky

SUMMARY

Shelter is near the top of the list when it comes to basic human survival needs. In extreme conditions, it is your number one priority. Within a safe, protected area, shelter provides both physical and mental security. Disasters can devastate a person's mental and emotional sense of nor-mality, and a simple shelter can be a huge morale boost in a time of chaos and disorder. Regardless of which shelter and bedding system you and your family choose, it's extremely important to test it out and make sure everything functions as you intend—inside and outside of your BOB. If it doesn't, rethink your choice.

COMMON DISASTER CONSIDER-ATIONS

If you live in an area prone to heavy snowfall or winter storms, a tent shelter will be preferred over a tarp shelter because of the added protection.

SURVIVAL QUICK TIP

If you don't have access to a store-bought sleeping pad, an excellent natural alternative is a bed of pine boughs. To create this bed, pile eight to twelve inches of pine boughs on the ground in the rough shape of your body. This creates a sur-prisingly comfortable sleeping pad that helps to insulate your body and bedding from the cold ground. Most evergreen trees such as juniper, cedar, and pine work great.

Natural Tree Bough Sleeping Pad

7 FIRE

THE ABILITY TO CREATE FIRE is quite possibly the most important survival skill on earth. Fire has been the core of survival since the beginning of time. It allows a survivalist to accomplish a huge variety of life-sustaining tasks. Bugging out can present a family or an individual with a myriad of ways to die. Below are several ways you can use fire to help stay alive.

Heat

In certain situations, fire may be your only way to stave off severe cold and control your body's core temperature. The heat from a fire not only provides warmth, but it can be used to dry clothes, shoes, and gear. Wet clothes and cold temperature is a recipe for death. As I mentioned earlier, hypothermia is the number one outdoor killer. Fire is the best way to battle hypothermic conditions.

Cooking/Boiling

Fire can be used to cook and heat food. It is also necessary to boil and purify drinking water.

Signaling

Creating smoke signals by day and signal fires by night are two effective and proven methods of signaling for rescue. Both have saved the lives of countless lost survivors.

Morale

In a disaster, 90 percent of survival is dependent on a person's mentality. As I tell all of my students, the *will* to survive is greater than the *skill* to survive. Fire can go a long way in boosting one's morale in a disaster scenario. The warmth and light a fire provides is calming, uplifting, and empowering. Building a fire gives you a sense of control and accomplishment in a

Drying Out Wet Boots

Cooking Food With Fire

Sample Fire Kit

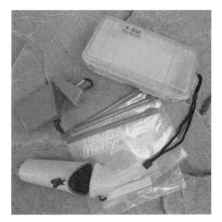

Pelican Case and Resealable Bags

Strike Anywhere Matches and Waterproof Match Container

very defeating environment. Staying positive is absolutely critical to surviving a situation where the odds are stacked against you. Fire can help sustain a positive mindset.

YOUR FIRE KIT

Kit simply means a smaller compartmentalized container within your BOB. As I mentioned earlier in the book, keeping category items compartmentalized in their own kits makes the items easier and faster to find when you need them. Fire items should be stored in their own waterproof kit to protect them from water and moisture. You can use a vast number of containers for your fire kit. Several practical examples are:

- sealed aluminum containers with o-ring
- watertight bags, boxes, and tubes
- non-watertight containers with contents packed in resealable bags

Regardless of the container style and size you choose, practice identifying this kit inside of your BOB in complete darkness or while blindfolded. You could very well need to find and use this kit in low-light circumstances. Again, disasters don't present ideal environments. Prepare for the worst and anything better is a bonus.

Because fire is such an important survival resource, I encourage redundancy when it comes to packing fire-making tools and supplies in your BOB. Your BOB fire kit should contain two main fire-making components:

1. ignition sources
2. fire-starting tinder

IGNITION SOURCES

Pack a minimum of three ignition sources. I can justify this redundancy because the cost and weight of each one is very minimal.

Ignition Source 1: Cigarette Lighter

Lighters are cheap, lightweight, reliable, easy-to-use, long-lasting and extremely effective. I carry one lighter in my waterproof fire kit and two more in separate spots on my BOB. Lighters do have certain limitations. They don't function well in extreme cold or when wet.

Ignition Source 2: Waterproof Strike Anywhere Matches

Regular matches are just too vulnerable to moisture. Be sure to pack a dozen or so waterproof strike anywhere matches stored in a sealed match case. You can purchase both in the camping section of any outdoor store or even a big-box discount retail store.

Ignition Source 3: Fire Steel Striking Rod

The technical name for this product is a ferrocerium rod. Many people also use the name ferro rod or metal match. A fire steel can generate sparks at over 2,000˚F when scraped with a metal striker or the back of your survival knife. There are many different styles of fire steel sparkers. Generally, they all work using the same principle.

SURVIVAL QUICK TIP

Make strike anywhere matches waterproof by dipping them in fingernail polish. Dip twice for a waterproof seal. Dip a third time for peace of mind.

Waterproofing Matches in Fingernail Polish

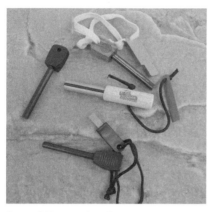

Several Ferrocerium Rods Including Kodiak Firestarter

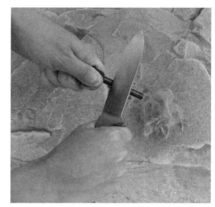

Striking Sparks With Knife

A fire steel can generate sparks even in damp and wet conditions. An average fire steel can be used thousands of times and is an excellent survival ignition source. Striking these sparks into prepared fire tinder is a very effective fire-starting technique and one that I use almost exclusively while in the bush. The fire steel I carry is one made by Kodiak Firestarters. They manufacture a fire steel that is mounted to a small bar of magnesium. Of course, you can use the fire steel alone to ignite dry tinder in reasonable conditions just as you would any ferro rod. However, if your conditions or fire-starting tinder aren't ideal, you can scrape off shavings from the built-in magnesium bar into a small pile with your knife or the included striker tool and use these shavings as tinder. Magnesium shavings ignite with just a spark and burn

at over 5,000°F. It's hard not to get a fire going with a small burning pile of metal! These integrated fire steels are a little pricier but the added bonus of built-in magnesium fire-starting material is worth the extra few dollars and ounces. This is an ignition source and fire-starting tinder in one compact package.

FIRE-STARTING TINDER

The ignition source is only half of the fire-starting equation. In a Bug Out scenario, I want *guaranteed* fire. This means I need a guaranteed ignition source and some fire-starting tinder that is guaranteed to light when I hit it with one of my ignition devices. The only *guaranteed* fire tinder is the tinder that you pack with you. Although natural fire-starting materials exist, certain weather conditions can make finding dry, flammable fire tinder very difficult. Below are several great BOB fire tinder options. I recommend you pack at least two of these.

WetFire Fire-Starting Tinder

WetFire is a brand name, store-bought fire tinder available at most outdoor retailers. It is undeniably the best fire starter available. It will light with just a spark in almost any weather condition. It will even light and burn while floating in water.

Package of WetFire

It's a remarkable product and makes a very reliable BOB fire-starting pack item. WetFire tablets will burn approximately two to three minutes and come individually wrapped in a waterproof package. With this burn time, you can even burn a Wet-Fire tablet as the fuel source in an Esbit stove mentioned in chapter four, making these tablets a good multi-use item.

A tablet of WetFire also fits into the handle of the StrikeForce Fire Starter. This is an excellent tool that includes a ferro rod and striker built into a durable plastic housing with a compartment that fits one cube of WetFire. This makes for a very compact all-inclusive, fire-starting package.

WetFire Burning in Water

Steel Wool

Common steel wool is one of the best fire-starting materials available. The

WetFire Cube in Esbit Stove

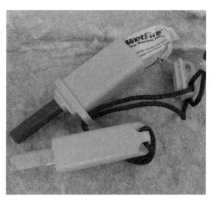

StrikeForce Fire Starter From
ForgeSurvivalSupply.com

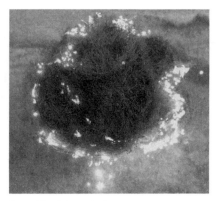

Steel Wool Smoldering

smallest spark will ignite the thin metal fibers into a smoldering ember that burns at a very high temperature. The smoldering steel wool can then be used to ignite combustible tinder, such as dried grass, leaves, paper, etc. Steel wool is readily available at any hardware and grocery store. It is also very cheap.

Like WetFire tinder, steel wool burns even when damp. Even if it's soaking wet, you can shake it out and ignite it within a few seconds. You can pack a good amount of steel wool in a very small container and it doesn't have an expiration date. Steel wool will ignite and smolder even in freezing conditions.

PET Balls

One of best fire starters I've ever used can be made at home in just a few minutes and costs virtually nothing. This homemade tinder only requires two ingredients: petroleum jelly and either cotton balls or dryer lint. (PET is short for petroleum—hence the name PET Balls.)

These are very easy to make. Simply saturate a cotton ball or comparable-sized chunk of dryer lint with a quarter-sized scoop of petroleum jelly.

Then, mix it in thoroughly so that all of the fibers are coated.

Lastly, roll each chunk into little balls and store them in a watertight container or resealable bag.

The petroleum jelly acts as a fire extender. It becomes a fuel source and turns the cotton/lint into a makeshift wick that will light with just a spark and then burn for several minutes. Without the petroleum jelly, the burn time would be just a few seconds—drastically reducing your window of opportunity to get a healthy fire going. In addition, the petroleum jelly

Dried Grass, Cattail Down, and Milkweed Down

Flat Rock Fire Platform

helps to waterproof the cotton/lint as well. Petroleum jelly can also be mixed with natural tinder such as dried grass, cattail down, or milkweed down with similar success.

For this reason, I always travel with a tube of Carmex lip balm, a petroleum-jelly-based product that can easily be used as a fire extender in an emergency.

To use a PET Ball, pull it apart to separate and expose the fine fibers. This increases surface area and facilitates airflow. Then, simply strike it with a spark from a fire steel or light it with a match or lighter and get ready to place small kindling on the flame.

BUILDING A FIRE

Igniting flammable fire tinder is one thing; building a fire and keeping it burning is a practiced skill in and of itself. Allow me to stray from "building your Bug Out Bag" for a few minutes to outline a simple five-step system for building a successful fire. There are many different ways to build a fire. This is the one I use most often.

Step 1: Fire Platform

A good fire platform is a solid foundation for any successful fire—especially in damp, snowy, or wet environments. The purpose of a fire platform is to keep your dry tinder kindling and initial flame off of the ground. Even the slightest bit of moisture can affect your fire-starting material's willingness to burn. Your platform can be constructed from a huge variety of materials—natural or manmade. I've used everything from flat rocks to a metal trash can lid. Three fire platform ideas are:

- flat rock
- tree bark
- wood branch

Tree Bark Fire Platform

Wood Branch Fire Platform

Step 3: Toothpick Tepee

Step 2: Tinder Bundle and Ignition

It is very important to have the next three phases of the fire building process prepared in *advance* before lighting your fire tinder. Time will be working against you and your only defense is proper preparation—especially when working with quick-burning tinder material.

When your platform is ready and you have all the sticks ready, ignite your fire tinder. In the photo for step 3 I'm using a cube of WetFire as tinder. Your fire kindling materials need to be as dry as possible. The material should snap and crack when you break them, not bend.

Step 3: Toothpick Tepee

Once your tinder bundle is burning, pile toothpick-sized twigs and splinters of wood in a tepee fashion around the burning tinder. Give these small twigs and splinters enough time to start burning. Fire needs oxygen to burn. It may be helpful to fan and blow the small flame to help intensify the heat.

Step 4: Q-Tip Tepee

Your next layer of fuel should be slightly larger than the first—about the size of Q-Tips. Stack these around the small fire in the same tepee arrangement. Allow them time to burn. Fan and blow as necessary.

Step 4: Q-Tip Tepee

Step 5: Pencil Tepee

Pencil Tepee With Feather Sticks

Step 5: Pencil Tepee

As with before, your next layer of fuel should be larger—about the diameter of a pencil. They should also be stacked like a tepee around the flame. Carving these into "feather sticks" will drastically improve your rate of success. To create a feather stick, carve back thin strips from the stick. This creates more surface area to burn on the stick.

At this point, your fire should be steadily burning on it's own. You can continue to stack on larger limbs and branches.

SUMMARY

Your Bug Out fire kit is one of the most important additions to your BOB. Spend some time in your backyard using your fire kit to make fire in a variety of weather conditions. If you don't know how to use the kit, it will be worthless in an emergency situation.

COMMON DISASTER CONSIDERATIONS

If you live in an area prone to heat waves, droughts, or wild fires keep at least 36" diameter of bare earth or noncombustible material around any open flames. Working with fire in areas prone to these natural disasters can be extremely dangerous. Prepare your fire/cooking area accordingly.

8 FIRST AID

IN A DISASTER EMERGENCY, you are almost guaranteed to be confronted with some kind of first aid need. From bee stings to broken bones and everything in between, anything is possible. Combine the disaster environment with fatigue, panic, hunger, fear, and disorder and you are exposed to all kinds of ways to be injured. Add "field medic" to your list of responsibilities during a Bug Out.

Insufficient first aid supplies during a chaotic disaster evacuation can make an already very bad situation worse. Proper treatment materials are must-haves in a first-aid emergency. There are no ideal substitutions. Pack size and weight restrictions will limit how much you can bring, but the goal is to pack enough first aid supplies to cover the majority of what could happen. Beyond this, you will have to improvise or wait.

First aid is a compartmentalized kit within your BOB. It should be easy to recognize by both sight and touch. This is the one category within your BOB that I actually recommend starting with a prepackaged kit—then supplement and customize it with additional items. Buying a "starter" kit saves time in collecting many of the basic first aid items. You can certainly build your own kit from scratch as well.

PREPACKAGED FIRST AID KITS

Prepackaged first aid kits are available in almost every grocery store, pharmacy, and general merchandise store. And all of these are inadequate for your Bug Out needs. For most of these kits, you'll find the manufacturers put more thought into the fancy packaging than actually assembling the contents. *Don't buy one of these generic*

Several Generic First Aid Kits

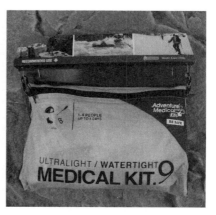

Specialty Four-Person First Aid Kit by Adventure Medical Kits

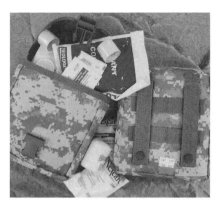

Military-Style Specialty Kit

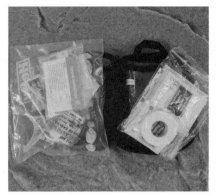

First Aid Kit Supplies Packed in Resealable Bags

first aid kits! You need to start with a more substantial base kit designed specifically for outdoor enthusiasts.

Most outdoor sports stores (and related retail websites) have a first aid section within the camping and backpacking department. Two great sources for emergency first aid kits are Nitro-Pak (nitro-pak.com) and Adventure Medical Kits (adventuremedicalkits.com).

Camping and backpacking pre-packaged first aid kits are the kind you want to use as your base kit. Off the shelf, they are still too inadequate for a BOB, but these kits are more substantial and specialized than general-purpose kits. Many of these kits are also designed to contain enough material to adequately treat a specific number of people, which can really save you time in putting together the first aid kit for your family or Bug Out team.

Purchase a kit designed for the number of people in your household and modify it by adding items from those listed in this chapter.

FIRST AID KIT CONTAINER

The first step in assembling your final kit is choosing a container. If you purchase a premade specialty kit, its container will probably work just fine. The only important factor about your first aid kit container is that it must be waterproof. If the container it not watertight, you will need to package the items in several watertight resealable bags. Water and moisture will completely compromise the efficacy of many items in your kit including bandages, gauze, and pills.

In addition to packing groups of items in resealable bags, I pack my entire kit in a watertight flexible map case that can be purchased in the kayak department of most outdoor retailers.

These plastic cases are durable, flexible, and made specifically for keeping items dry. As you'll see in chapter twelve, this is the same style case I use for my important documents.

KIT CONTENTS

Following is a list of contents that should be included in your BOB first aid kit. For applicable line items, I break down the quantities for one-to-two person kits and four-to-six person kits. Many of these items can be purchased in small quantities from the travel-size section at any pharmacy.

Cut and Wound Items

- **Antiseptic Wipes**
  1–2 persons: 10
  4–6 persons: 15
- **Adhesive Bandages** (1"×3")
  1–2 persons: 12
  4–6 persons: 18
- **Adhesive Bandages** (Knuckle & Elbow)
  1–2 persons: 3
  4–6 persons: 5
- **Adhesive Wound Closure Strips**
  1–2 persons: 5
  4–6 persons: 8
- **Sterile Gauze Pads** (3"×3")
  1–2 persons: 4
  4–6 persons: 8
- **Sterile Gauze Roll Bandage** (2", 2 yards)
  1–2 persons: 1
  4–6 persons: 2
- **Medical Tape** (1", 10 yards)
  1–2 persons: 1
  4–6 persons: 2

First Aid Kit Packaged in Waterproof Map Case

Antiseptic Wipes and Adhesive Bandages

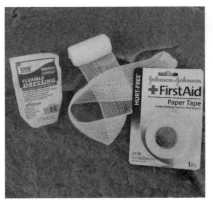

Gauze Roll and Medical Tape

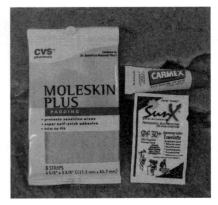

Moleskin, Sunscreen Towelettes, and Lip Balm

Blister/Rash/Burn Treatments
- **Moleskin Patches** (4"×5")
  - *1–2 persons:* 2
  - *4–6 persons:* 4
- **Sunscreen:** Small tube or towelettes
- **Lip Balm:** Petroleum-based lip balm can be mixed with fire tinder and used as a flame extender to help start a fire

Support
- **Elastic Wrap Bandage** (3", 2 yards): For wrapping sprained and or strained joints

Medicines/Ointments/Washes
- **Antibiotic Ointment**
  - *1–2 persons:* 1 small tube or 2 single-use packets
  - *4–6 persons:* 1 small tube or 4 single-use packets

- **Alcohol Swabs**
  - *1–2 persons:* 4
  - *4–6 persons:* 6
- **Ibuprofen Pills:** Reduce fever and treat pain or inflammation
  - *1–2 persons:* 5 200mg pills
  - *4–6 persons:* 8 200mg pills
- **Antihistamine Pills:** Reduce cold and allergy symptoms
  - *1–2 persons:* 4 25mg pills (diphenhydramine hydrochloride)
  - *4–6 persons:* 6 25mg pills (diphenhydramine hydrochloride)
- **Acetaminophen Pills:** Reduce fever and treat general aches and pains
  - *1–2 persons:* 5 200mg pills
  - *4–6 persons:* 8 200mg pills

- **Aspirin Pills:** Reduce fever and treat pain and inflammation
    - *1–2 persons:* 3 325mg pills
    - *4–6 persons:* 6 325mg pills
- **Imodium pills:** Antidiarrheal medicine
    - *1–2 persons:* 2 125mg pills (simethicone)
    - *4–6 persons:* 4 125mg pills (simethicone)
- **Antiemetic (Dramamine):** For motion sickness
    - *1–2 persons:* 3 50mg pills (dimenhydrinate)
    - *4–6 persons:* 6 50mg pills (dimenhydrinate)
- **Baby Vitamins**
- **Visine Eye Wash**

Small aluminum and plastic pill containers are available at any pharmacy for just a few dollars. These are perfect for storing a variety of medicines within your first aid kit. They are crush resistant, compact and waterproof. I use several of these containers in my BOB for a variety of mini-kits, one being my mini fishing kit.

MISCELLANEOUS MEDICAL ITEMS

- **Rubber Gloves:** Can also be used as water containers, and to keep items dry, such as fire tinder
- **Tweezers:** For splinters and ticks
- **Safety Pins:** Quantity of five in a variety of sizes—for gear repairs and/or emergency sutures
- **Insect Repellent:** 100-percent DEET is most effective. Many insect repellents are also flammable and can be used as a fire-starting aid in damp or windy conditions (available in small single-use packets or small spray bottles).

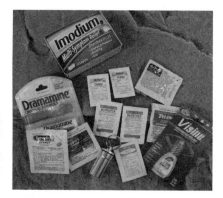

Variety of First Aid Medicines

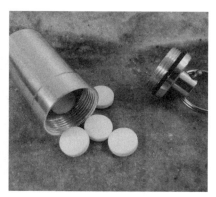

Aluminum Pill Capsule

Rubber Gloves, Tweezers, and Safety Pins

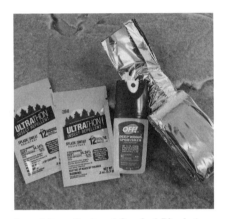

Insect Repellent and Survival Blanket

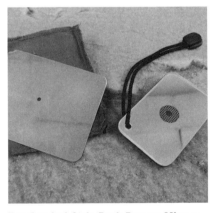

Two Survival-Style Pack Rescue Mirrors

Mirror

A mirror can be a very useful first aid and hygiene tool, especially when traveling alone. It's useful when self-treating any type of injury to your eyes, face, head, or back. Once while back-country camping, I nearly had to cut my trip short because of something in my eye. Since that experience, I always camp with a small survival mirror regardless of how lightweight I'm trying to pack. I also include one in my BOB.

A mirror is also a proven signaling tool. Sunlight reflected by a mirror can be seen for miles, and it's perfect for trying to signal a rescue plane, vehicle, or team. A specially designed signal mirror has a "sighting hole" in its middle to help the reflected sun rays directly at your target. The two mirrors in the photo are both signal mirrors. I carry a small dog-tag sized signal mirror in my BOB that doubles as a first-aid and hygiene mirror. It's small but mighty.

Emergency Survival Blanket

Survival blankets are windproof and waterproof and reflect 90 percent of your body heat. They are a very flexible multi-use survival product. In cold weather, you can wrap yourself in the blanket to stay warm by conserving as much body heat as possible. In full sun, the blanket can be set

MULTI-USE ITEM: EMERGENCY SURVIVAL BLANKET

★★★★★ FIVE-STAR RATING

An emergency survival blanket can be used for a variety of survival related functions. They make excellent signaling devices. They can also be used as a makeshift poncho, a quick waterproof shelter, a ground tarp or gear cover. All of these features from a product that weighs only 3.2 ounces.

Used in the Traditional Method as a Survival Blanket

Survival Blanket Poncho Wrap

Makeshift Lean-To Shelter

Waterproof Gear Cover With Log Weights

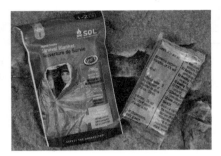

Dog Tag Rescue Signal Mirror

Adventure Medical Kit Heat Sheet Survival Blanket

in reverse as a shade shelter to reflect the sun's rays. My survival blanket of choice is the Heat Sheet by Adventure Medical Kits. The Heat Sheet survival blanket is thicker and more durable than the average silver mylar blanket.

One side of the Heat Sheet is a bright orange color, making it a very useful emergency rescue signal. It also has survival instructions and diagrams printed directly on the blanket for quick reference. At 60"×96",

the Heat Sheet is large enough to accommodate two adults, which is really a nice feature.

PERSONALIZING YOUR FIRST AID KIT
Medications

Each individual has his or her own very specific medical needs. You must consider each of these needs when assembling your first aid kit. Below are areas for consideration:

- daily prescriptions

SURVIVAL QUICK TIP

Survival blankets don't come with tie-down points, such as grommets. This can make them tricky to tie down when using them for shelters or gear covers. A quick tip is to put a small rock in the corner and tie your rope around this rock. This creates a very solid tie-down point that will not tear the blanket.

Rock in Corner of Survival Blanket for Tie-Down Point

- allergy medicines/emergency allergic reaction medicines
- asthma inhalers
- medical instruments, such as syringes, blood sugar testers, etc.
- special baby and children's medicines

Consider keeping full prescriptions in your BOB if possible. It may be difficult to get a refill even after you reach safety. To keep the medication fresh, rotate the prescriptions in your BOB on a regular basis. When you refill the script, put the new one in the BOB and take the old one out for your use. This system should allow you to use up all your medication before it expires.

Glasses and Contacts

If you wear prescription glasses, keep a backup pair in your BOB. One of your older prescriptions will work just fine. Otherwise, breaking or losing your primary pair can leave you very vulnerable and dependant—neither being ideal in a Bug Out environment. You want to be a resource to your crew, not a liability.

Don't rely on contacts as your only vision source. Pack a backup pair of glasses even if you pack a backup pair of contacts. Also be sure to pack a travel-size bottle of contact solution and a contact case.

SUMMARY

Remember, this is a 72-Hour BOB. It's easy to get carried away and over-pack only to realize at the end of the project that you need to reevaluate your contents. Be thorough but not excessive when it comes to first aid. I've seen guys pack entire surgical kits with IV drips and anesthesia medications in their Bug Out Bags. I choose to keep it fairly simple. You will have to draw your own limitations.

COMMON DISASTER CONSIDERATIONS

If you live in an area prone to nuclear attack or fallout, please take note of these special considerations and/or pack items.

Potassium iodide pills taken before exposure to nuclear fallout can provide almost 100 percent protection from thyroid damage associated with radiation exposure. High-risk nuclear areas would be large cities prone to military attack, coastal states at risk of exposure from overseas trade winds, and areas near nuclear power plants. Plan on a ten-day supply of potassium iodide pills per person. A vast amount of information about nuclear threats can be found on www.ki4u.com. Potassium iodide pills can be purchased online at www.campingsurvival.com.

9 ▸ HYGIENE

PEOPLE OFTEN UNDERESTIMATE the importance of personal hygiene when preparing for disaster survival. It's an easy category to overlook. In reality, hygiene-related issues are some of the most critical and complicated concerns in the aftermath of a disaster. We take so many modern conveniences for granted:

- running water
- working restrooms
- clean clothing
- clothes washers and dryers
- access to cleaning supplies
- regular trash-removal service
- electricity

Most, if not all, of these luxuries will be off-grid or unavailable during and after a large-scale disaster. There are two areas of hygiene to consider in disaster survival: public and personal.

PUBLIC HYGIENE

An incredible network of people, facilities, and machines organize each day to relocate, dispose of, disinfect, and treat our insane amount of garbage, raw sewage, hazardous materials, and medical waste. Removal and proper handling of animal and human corpses is included in this orchestra of daily events.

Historically, large-scale disasters cripple the normal waste removal and treatment services that we depend on to keep our cities clean.

The inability to properly deal with unclean waste presents life-threatening challenges.

During this time there is a much higher risk for the spread of disease and illness. Your countermeasures against this risk are to keep your personal hygiene and waste removal in check.

PERSONAL HYGIENE

Everything becomes less efficient and productive when dirty or soiled—including the human body. Not only is personal hygiene important to prevent the spread of disease and infec-

Trash Dumpsters

Sewage Treatment Plant

tions, but it also impacts morale. Keeping your spirits high and maintaining a semi-sense of normality is very important. When survival is 90 percent mental, anything you can do to boost your morale goes a long way. This starts with packing items in your BOB to maintain personal hygiene.

BOB PERSONAL HYGIENE PACK ITEMS

Create a mini-hygiene kit within your BOB to keep these items together and easy to find.

All-Purpose Bar of Soap or Packaged Soap Sheets

Soap is the recommended cleaning agent for open wounds until you can access medical treatment. You can obviously also use soap to bathe and wash other items, such as clothing and cooking utensils. Dirt and body oils can clog the breathable fibers of your clothing, reducing its insulating properties. Washing soiled garments keeps them functioning at peak performance. My BOB hygiene kit includes a hotel-size bar of soap in a resealable bag. There's no way you would use up this much soap in a 72-hour time frame.

Coleman makes a pretty cool soap product called Soap Sheets. I found the ones photographed at Wal-Mart. Fifty little soap sheets come packaged in a small, compact flip-top container. The sheets dissolve into a sudsy lather when they come in contact with water. The container is not watertight, so be sure to pack these in a resealable bag if you choose this option.

Tampons and Sanitary Napkins

Besides their intended purpose, tampons and sanitary napkins have a

Travel-Size All-Purpose Soap or Packaged Soap Sheets

Sanitary Napkin Used as Emergency Bandage With Duct Tape

variety of survival uses. They can be used as gauze-like first aid bandages and secured with duct tape or medical tape.

They can also be used to pre-filter cloudy/dirty water.

In addition, they make excellent fire tinder. You can mix the cotton-ball-like material with your Carmex lip balm to create a fire starter that will burn for several minutes.

These items are an excellent multi-use BOB survival pack item.

Disinfecting Wet Napkins

Antibacterial wet naps are available in grocery stores. Find them in the paper product aisle. (Be sure to buy brands specifically designed for use on skin. Don't buy the surface-cleaner wipes—they're too harsh and may cause damage to your skin.) These are a perfect bathing alternative. A quick "spit-bath" with a couple of wet naps will help to clean your body of bacteria, grime, and body oils. These are especially useful when water is scarce or in cold weather. Wet naps can also be used to clean and maintain survival gear such as your cooking pot and utensils.

Travel-Size Hand Sanitizer

Hand sanitizer has a high alcohol content, which makes it perfect for quickly disinfecting your hands and other body parts if necessary. And it does not require precious water to be effective. It can also be used to disinfect small scrapes and cuts. However, any open wounds should be washed only with soap and water. The alcohol content in hand sanitizer also makes it a viable fire starter. It burns fast but could be useful as a fuel source in less-than-perfect fire-building conditions.

Sanitary Napkin as Water Filter

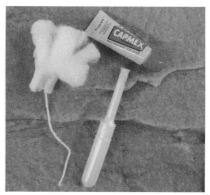

Tampon With Carmex Lip Balm

Lightload Towels Opened and Two Compressed Towels

Sample Specialty Car Shammy

Diapers

If you will be traveling with a young child who isn't potty trained, you'll need an ample supply of diapers for 72 hours. This is critical to group hygiene. Pack disposable diapers, even if you use cloth diapers at home. Update the diapers in your BOB as soon as your child moves up in size. (You may need to do this every two to three months if the child is under one year of age. This is also a good time to update clothes you have packed for the baby.) An additional stock of wet napkins and a small container of baby powder and diaper cream (to prevent diaper rash) is also recommended.

Small Pack Towel

Do *not* pack a normal cotton bath or beach towel. Items made of 100 percent cotton take forever to dry. Plus these are way too heavy and bulky, and you don't need a full-sized towel.

You need a towel made from a super-absorbent material that is lightweight, easy to ring out, and quick to dry. The Lightload Towel is a very popular brand of this style towel and is available at ultralighttowels. com. These towels are made from a 100 percent viscose material and can double as a water filter, first-aid bandage, strainer, fire starter, diaper, mask, and scarf. They're compacted into a small, waterproof puck that is the perfect size for a BOB. Even when opened, they can still be squished into very small spaces. I carry two of the 12"×24" towels in my BOB. They're small, but if using it to dry off your body, you can ring it out several times in the process.

Car shammies/chamois are another great BOB towel option. Made from absorbent, sponge-like fabric, they are durable, washable, lightweight, and quick to dry. Find them

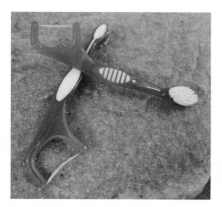

Two Mini Travel Toothbrush/Pick

Travel-Size Toilet Paper

in the auto detailing section in any discount department store.

Any of these camp towels can be disinfected by boiling in water. Ultra-light packers can use their bandana as a camp towel.

Mini Travel Toothbrush/Pick

You can certainly survive for 72 hours without a toothbrush, so this item is optional. However, miniature travel-size toothbrush and floss combination items are cheap and weigh almost nothing. They are also disposable.

With two functions in one tool, this is a smart item to carry. It is one of those morale-boosting items. This is more a mental than physical exercise that reminds you that "normal" is still possible.

Toilet Paper

Be sure to pack a few yards of toilet paper unless you want to use leaves and/or scavenged paper. Prepackaged travel rolls like the one shown are available for a couple of bucks, or you can just roll some up and store it in a resealable bag like I do.

SUMMARY

Even in a short-term 72-Hour Bug Out, hygiene has mental and physical repercussions that affect your ability to survive. Taking simple steps towards maintaining cleanliness can prevent the onset and spread of disease as well as make bugging out more comfortable.

COMMON DISASTER CONSIDER-ATIONS

If you live in an area prone to heat waves or droughts, pack extra wet naps. When water is scarce, personal hygiene can become more difficult.

10 TOOLS

INDEPENDENT "OFF-GRID" SURVIVAL requires us to perform tasks that are completely out of the normal daily routine for the vast majority of modern society. Without the proper tools, even the simplest of survival duties can be extremely difficult, time-consuming, and labor-intensive. A small assortment of specialized tools is a critical addition to every BOB.

BUG OUT TOOL 1: SURVIVAL KNIFE

Your survival knife is without question one of the top three most important items in your BOB. (An ignition device and a metal container are the other top two.) For many, choosing a survival knife is a very personal decision. With thousands of knives in the marketplace, the choices can be somewhat overwhelming. Don't be fooled by what you see in the movies. The fancy knives seen in survival movies are more for prop collectors than for real survivalists. By design,

a survival knife should be fairly simple. It should be about function not "flash." In this section, I will discuss why a survival knife is so important as well as the attributes of a good survival knife. I will also give you my top four survival knife picks to help get you started in your knife search.

Functions of a Survival Knife

Your knife is probably the most multifunction piece in your entire BOB. Its list of survival uses are endless. You don't know how much you need a good, sharp cutting tool in a survival situation until you don't have one. I learned this first hand on a three-day survival trip in which I was not able to bring a modern knife. I will never take my knife for granted again. Below is a short list of tasks a knife can assist you with:

- cutting
- hunting
- dressing game

Survival Knife on Belt

Using Pommel to Hammer Tent Stake

Carving Feather Sticks for Fire Building

Carving Frog Gig

Rescue Signal With Reflection From Sun

Survival Knife Strapped to Bug Out Bag

- hammering shelter anchors
- digging
- self defense
- splitting/chopping
- making fire
- carving
- signal mirror (if blade is polished steel)
- building shelter
- food preparation

You will use your knife often. Keep it very accessible. I actually store my survival knife strapped to the outside of my BOB.

In a BOB situation, I plan to immediately secure my knife on my belt where it will be ready for quick deployment.

I have no interest in digging through my pack to access my knife.

Fixed Blade Knife and Folding Knife

Spyderco Native Knife

Rat Tail Tang (left) and Full Tang Blade (right)

ATTRIBUTES OF A SURVIVAL KNIFE

Fixed Blade

Your survival knife should have a fixed blade—not a folding- or lock-blade style. True, folding knifes can be more convenient to carry, but strength is compromised at the folding joint. If the knife breaks during rigorous use, you are SOL. If you really like folding knives, carry one as a backup but not as your primary survival knife. I carry a Spyderco Native locking folder as my everyday-carry knife and it will be my BOB backup knife as well.

Full Tang

The phrase *full tang* means the metal knife blade and handle are made from one solid piece of metal. The metal handle is then sandwiched with knife scales to form a grip. Full tang construction is much more substantial and less likely to break during hard use. The alternate to a full tang is a rat tail tang. A rat tail tang is much smaller and narrow.

A full tang blade is much more robust and stable. It can withstand incredible abuse from demanding tasks, such as splitting wood—often called batoning in the survival community.

I own many non-full tang knives and love them all. However, they aren't my first choice in survival knife picks.

Using Survival Knife to Split Wood (Batoning)

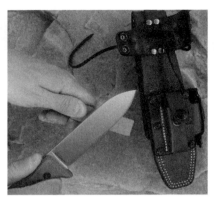

Sharpening Knife on Whet Stone

Sharp

Your survival knife should be razor sharp. It should shave the hair off your forearm. If it doesn't, buy a whet stone and hone the blade until it does. You should take pride in your knife's razor edge. A dull knife is more difficult and cumbersome to use effectively. It requires more effort and pressure to perform tasks, which leads to erratic carving and cutting. A sharp knife is actually safer to use and is a more precise cutting tool that requires less energy and time as compared to using a dull knife.

Size Does Matter

As a rough estimate, the overall length of your knife should be in between 7" and 11". A knife that is much larger that 11" isn't practical for delicate and detailed tasks. However, a knife smaller than 7" is less capable of performing tasks that require a larger blade—especially demanding jobs.

Pointed Blade/Single Edge

Your knife needs to have a pointed blade tip. The point comes in handy for all kinds of chores. I broke the point off of my favorite survival knife and it drastically impacted the knife's effectiveness as a useful tool. I eventually had to replace it.

Also, the knife blade should not be double-sided. Choose a single-edged blade only. You won't have a need for two sharp edges. The flat back ridge of a knife blade can actually serve several functions. Below are some of the most common:

- striking a fire steel
- used as a stabilizing platform for thumb or hand
- pounding surface while splitting or batoning wood

Stabilizing Knife With Thumb While Carving

Two Kydex Knife Sheaths

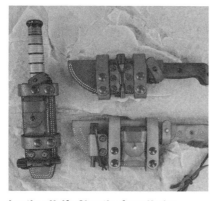

Leather Knife Sheaths from Hedge-hogleatherworks.com

I use the back ridge of my knife in these ways all of the time. A sharp, double-edged blade makes these important functions impossible.

Quality Sheath

There is nothing I hate more than a substandard knife sheath. Many knife enthusiasts feel the same way I do about quality sheaths. Poorly designed and cheaply made sheaths can be frustrating and dangerous to use.

A quality sheath should hold your knife in place snugly and securely. Your knife should not fall out when the sheath is shaken or turned upside down. At the same time, though, the knife should be easy to put in and take out of the sheath. You should be able to comfortably remove and insert the knife single-handed. Personally, I prefer molded Kydex or leather sheaths. Both are rugged materials that can handle extreme environments.

Even some great knifes come with horrible sheaths. I've lost knives in the field due to poor sheath retention. A knife is an investment. If you find a great survival knife but hate the sheath, there are several companies that can make custom kydex or leather sheaths specifically for your knife. Hedgehogleatherworks.com in St. Louis is one such company; they make aftermarket leather sheaths for several very popular survival knives including the Blackbird SK-5 and the Becker BK2 listed in my top survival knife picks. I own several Hedgehog Leatherworks knife sheaths and can attest to their quality and workmanship. Another company, SharkTac, specializes in custom-molded kydex sheaths.

FOUR GREAT SURVIVAL KNIVES

Blackbird SK-5 Survival Knife

The Blackbird SK-5 has been meticulously designed by survivalist Paul Scheiter. It meets all of the survival-knife criteria listed earlier in the chapter. It is extremely well suited for any kind of survival environment or disaster-emergency scenario. The Blackbird features a very solid spear point tip and an abrupt angle grind on the back of the blade that is out-standing for striking a fire steel rod. The leveled pommel provides enough surface area for light-duty pounding. It also has a slot on the handle for attaching a lanyard or wrist leash. As an added bonus, the ergonomic grip prevents hot spots and blisters that form on the hand after repeated handling of the knife. The blade is made from 154CM, a high-grade stainless knife steel requiring relatively no field maintenance when on the go. This is a plus, especially in tropical, wet, or humid environments when lesser-grade steels might corrode and rust. 154CM grade steel also holds a very good edge even during strenuous cutting.

Blackbird SK-5 Specs:
- Overall length: 10"
- Blade length: 5"
- Blade thickness: .13"
- Price: $149.00

Blackbird SK-5 Survival Knife

Becker BK2 Knife Shown With the Black Nylon Sheath That Came With It and Also a Custom Hedgehog Leatherworks Leather Sheath

- hedgehogleatherworks.com to order

Becker BK2 Companion Knife

The Becker BK2 is very simple but incredibly functional. It includes everything you need and nothing you don't. This is an example of a classic, no frills, workhorse survival knife. One very cool feature many people aren't aware of is that the knife handles can be removed with a small allen wrench. The handles have recessed cavities on the inside that allow you to store small kit items such as fish hooks and line or fire tinder. The tang also protrudes from the bottom and can be used for pounding and batoning.

BK2 specs:
- Overall length: 10.5"
- Blade length: 5.25"
- Blade thickness: .25"

- Price: approximately $70
- Where to order: www. willowhavenoutdoor.com

Gerber Big Rock Camp Knife

I realize that not everyone can afford to spend seventy dollars or more on a survival knife for their BOB. If you are budget conscious. Gerber makes several excellent full tang, fixed-blade knives. For example, the Gerber Big Rock pictured here is available online and at many outdoor retailers. It is a very solid full tang knife that performs very well with demanding use. It has a nonslip rubberized textured handle for a sure grip in almost any condition. It also has a lanyard hole and a half serrated blade for dual purpose cutting and ripping. I've used this knife on many occasions and have not been disappointed.

Gerber Big Rock Camp Knife

Mora 840MG Camp Knife

Schrade Tough Multi-Tool

Knife Blade on Leatherman MUT Multi-Tool

Big Rock specs:
- Overall length: 9.5"
- Blade length: 4.5"
- Blade thickness: .19"
- Price: $34.99
- Where to order: www.rei.com

Mora of Sweden 840MG Clipper

The Mora of Sweden knife company has a rich history in manufacturing outdoor lifestyle knives. While not a full tang blade, you won't find a better knife for the money spent—only around fifteen dollars. I've used and abused this knife on countless adventures and have yet to destroy one. Because it does not meet all of my survival knife criteria, I wouldn't recommend it for your primary BOB knife, but it is an excellent backup blade.

840MG specs:
- Overall length: 8.5"
- Blade length: 3.88"

- Blade thickness: .08"
- Price: $15
- Where to order: www. willowhavenoutdoor.com

BOB TOOL 2: MULTI-TOOL

A good multi-tool is like having a compact, lightweight toolbox in your BOB. Many multi-tools have up to ten different tools built into one unit. Like your knife, these tools can and will be used for countless tasks in a survival environment.

Following is a list of tools that should be integrated into any multi-tool that you purchase for your BOB.

Knife

I know, you've already chosen a survival knife. The multi-tool knife is not your survival knife. This one is your backup knife just in case something happens to your primary. The knife blade in your multi-tool will be much

Saw Blade on Leatherman MUT Multi-Tool

Leatherman MUT Sawing Branch

Pliers Tool on Schrade Tough Multi-Tool

Multi-Tool Pliers Holding Hot Cooking Pot

smaller than the blade on your main knife and might be better suited for certain detail-oriented tasks. Regardless, having redundancy in the cutting tool department is never bad practice. No knife is bad news.

Mini Saw Blade

A mini saw blade can buzz through 2"–3" limbs and small trees in no time. This can certainly be helpful when collecting fire wood or building makeshift shelters.

Pliers

When you really need a set of pliers, nothing else will quite do the trick. It's one of those items that you don't think about until you need it. Among other tasks, pliers can be used to loosen or tighten nuts and bolts, bend metal or wire and hold hot cooking pots. In

Cutting Fence With Multi-Tool Wire Cutters

Repairing Vehicle With Multi-Tool

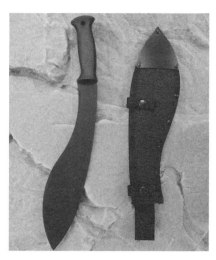

Kukri Style Machete

cold weather, pliers can be more useful than your own hands with many mechanical tasks.

At the base of your pliers should be wire cutters. These can be used to strip wire if necessary. They can also be used to cut snare wire or fencing. You never know what kind of crazy situation you are going to be faced with. Rather than dull and damage your knife blade, use a tool designed to get the job done quickly and with less energy.

Cross-Point and Flat-Head Screwdrivers

Both styles of screwdrivers are a must. These two screw bits will fit 95 percent of all the screws you might encounter. They can be used with your own gear repair and for a myriad of potential tasks along the way. I've used my flat-head screwdriver on several occasions as a mini pry bar.

MACHETE (OPTIONAL)

If you anticipate going through or into any kind of wilderness area during a potential Bug Out, a machete can be an incredibly useful too. Machetes make fast work of chopping and gathering wood. They are also useful when clearing thick brush and blazing trails through dense undergrowth. A machete can be used to carve out snow blocks for building

Latin-Style Machete

Latin-Style Machete inside of BOB

wind shelters. It makes a very efficient digging tool as well.

Personally, I like the added benefits a machete offers and have chosen to pack one in my BOB. Many tasks can be performed faster and with less energy with the use of a machete instead of your survival knife. It certainly isn't a necessary piece of Bug Out gear. This is a luxury item.

SUMMARY

The sky is the limit with all of the situations you could face during a disaster Bug Out. Having a small assortment of tools on hand can save you valuable time—not to mention wear and tear on your body. I've always tried to live by the phrase "work smarter, not harder." Tools allow you to do this.

COMMON DISASTER CONSIDERATIONS

If you live in an area that experiences heavy snowfall, you might consider packing a lightweight collapsible snow shovel in your BOB during the winter months. Remove it in your summer season review. The ability to shovel deep snow may prove to be an invaluable survival option. Several manufacturers sell pack shovels designed for climbers and mountaineers that are surprisingly compact and lightweight. A good collapsible shovel for this is the Black Diamond Deploy.

11 ▶ LIGHTING

IN A BUG OUT SCENARIO, the electricity will almost certainly be off-grid. Besides the sun and moon, your only light source might be inside your Bug Out Bag. Not having a flashlight of some kind can stop you dead in your tracks during low-light or dark conditions. There are countless reasons to include a light source. The most obvious are listed below.

LOW-LIGHT OR NIGHTTIME TRAVEL

Traveling at night can be advantageous in some instances. In desert regions, for example, traveling by night is cooler and conserves precious water versus traveling under full-sun by day. Depending on the circumstances, you may want to avoid interaction with other survivors by traveling at night and remaining low-key. Regardless, traveling in nighttime or low-light conditions without a flashlight can be very dangerous. Even a very minor injury can be a devastating setback and travel burden.

SETTING UP CAMP IN LOW LIGHT

If you do travel during daylight hours, you'll get farther faster if you can begin traveling at first light and stop after twilight. This means you'll be setting up and breaking up camp in low light. For ease and safety, you'll need to be able to see what you are doing. Carrying a light source increases your productive time on your route and in camp settings.

SIGNALING

A high intensity flashlight makes an effective signaling device. It can be used for a variety of applications.

Signaling Within Your Bug Out Team

The members of my Bug Out Team and I have developed a very simple communications code using flashlights. We can use "flashes" of light to relay basic messages should the need arise to communicate from afar or in silence. Each of us keeps a small laminated note card in our BOB with the signal codes. Below are a few from our list:

- 1 short flash: *Safe*
- 2 short flashes: *Come to our location*
- 3 short flashes: *Meet you at the BOL (Bug Out Location)*
- 4 short flashes: *Leave me or Keep moving*
- 1 short, 1 long flash: *Danger*
- 1 short, 1 short, 1 long flash: *Affirmative*
- 1 long, 1 short, 1 short flash: *Negative*

Signaling for Rescue

A flashlight can also be used to signal for rescue. Besides just waving it around to get a rescue team's attention,

Ultralight Head lamp: Black Diamond ION

Mini Maglite

there are internationally recognized distress signals. The most popular is Morse Code for the letters SOS. In Morse Code, the letter S is three dots and the letter O is three dashes. Thus, using your flashlight, the SOS distress signal would be three short bursts of light then three longer bursts of light then three shorts bursts of light. Then, this pattern is repeated. Typically, the longer burst should be equal in length to the three short bursts combined.

LIGHTING OPTIONS

When it comes to the lighting category, I suggest packing one main flashlight, one very small backup light, and one alternative light source.

Main Flashlight: LED Headlamp

Get a hands-free LED headlamp. Don't bother with any other styles for your primary BOB light source. The most obvious benefit of a head-lamp is that both of your hands are free to work. They are also extremely lightweight and the LED models last a very long time before new batteries are needed. Some models weigh in at only a few ounces. There are a huge variety of headlamps on the market at varying price points. Regardless of your budget, I'm sure there is one to meet your needs.

Headlamps provide ample light for normal tasks such as setting up camp, preparing meals and traveling. These are the perfect BOB lighting source—compact, lightweight, bright and long-lasting.

Two Great Backups

1. Mini Maglite LED. The mini Maglite LED is a perfect backup BOB flashlight. Below are some reasons why I love it:

- durable
- waterproof

Photon Brand LED Mini Light

Photon Light as Zipper Pull

- shines an impressive light beam for its size
- small and compact
- lightweight
- long-lasting battery life
- extra bulb stored inside handle

I've gone on many overnight camps when I've used the Mini Maglite exclusively. It is a good, reliable tool.

2. Mini Keychain LED. These little keychain-style LED lights are surprisingly bright for their size. They are also very cheap, typically around five dollars. If you are a minimalist packer, then these are an excellent solution. They can be attached to zipper pulls or tucked into almost any small space. I keep mine as a zipper pull on one of my smaller kits. They are also virtually indestructible. The Photon brand (my choice) has a crush-proof bulb and is visible over one mile.

ALTERNATE LIGHT SOURCES

While neither of the following options are completely necessary, they are both small and lightweight with unique benefits in a survival/rescue scenario. Because of this, I have included them as recommended pack items.

Candle

Any small candle will work just fine. The one I use is 1" in diameter and 4" tall. The brand is 9-Hour Candle and it's designed specifically for survival and preparedness applications. It has a long, steady burn time (nine hours).

A candle can be used for light in a base camp or shelter but also can be helpful while starting a fire in less-than-perfect conditions. If you find yourself working with damp fire tinder, you can light the candle first and use it to ignite your tinder. This is a much more efficient way to start a fire

9-Hour Candle

Glow Sticks

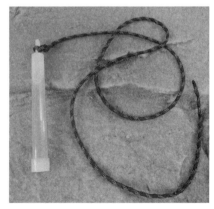

Glow Stick Fitted With 36" Length of Paracord

and helps to conserve your ignition source. In a small, protected shelter, the flame from a candle can also be used as a heat source to raise the temperature a few degrees if necessary. This is especially true in a snow-cave-style shelter.

Glow Sticks

Snap-style glow sticks typically last anywhere from two to four hours and can be an excellent overhead lighting solution when hung from the ceiling of a shelter or tent. They also make a highly visible nighttime signaling device. There are two important attributes to a good visual rescue signal. The first is motion. The second is that it looks out of place from its surroundings. This can be accomplished with shape, color, or both. The best way to signal using a glow stick is to attach a 36" length of cord onto one end and swing it in circles as fast as you can while facing your target.

The produces a very unique circular motion of light that can be seen for miles.

SUMMARY

Just for kicks, I weighed all of my lighting tools:

- one headlamp
- one Photon keychain light
- one 9-Hour Candle
- one glow stick

Glow Stick Rescue Signaling Technique

All Lighting Items Fit In Your Palm

The total weight came in at 7.2 ounces—not even half a pound! And all of them combined fit into the palm of my hand.

Just these few ounces can make such a huge difference in a disaster survival scenario. They can drastically impact your chances of a successful Bug Out and rescue.

12 COMMUNICATIONS

THE COMMUNICATIONS CATEGORY encompasses a variety of topics. Ultimately, communication deals with anything related to:

- sending information
- receiving information
- recording information
- navigation

When large-scale disasters strike, you can no longer depend on normal communication services. "Normal" will not exist for hours, days, and maybe weeks. Most, if not all, communication services will go off-grid. Cell phones and landline phones probably will not work. Local radio and TV stations will most likely not be broadcasting. And digital GPS systems may be inoperable. Lastly, you can forget about getting an internet connection. A large-scale disaster will completely disconnect you and the affected area from the rest of the world for an undetermined amount of time. This will inevitably lead to a great deal of chaos, panic, and disorder. To successfully navigate through this chaotic aftermath, you need to make preparations in advance. Below are several communications-related topics that need to be considered when assembling your Bug Out Bag.

CELL PHONE

It's almost guaranteed that your cell phone will not be working during a disaster Bug Out. Either local towers will be destroyed or the networks will be overwhelmed with volume. Despite this, you need to bring your cell phone with you just in case. In past recorded disasters, survivors have had more success sending and receiving text messages than actual phone calls. Even a sporadic text message could be very instrumental in communicating with friends and loved ones. In the remote chance that your cell phone can send/receive calls or texts, it will be your main point of contact—making it an incredibly valuable asset.

Many cell phones will not last seventy-two hours on one charge. I recommend packing either a second fully charged battery or a manual hand-crank charger. There are several affordable hand-crank chargers on the market with optional adaptors to fit virtually any cell phone make

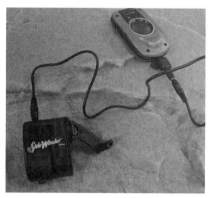

Sidewinder Hand-Crank Cell Phone Charger

and model. I picked up the one in the photo for fifteen dollars on Amazon. It charges a cell phone and also has a built-in LED light for emergency lighting. My Etón FR300 Emergency Radio (detailed in the next section) also has a hand-crank cell phone charger port. This is an awesome built-in feature.

If bugging out by vehicle, be sure to have a car charger.

There are also solar chargers. These, however, are useless without sun, so don't rely solely on them. Even in a typically sunny environment, disaster conditions may block the sun.

Etón FR300 Multi-Purpose Emergency Radio

EMERGENCY RADIO

An emergency radio is a great communications addition to your BOB. This may be your only source of incoming news while on your Bug Out journey. Knowing disaster updates can help you coordinate your travel and plan your routes. Radio updates can also provide information about safe and/or dangerous areas as well as rescue points, supply schedules, or imminent threats.

There are many makes and models of emergency radios available. The one pictured above from Etón Corporation (etoncorp.com) has a built-in hand-crank cell phone charger and an LED flashlight. The hand-crank can also power the radio should the

batteries and built-in battery pack die. There are small emergency radios available with fewer options. In my opinion, though, the hand-crank power option is a must.

When selecting an emergency radio, it is critical to choose a model that is equipped with NOAA Weather Radio. National Weather Radio (NWR) is a public service from the National Oceanic and Atmospheric Administration (NOAA). The NOAA broadcasts weather alerts, warnings, and disaster information twenty-four hours a day through more than a thousand transmitters that cover most of the United States. Even when local radio and TV stations are not broadcasting, you should be able to get a NOAA signal. Radios must be equipped with special receivers to receive this NOAA signal, and, typically, this station is clearly marked on emergency radios that have this feature.

In addition to weather-related information from the National Weather Service, the National Weather Radio stations can also transmit a variety of other disaster-related information by collaborating with other government entities, such as the Federal Emergency Management Agency (FEMA) and the Emergency Alert System (EAS). This can include state and local emergencies, hazards, environmental threats and even Amber alerts. Each state has its own Emergency Alert System in place. Get familiar with your state's EAS policies and plans. You can find that information on the FCC's website www.fcc.gov/encyclopedia/state-eas-plans-and-chairs.

IMPORTANT DOCUMENTS

I could probably write an entire chapter on how and why to carry important documents. While dealing with this paperwork may seem boring, it's vitally important to carry this information in your Bug Out Bag, so don't overlook this section.

If you've decided to bug out, it's safe to assume that there is a risk your house will be destroyed and/or looted and robbed. Sorry to be pessimistic, but the reality of a disaster is that *both* do happen. Unfortunately, the house you leave behind is not only at the mercy of the disaster but also people who take advantage of horrible situa-

Important Documents in Waterproof Map Case

tions. This is a fact rarely covered in the news. You must prepare in advance a portfolio of your most important personal documents.

These documents are critical to getting your life back in order during the "recovery stage" after the dust has settled. They can also be extremely useful during the actual Bug Out as well. Authorities may require proof of identification or other documents and you don't want *anything* holding you up once you've decided to move. Don't let something as simple as a passport or driver's license delay your travel. In the event of a Public Health Emergency it's likely you will be required to provide medical documentation to clear check-points. There are countless reasons to prepare and pack your Survival Document Portfolio (SDP) in your BOB.

If the documents listed below are destroyed, replacing them can be a very difficult, time-consuming, and costly process. Acquiring duplicate or replacement copies can take weeks or months and can really affect your ability to react quickly and efficiently to the logistical aftermath of any disaster. Organizing your SDP ahead of time and taking it with you can save a lot of heartache and money in the future.

Identification Documents

Below is a list of documents that might be necessary for identification:

- driver's license
- birth certificate
- Social Security card
- passport
- military ID
- marriage license

Insurance Documents

It is important to be able to provide proof of insurance during and after a Bug Out. These should include account numbers and contact information. Your insurance documents might include some of the following:

- property insurance
- auto insurance
- life insurance
- rental insurance

Medical Documents

Proper and current documentation can make life so much easier in the event of a Medical or Public Health Disaster. Below are the most important medical related documents:

- health insurance cards
- record of immunizations
- list of prescription medications
- documentation related to disabilities
- allergy information
- will

Financial Documents

Having account information and contact numbers for the following items can be incredibly useful if you are displaced for a period of time following a disaster:

- bank accounts
- credit cards
- loan accounts
- mortgage

Document Security

Even if you are not preparing for a Bug Out at all, it's good practice to keep the above documents (or duplicate copies) together in a safe and secure place at home. A shoe box hidden in the closet is not sufficient. Invest is a good quality water-tight and fireproof safe that can be bolted to a wall or floor—preferably to the concrete foundation of your home. I keep my SDP inside a safe and also sealed in a water-tight map case.

Similar map cases can be found in the camping or kayak section of most outdoor retailers. These cases are typically larger and much more durable than an average resealable bag.

I do *not* keep my SDP in my BOB year-round. This is the one item I will grab in addition to my BOB during a Bug Out. In the photo, you might notice that I also keep *cash* stored with my SDP.

SDP With Cash in Small Fireproof Safe

CASH MONEY

Don't expect to swing by the ATM on the way out of town while a hurricane is tearing through behind you. First, all the "unprepared" will be doing the same thing, so prepare to get in line. Second, the ATM probably won't work anyway. Don't plan on accessing your safe deposit box either. Carry *cash* in your BOB!

Pack five hundred dollars minimum—preferably one thousand dollars. This cash should be in small denominations—ones, fives, tens and a few twenties. Keep this cash in your safe with your SDP. In a Bug Out situation, as soon as you remove the cash from your safe the cash should be split up and kept in five different places on your person. If and when you do need to take out some cash, it's important not to display everything you have. There will most certainly be a need for money at some point along your Bug Out journey. A handful of quarters is also a good idea. You might have a need for coins, i.e., vending machine or pay phone.

AREA MAP

Knowing where you are going is one thing. Getting there in the wake of a disaster is something totally different. Disasters have a bad habit of completely destroying and/or blocking roads. If the roads aren't destroyed, they are often jammed with other vehicles "getting out of Dodge". Navigating out of a disaster field can be very frustrating and difficult.

Please, please, please, don't depend on your GPS or SmartPhone to provide you with alternate escape routes. Most likely, neither will work. Remember that ancient thing called a map? Buy one for your local area and keep it in your BOB!

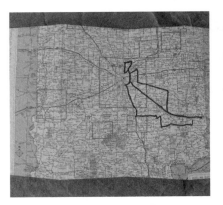

Local Map With Highlighted Routes to BOL

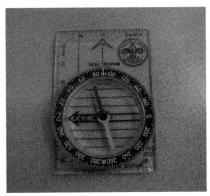

Compass

Highlight at least three routes on the map from your home to your Bug Out Location (BOL). Expect blockages and have contingency plans in place. If you travel to your BOL throughout the year, explore alternate routes.

COMPASS

A reliable compass is a necessity for any traveling survivalist. Add one to your BOB. My compass is an old Boy Scout model that I've had for about twenty years.

TWO-WAY RADIOS

I personally don't carry two-way radios, and they aren't a necessity. However, if you plan on bugging out with a large family or team, these are worth your consideration. If there was ever a reason to split up, a set of two-way radios would be a very valuable piece of kit. Pack a set only if they make sense for your Bug Out needs.

NOTE PAD AND PENCIL

The ability to record important information and leave notes is an important facet of the communication category. Both are very applicable in a Bug Out scenario. A company called Rite in the Rain makes a very unique all-weather writing paper created to shed water and enhance the written image. Their paper is widely used throughout the world for recording critical field data in all kinds of weather. I carry one of their 4"×6" notebooks in my BOB. I cut a pencil in half and keep it in the top spiral binding. I recommend you do the same.

SIGNALING TOOLS

In a Bug Out scenario, it is critical that you can signal for rescue. Signals

Two-Way Radio Walkie-Talkies

Rite in the Rain Water Proof Note Pads

are a very important component of a BOB communication kit. During the 2011 Tohuko earthquake in Japan a man was swept eleven miles out to sea on the roof of his house. He was eventually found, but a signaling device could have shortened his time lost at sea. I've highlighted several ways to signal for rescue in previous chapters. Some of these include:

- signal mirror (chapter eight)
- survival blanket signal (chapter eight)
- flashlight (chapter eleven)
- glow stick (chapter eleven)
- signal fire (chapter seven)

In addition to all of these, I also suggest packing a small whistle. The brand I use is Fox 40 available from fox40world.com. This whistle is made from a durable polycarbonate that is water and rust proof. It has no moving parts to jam or freeze and can even be blown underwater. The 120-decible blast travels for miles.

Signal whistles are far more effective than using your own voice. The whistle blast is *much* louder and travels *much* farther than any sounds you can make by screaming. It also takes far less energy to blow a whistle than to scream.

SUMMARY

This chapter is about sending and receiving *information*. Whether providing identifying documents, writing down emergency data or listening to disaster radio broadcasts, the ability to exchange information is critical. It is necessary to have a variety of alternative tools on hand to send and receive information.

13 ▶ PROTECTION & SELF-DEFENSE

TO APPRECIATE THE INFORMATION in this chapter you must read it with a different mindset. You have to imagine yourself actually in a disaster Bug Out—picture yourself really there. Your family is scared and you are just trying to get somewhere safe. Traffic was at a complete stand-still so you were forced to abandon your vehicle and travel by foot to your destination. As dawn approaches, you notice the silhouettes of three or four guys swiftly approaching your family from behind. You get an uneasy feeling in your gut and instinctually know that this is not going to end well. Maybe their intent is to take your food and water or your shelter. That would be a best-case scenario. Or, maybe they just want to borrow your daughter for a while. Their strategy might also be to beat everyone unconscious, take everything you have and leave you for dead. Regardless, you have some very serious decisions to make in about thirty seconds.

I am not crazy, and this is not fiction. Scenarios just like this happen in the wake of *every* disaster in *every* country and in *every* neighborhood. I told you in the very beginning of the book that this was going to be a complete and thorough guide about how to build a Bug Out Bag. This is a chapter that will make some people uncomfortable. I can't in good conscious give you a product that is not complete. A Bug Out Bag is *not* complete without inclusions for self-defense.

THE UGLY TRUTH

Disasters have devastating consequences and can leave people, cities, and regions with horrific and unimaginable circumstances. I am always amazed at how generous my fellow Americans are when responding to help victims of disaster. It seems that disaster sometimes brings out the absolute best in people. Whether it be in the form of donations or hands-on labor, it is very moving to see people rally behind those who have suffered so much loss. These efforts are always covered by news outlets weeks and months after a disaster strikes.

Unfortunately, however, there are people in this world who do not share the same sentiment about helping our brothers and sisters who are hurting. For some, disasters bring out their worst qualities. These predators use the chaos and disorder that surround disasters to further victimize people through looting, robbing, violence, and rape. These events are rarely, if ever, mentioned by news outlets—leaving many unaware of the potential dangers. This reality is the darkest side in any disaster situation and is rooted in selfishness, greed, and sometimes desperation.

It's no mystery that large-scale disasters overwhelm normal public-safety operations—at least temporarily. It's during this time when most violent crimes occur. You must be prepared to defend yourself and your family from individuals and gangs should the need arise. Whether you like the idea or not, you would be naïve and foolish not to take this category seriously—especially if traveling with women and small children.

SELF-DEFENSE MENTALITY

Self-defense is a very touchy subject. I am not an expert on the laws surrounding self-defense or the use of lethal force. I do know, however, that there is a very fine line between defending yourself or your family and attempted murder, manslaughter, or homicide. Legally, you can only respond to an attack with an equal amount of lethal force.

I know what I would do to protect myself and my family. Everyone has his or her own comfort level, limitations, morals, and boundaries. It's not my place to tell you how you should act if threatened. That's your business. What I can do is provide you with some basic self-defense guidelines and list what I think are a few practical self-defense tools to keep in your BOB. How you use this information is your call.

Bottom Line

You can only use lethal force when you or your family are faced with an absolute and unavoidable act of injury or death from someone else. It must be your last and only option. The laws of this country and your state apply before, during, and after a disaster.

SELF-OFFENSE

The best self-defense is self-offense. Self-offense is taking every precaution possible to avoid any kind of confrontation. This includes evading from and removing oneself from dangerous, confrontational, or questionable situations.

There is absolutely *no* benefit in trying to prove yourself. Confrontation is a *lose-lose* scenario. No one wins.

Below are self-offense tips and guidelines that can help you avoid using self-defense options:

- Check your ego and pride at the door. They have no place here. The desire to prove yourself will only get you in trouble. Embrace humility.
- Be observant.
- Don't flaunt your tools and supplies. Keep your behavior low-key.
- Never travel alone unless you have no choice. There is safety in numbers.

- Never assume anything. Make decisions based upon facts.
- Don't just acknowledge your gut feeling—follow and act on it.
- Question everyone.
- Trust no one.

These guidelines may seem to border on paranoia, but who cares? In the midst of lawlessness and pandemonium, it's okay to behave a little bit paranoid and cautious. Let your survival instinct guide the decisions you make. Below are some words that should describe your mental state of self-offense:

- steady
- observant
- calculated
- attuned
- methodical
- aware
- cautious
- humble

You are only one side to this delicate equation. You can control yourself but you cannot control other people. Conflict is sometimes unavoidable. When faced with conflict, you must know your self-defense options. You need to prepare these options ahead of time. These tools need to be accessible. And as with any Bug Out survival skill, training, practice, and experience drastically increases your odds of successful deployment.

SELF-DEFENSE OPTIONS
Your Body

If trained properly, your body can be an effective defense weapon. I completely endorse and recommend taking a local self-defense course or enrolling in regular self-defense training classes. Knowing how to effectively strike an attacker with specific targeted blows takes professional training and experience. A demobilizing strike doesn't just happen randomly. It is intentional and premeditated. If properly executed, powerful strikes to the throat, groin, and knees can instantly neutralize an attacker. If possible, it is best if these strikes are made proactively and offensively to catch the attacker off guard. Defense is reacting to an event. Offense is acting before an event happens. It is much more effective to make an offensive strike than a defensive one. Offensive strikes are also more controlled and precise.

Hand-to-hand combat should be your absolute last option of self-defense or self-offense. It is incredibly risky and dangerous. If your attacker wields a weapon, or if there are multiple attackers, your chances of successfully defending yourself with your bare hands go *way* down. Unarmed self-defense skills are very important and should be a part of your disaster preparedness training regimen. However, you would be completely

Cold Steel Inferno Pepper Spray

Inferno Secured to Shoulder Strap

misguided and naïve to depend on these skills as your sole self-defense options.

I don't like or condone violence. However, protecting myself and my family from harm is an exception. You *must* pack self-defense weapons in your BOB.

Pepper Spray

There is a reason why military, police, and security professionals carry pepper spray—it works! I have chosen to carry a canister of Cold Steel Inferno pepper spray as a part of my BOB rig. I applied an adhesive Velcro strip to the side of the canister and applied another Velcro strip to the padded shoulder strap on the front of my BOB. This keeps the pepper spray secure, but easily accessible. I can detach and deploy this spray in under two seconds.

Following are my general guidelines when it comes to purchasing and using pepper spray:

- Buy a pepper spray that has the active ingredient Oleoresin Capsicum. Oleoresin Capsicum is derived from pepper plants and is extremely effective in irritating the eyes, airways, and lungs of an attacker. The spray you choose should have around 5 to 8 percent Oleoresin Capsicum. A pepper spray's strength is measured by Scoville Heat Units (SHU). My pepper spray is 2,000,000 SHUs. Anything in this range is sufficient.
- Buy a pepper spray that sprays in a *stream* pattern as opposed to a *fog* or *mist* spray. A *stream* pattern typically sprays the farthest distance and performs better in outside conditions. *Fog* and *mist* sprays are considered very effective in terms of stopping power because they have better disbursement

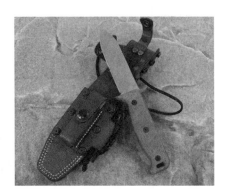

Self-Defense Knife

of active ingredients, but they are drastically affected by wind strength and direction, so for a disaster Bug Out, I suggest *stream* spray. For all effective purposes, I consider a *foam* to be in the *stream* spray category because it shoots straight and fast. My pepper spray is a *foam* that dissolves on contact.

- Spray and retreat! Don't hang around to watch what happens. The entire purpose of pepper spray is to disorient and demobilize an attacker long enough for you to escape. Spray your attacker and, after you confirm a direct hit, retreat immediately. Any decent pepper spray should buy you enough time to get away safely.

Pepper spray is legal in all fifty states, but some states have imposed certain restrictions. Be sure to check your local and state laws to see if they have any that apply specifically to the purchase and use of pepper spray. You can review your state laws and purchase Cold Steel Inferno at www. coldsteel.com/pepper-spray.html.

Survival Knife

Remember your Survival Knife from chapter ten? This knife is an excellent self-defense weapon. Again, however, this is certainly considered close quarters, hand-to-hand combat. Even with training, self-defense with a knife can be very dangerous. The most obvious is the risk of your knife being taken from you by an attacker. Attackers typically don't give fair warning. Like animal predators, they prefer to stalk and surprise their victims to prevent retaliation. Consequently, the chances of unsheathing and using a knife for defense is fairly remote. Regardless, it is still a viable self-defense option that has it's place in this chapter.

When you call around to local organizations offering self-defense classes, ask if they teach knife courses. You may want to consider this training.

Machete or Other Long Reach Tool

Machetes and the like have been used as self-defense weapons for centuries all over the globe. If you've decided to pack a machete in your BOB, it is not only an effective deterrent, but it can

Machete in Bug Out Pack

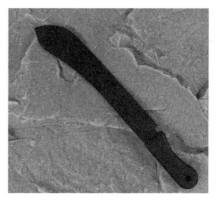

Cold Steel Bolo Machete

be an incredibly effective weapon to keep an attacker at bay. It has reach and chopping force—a deadly combination. I'll admit, it sounds like something out of a Mad Max movie. However, if I were an attacker looking for victims, I probably wouldn't go after the guy with a machete if there were other targets; would you?

There are countless other items that can be found on location that make excellent self-defense weapons. Just to name a few:

- hammer
- pipe
- chain
- bat
- pry bar
- axe

Anything that can be swung, thrust, thrown, chopped, hacked, slammed, pounded, shoved, slashed, whacked, smashed, thrashed, or bashed can be used as a self-defense

weapon. Remember, though, it can also be forcefully taken and used against you as well.

If a true life-or-death violent attack actually did occur in a Bug Out Scenario against me or my family, there is only one self defense weapon I hope to have. That weapon is a gun.

BUG OUT GUN

Guns aren't for everyone. In the wrong hands, guns can cause more harm than good. Ownership of any deadly weapon is a huge responsibility and should be taken very seriously. If ever faced with a Bug Out Scenario, I will be taking a gun. I have a gun packed with my BOB. I will discuss what kind of gun a little later. I know several people, however, who I hope will not be taking a gun. They don't have the proper training; they aren't practiced or experienced with firing a gun; and they don't have the calm resolve that is needed to make good, solid decisions in a scary and chaotic environment. These individuals are best *traveling with* someone who knows and understands firearms.

What type of person are you? Do you have firearms training or experience? Are you an accurate marksman with a gun? Only you know the answers. Be honest and responsible. Don't carry a gun unless you can back it up with knowledge and know-how. If you don't feel prepared to travel with a gun right now but you see its place in a Bug Out Survival situation, then get some training under your belt and start building competence and confidence with your weapon of choice. Almost every large city has a firing range that offers gun ownership classes.

Handgun vs. Shotgun vs. Rifle

I love handguns. I love shotguns. And I love rifles. I own several of all three types. In a disaster, you can't take all of them or even two of them—it just isn't practical. What fits into your Bug Out Bag the best? The primary use is self-defense. Theoretically, your BOB contains 72 hours worth of food, so it's not necessary to pack a hunting weapon. Ideally, your gun can be hidden and concealed from the view of others. Remember, you don't want your stuff to make you a target. You also don't want to become a target of authorities or law enforcement. Carrying a gun during chaotic disaster emergencies does not settle well with authorities and they *will* stop you. They don't know each individual and are looking out for the best interest of the community, so the general rule of thumb is that anyone running around with a gun in the midst of a disaster is dangerous. If you want to keep your gun, it must be concealed.

Given these considerations, I believe the best type of Bug Out gun

SURVIVAL QUICK TIP

Know your local and state gun laws! Each state has it's own unique set of gun ownership, carry and transport laws. Find out the answers to the following questions by contacting your local police department.

- Can I travel with a gun?
- What kind of guns can I travel with?

- Do I need a permit to travel with a gun?
- Can I carry a concealed weapon?
- What else do I need to know about traveling with a gun?

is a pistol. Handguns are very easy to conceal. They are also fairly light-weight, which is certainly a concern. The ammo is small and packable as well. A pistol is an incredible self-defense weapon. Depending on the model, a typical handgun holds between five and nine rounds of ammunition—giving the user multiple shots before reloading. Some high-capacity magazines can extend this number to upwards of thirty rounds. Though no maintenance should be necessary in a 72-hour Bug Out, most handguns are fairly simple to maintain. Narrowing the gun choice down to a handgun is only half of the decision-making process. There are literally hundreds of different handgun makes, styles, and calibers.

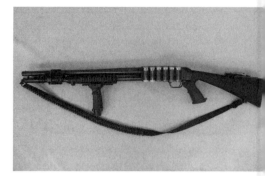

Survival Shotgun

Ruger 10/22 Rifle

Revolver vs. Automatic

I am certain to ruffle some feathers with my opinions about whether you should pack a revolver or a semi-automatic pistol. First, let me say that there are excellent revolvers and excellent semi-auto pistols. I would be happy to carry either one in a Bug Out. However, I choose to pack a revolver in my BOB for two main reasons:

Reason 1: Simplicity. I like how simple a revolver is. There's a barrel, a bullet, and a hammer. It's pretty hard for something to go wrong or jam. They are also very easy to load

Glock Pistol

and unload. Semi-auto pistols have several moving and sliding parts. And, as much as hard-core semi-auto die-hards don't want to admit it, these guns occasionally jam. I've shot thousands of rounds through both revolvers and semi-autos. I've never had a revolver jam on me. I have had semi-autos jam on several occasions. I remember one instance vividly.

Revolver Cylinder With 5 Rounds

Reason 2: Caliber Flexibility. When it comes to choosing a caliber, I want something with knock-down power. If the situation has called for me to aim and fire my weapon at an attacker, I don't want to just injure him. I want to *stop* him—period. For this reason, I have chosen to carry a .357 Magnum 5-shot revolver in my BOB. .357 caliber revolvers will also fire .38 caliber rounds, which gives you some flexibility in sourcing ammo. If you're in a pinch, trying to find two popular calibers is easier than trying to find one.

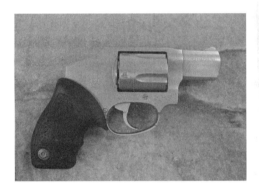

Taurus .357 Magnum

SUMMARY

Remember, self-offense is the best self-defense. Use your wits and gut feelings to keep out of potentially dangerous situations. And, just because it's a disaster environment doesn't mean that normal laws do not apply.

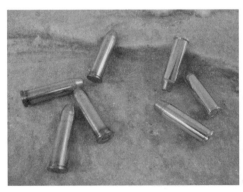

.357 Bullets (left) and .38 bullets (right)

14 MISCELLANEOUS SUPPLIES

THIS CHAPTER IS DEDICATED to BOB items that don't necessarily fall into the first eleven supply categories. Some are luxury items based on pack size and weight. Others are items that I would consider necessities. I will indicate importance in each description.

RESEALABLE BAGS

Resealable bags are excellent disaster survival tools. They have a plethora of survival-related uses. In a pinch, they can be used as water storage or carrying containers.

They also make excellent waterproofing containers for moisture-sensitive items in your BOB, such as first aid kits and fire-starting implements. I double-bag anything I want to protect for an added layer of protection. I also keep three to four extra empty one-gallon bags in my BOB just in case I need them.

CONTRACTOR-GRADE TRASH BAGS

As mentioned in chapter two, contractor-grade 55-gallon trash bags can be used for all kinds of survival related tasks.

To recap, here is a short list of uses below. Pack two of these in your BOB if space allows.

- waste storage and disposal
- BOB water-proof pack liner
- ground cover
- poncho
- flotation device
- shelter canopy
- rescue signal
- water container/collection

N95 DUST MASK

N95 is a nationally recognized rating given to indicate that a mask filters airborne particles that are .3 microns or larger in size. N95 masks are made by a variety of manufacturers. When

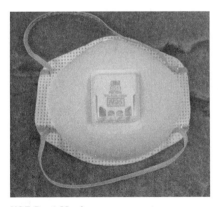

N95 Dust Mask

Mask as Crude Pre-Filter

Ten-Yard Hank of 550 Military-Spec Parachute Cord

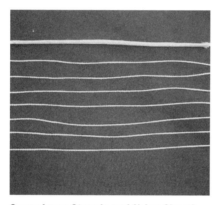

Seven Inner Strands and Nylon Sheath

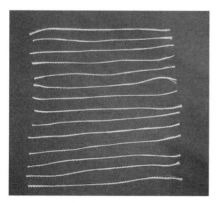

Seven Inner Strands Unraveled Into Fourteen Strands

selecting a dust mask, remember it's the rating that is important, not the brand.

The Centers for Disease Control (CDC) recommends the use of an N95 rated mask to prevent the spread of airborne viruses, such as H1N1. The mask basically traps particles, bacteria, and viruses that would otherwise be inhaled. I can think of several Bug Out scenarios when there would be a need for an N95 mask:

- volcanic eruption with plumes of dust, smoke, ash, and debris
- terrorist attack, nuclear attack, or bomb with explosions, smoke, ash, debris, dust
- pandemic, disease, or plague
- wild fire with airborne ash and smoke

When using an N95 mask, there are some tips to improve results:

- **Tight Seal:** A nice tight seal against your face improves performance. Be sure to form the aluminum nose guard to the contour of your nose. Thick facial hair prevents a good seal.
- **Exhalation Valve:** In the photo, this valve is the small, plastic square on the center of the mask. It allows for quick release of the carbon dioxide and moisture you expel when you exhale. The valve helps to prevent moisture from clogging

Creek Scanning Horizon

Fishing Kit

the fibers of the mask. It also helps to prevent glasses from fogging up as you breath.

N95 dust masks can also be used as crude water filters to filter out floating particulates.

550 PARACHUTE CORD

550 indicates that this rope has a tensile strength of 550 pounds. True military-spec paracord is comprised of seven inner strands encased in a woven nylon sheath. The tensile strength of these seven inner strands is 35 pounds. Even these seven strands are comprised of two twisted strands. In reality, a length of 550 paracord can be broken down into fifteen separate ropes—the fourteen inner strands and the woven sheath. Thus 10 feet of paracord can equal 150 feet of cordage if absolutely necessary.

This versatility combined with its strength makes 550 parachute cord a very popular cordage choice for disas-

ter preppers and survivalists. It can be used for thousands of survival-related projects. Below is just a small list:

- shelter building
- snares
- repairs
- fishing line
- emergency climbing rope
- belt

I suggest carrying fifty feet minimum of 550 Paracord. I carry two hundred feet cut down into the following more manageable lengths:

- quantity 2: 5-foot sections
- quantity 10: 10-foot sections
- quantity 2: 20-foot sections
- quantity 1: 50-foot section

BINOCULARS/MONOCULAR

These are certainly a luxury item but can be very useful if you have the extra space in your BOB. The ability to clearly see into the distance can give you several advantages. Some of the most notable are to:

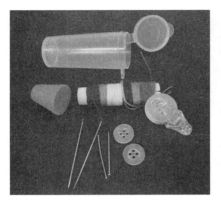

Sewing Kit and Container

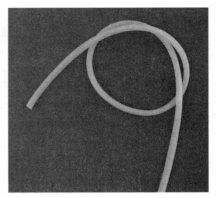

36" Length of Latex Surgical Tubing

- avoid threats
- inspect Bug Out Location before approach
- look for rescue or help
- look for best travel routes
- observe groups of people from afar
- read signage
- keep track of team members

SMALL FISHING KIT

Again, you have already planned for 72 hours worth of food, so this is not a BOB necessity. However, a small fishing kit can be packed into an extremely small container and weighs very little. In my opinion, it is a worthy addition.

A fishing kit should include the following items:

- 30'–50' of 30lb.+ test line
- 3–5 hooks in a variety of sizes
- 3–5 sinkers

I pack my fishing kit into a small aluminum pill case that I purchased at a local pharmacy.

SMALL SEWING/REPAIR KIT

Virtually weightless, a sewing kit can be useful to make necessary gear or clothing repairs while in route. It could also be used for emergency sutures. I purchased my kit from a local fabric store and keep it in the film-canister-style container in which it was packaged. It contains the following items:

- a variety of threads
- 2 sewing needles
- 2 push pins
- 1 button
- 1 needle threading tool
- 1 thimble

I also added about five feet of waxed dental floss. This thread is incredibly strong and perfect for repairs that need to be able to take some continued abuse, such as backpack straps or tarp tears.

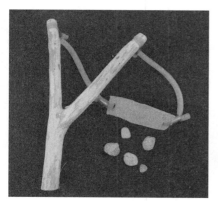

Slingshot Made With Surgical Tubing

Hawaiian-Style Fish Spear Made With Surgical Tubing

RUBBER TUBING

I mentioned this item in chapter three. Some pump water filter systems come with rubber tubing that you could use for other functions if needed. If you are not packing a system that contains rubber tubing, consider packing a 36" length of rubber latex surgical tubing. It can be used for many survival applications. Some include:

- tourniquet
- siphon
- drinking straw for hard to reach water supply
- makeshift slingshot
- makeshift fishing spear gun

DUCT TAPE

I also mentioned this item in chapter three. I wrap fifteen feet or so of duct tape around my Nalgene water bottle. I also wrap duct tape around several other items as well for easy storage. You can never have too much duct tape! For example, I also wrap my lighters and my backup Mora 840 knife sheath.

Between these items, I have approximately twenty-five feet of duct tape that can be used as needed. It is a multi-use product with uses only limited by your imagination. I've even seen videos and pictures of people making functional boats and rafts using duct tape. Several more practical noteworthy uses are:

- emergency first aid bandage
- cordage
- gear/clothing/shoe repairs
- makeshift emergency water container

SUNGLASSES

Besides protection from the sun, a good pair of shades can double as safety goggles. Take every precaution to protect your eyes—especially when you have limited access to medical

Lighters and Sheath Wrapped in Duct Tape

Bandana as Pot Holder

facilities and/or treatment. An eye injury can be a devastating blow to your Bug Out plans. Buy a cheap pair of sunglasses and a neck lanyard to prevent accidental loss.

TWO BANDANAS

It's amazing how something so simple and cheap as a bandana can have so many uses for a disaster survivalist. Bandanas literally have hundreds of uses. They are also nearly weightless and are very easy to pack—stuffing into even the smallest cracks of your BOB. I recommend packing two bandanas in your BOB. Below are some very practical Bug Out uses:

- face mask
- pot holder
- trail markers to leave signs of travel
- cordage—cut into strips and tied together
- crude water filter

- first aid bandage
- surface cover for food prep

INSPIRATIONAL ITEM

In every survival kit I build, I always include a small "inspirational" item. This item can be a source of motivation for when morale is low. It can be anything meaningful—something that keeps you going and reminds you that life is worth fighting for when the going gets tough. This item is different for everyone. It can be a family photo, a picture of your girlfriend or boyfriend, a small meaningful trinket or a religious item. Personally, I keep a small King James Bible in my BOB and a fun family photo. These two items inspire and motivate me not to give up.

For children, a toy, trinket, or stuffed animal can go a long way. Anything positive that can help distract them from the reality of a disaster en-

Strip of Bandana as Trail Marker

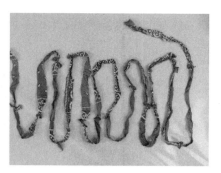

Bandana Cut Into Strips and Tied Together For 20' of Cordage

Bandana as Food Prep Surface Cover

Inspirational Item

vironment is a good thing. Familiar pleasures to a small child can represent hope, reassurance, and normality. A small comfort item even for tweens and teens can help reduce stress and maintain a sense of calm and normality amidst the chaos around them. Keep these comfort items packed in their bags ahead of time. Don't expect to be able to round up a favorite toy as you are bugging out. If your child is particularly attached to a specific toy, buy a duplicate to keep in the child's BOB so it's always ready to go.

SUMMARY

Use your best judgment when it comes to pack real-estate. You have to make decisions based upon space and how much weight you can carry. Inevitably, some items just aren't going to make the cut. That is okay and expected. The check-list in the appendix is actually organized in order of importance. If you are running low on space or coming close to your weight-cap, cut the items lower on the list first and work your way up.

15 BUGGING OUT WITH PETS

A FRIEND OF MINE who works in the veterinary business told me that more than 30 percent of American households own either a dog or a cat. She also said that more than 60 percent of households own some kind of pet. Consequently, this chapter is applicable for many readers. Whether or not your pet survives a disaster Bug Out has a lot to do with the steps you take to prepare in advance. Pets need to be considered when assembling your BOB if you plan on taking them with you. It might not be practical to take some pets if you are forced to Bug Out. This is a fact of life and a sad reality for many pet owners. This decision needs to be made in *advance*. If a disaster strikes and a Bug Out is necessary, you need to already know which, if any, pets you are taking with you. There is no time for arguments and thoughtful decisions in the middle of a crisis.

After you've made that decision, below are some BOB considerations for pets. Basic survival needs aren't really that much different between humans and animals—food, water, and shelter are the major concerns.

WATER

Just like humans, an animal's daily water requirements vary with size, weight, type, and environment. The best rule of thumb is that if you are thirsty, your pet is probably thirsty. It is a fallacy that dogs and cats are not susceptible to illness, vomiting, and diarrhea from water-born pathogens such as Giardia—especially those pets who are on very sheltered and strict in-house diets. Unfortunately, gone are the days in most parts of the world when humans or domestic pets can drink from natural water sources with no worries. It is certainly a risk, even for pets. If I had a pet, I'd probably still plan on them drinking from a natural source, but that is a personal choice.

Animals don't drink out of Nalgene water bottles very well. It's impossible not to waste water while trying to let them drink this way. For fifteen dollars, I bought a collapsible water dish made by Granite Gear. It's the perfect pet-watering container for a BOB.

FOOD

In addition to water, you will also need to pack pet food. The same guidelines apply that you used to pack your own food. Your pet's food must be lightweight, packable, and kept in a watertight container. I suggest dry pet food triple-packed in resealable bags. Pack seventy-two hours worth of pet food.

Granite Gear Slurpin Bowl

Dry Pet Food Packed in Resealable Bags

Leash on Small Dogs During Urban Bug Out

MEDICINE

If your pet takes medication you will also need to pack items related to this need: pills, droppers, syringes, etc. These items should be kept in a kit separate from your own first aid and hygiene kit.

LEASH & MUZZLE (IF NECESSARY)

Without a leash, keeping track of a curious or scared pet in a chaotic disaster environment can be a challenge. A leash is especially important if you are forced to travel by foot. In a pinch, a simple leash can be fashioned from your supply of paracord mentioned in chapter fourteen.

If you have a dog that is prone to snapping or biting, a muzzle should be included in your BOB. The last thing you need is your dog biting someone in a crowd.

PACK ANIMALS

Many animals have the ability to carry their own Bug Out Items. It's not at all uncommon for service dogs to carry items for their disabled owners in specially designed saddle-bag style dog backpacks. I've seen this on numerous occasions. This same concept can easily be duplicated in a Bug Out Scenario provided you have a pet capable of the task and you have prepared a pack for it in advance. Even smaller dogs can be fitted with small packs.

Maggie the Coon Hound Ready for a Bug Out

Pack Goat Fitted with Packs. Photo compliments of the North American Packgoat Association (www.NAPgA.org).

Ideally, though, this strategy is best suited for medium- to large-breed dogs and farm animals. Goats, for example, make excellent pack animals capable of carrying a quarter of their own weight. Many "pack goat" enthusiasts routinely take several day backcountry trips using pack goats to haul the supplies. Here is a photo of Charlie Jennings with goats purchased from Carolyn Eddy's herd at Eagle Creek Packgoats.

PAPERWORK/IDENTIFICATION

You need to also pack important documents and identification for your pet. Your pet should have an ID collar with your contact information and ra-

bies tag. You should also include vaccination records to prove your pet has had the proper shots within the previous twelve months. This documentation can help to ensure smooth travel if ever questioned by authorities.

SUMMARY

I always joke with my brother, who owns two miniature Doberman Pinschers, that they might as well be his children. That statement is especially true during a disaster Bug Out. If you are taking your pets, make preparations in advance. Try your best to make them as self-sufficient as possible.

16 BOB ORGANIZATION & MAINTENANCE

NOW THAT WE'VE DISCUSSED what belongs in your Bug Out Bag, it's time to think about packing the bag. From inside to out, every step of assembling your BOB should be methodically and strategically orchestrated. There should be nothing random or circumstantial about its content. Everything should be chosen with purpose and the way you organize the contents of your bag should be intentional.

When you are on the move in a disaster situation, you won't have time to dig through the entire contents of your bag to find what you are looking for. You need to be able to access and find exactly what you need at a moment's notice. Plus, your odds of losing items greatly increase if your bag is disorganized. Things will get scattered, dropped, or left behind.

The contents of your bag also need to be up-to-date. You don't want to face a Bug Out situation with a pack full of expired food and medication and out-of-season clothing. A regular maintenance schedule will keep you prepared year-round.

Below are the guidelines I use to organize and maintain my BOB.

WATERPROOFING

As I mentioned in the beginning of the book, the first piece of kit in my BOB is a 55-gallon contractor-grade trash bag. Even though my pack of choice is water resistant, I don't want to take any chances when it comes to getting my lifeline wet. After everything is in my pack, I fold up and tie off the top of the trash bag with a length of 550 paracord.

Trash Bag Liner Folded and Tied Off With Paracord

Sampling of Separate Compartmentalized Kits

COMPARTMENTALIZING

I've also mentioned the importance of compartmentalizing in previous chapters. I try to keep each supply category in it's own separate "kit" with a few exceptions. Compartmentalizing categories facilitates quick access to items when you need them. It also helps you to identify kits by touch in low-light situations. I tend to color code and label my kits as well.

PACK ORGANIZATION

Believe it or not, the order in which you pack a BOB actually matters. There are items that need to be packed for quick and easy access and then there are items that don't require a sense of urgency. I classify these two groups as "urgent" and "nonurgent."

Nonurgent items go into the pack first, thus taking longer to access. Urgent items go into the pack last and are easily accessed.

First-In Items

- extra clothing
- bedding
- hygiene
- first aid
- miscellaneous supplies

Last-In Items

- shelter
- water
- food (human and pet)
- fire
- cold weather clothing items

Finally, there is a small grouping of items I consider "Emergency Items."

These items should be either strapped to your body or in an easy and quick-to-access pack pocket. Sudden use of these items is likely necessary.

Emergency Items
- communication (except for radio)
- self-defense
- lighting
- tools—especially survival knife
- poncho

You will find that adopting this three-step priority system will make the most efficient use of your time, energy, and pack real-estate in a Bug Out Scenario.

Laminated Inventory Sheet With Noted Review Dates

BUG OUT BAG BIANNUAL REVIEW
I've mentioned the concept of a biannual review several times in previous chapters. There are two main reasons to conduct a review of your BOB twice each year:

1. Food/water: You should replace and replenish your BOB food and water storage at least every six months. This includes both human and pet items.
2. Clothing: If you live in a region with distinct seasons, as I do, it will be necessary to add and remove cold-weather clothing before and after the onset of winter.

I have categorized food, water, and cold-weather clothing as "last-in items" so they will be easy to access during your biannual reviews. Schedule your biannual review on or near holidays or annual events so they are easier to remember. If you have a long cold-season, Labor Day and Memorial Day could be your events. If you have a shorter cold season, changing to and from Daylight Saving Time could be your marker. Whatever schedule you choose, don't forget to mark it in your calendar.

Even if you don't get outdoors much to practice your survival skill sets, a biannual review can be the perfect excuse to brush up. Your review can also include a "skill review" where you take an afternoon to practice critical BOB skills such as fire making, shelter building, and food preparation. Having the tools does not make you proficient in using them. Practice does.

BOB Inventory Checklist

I've created an BOB inventory checklist that you can download for free at betterwaybooks.com/bobinventory. Keep this list with your pack to make it easier to conduct your biannual review. Write the date of each review on the checklist so you know at a glance when you need to change out the food and first aid equipment.

Lifestyle Review

A BOB review is also a time to evaluate any major life changes that can affect your BOB pack items. I call this a *lifestyle review*. Some life changes that could affect this review are:

- children (addition or loss)
- marriage or divorce
- location/environment
- weight/health/medications
- additional family member, such as live-in grandparent or live-in parent
- pets (loss or addition)

It's easy to forget items in your BOB after it has been sitting in wait for six months or longer. A lifestyle review can be very time-consuming if you have to go through your entire pack from start to finish. For this reason, I keep a laminated inventory sheet attached to the outside of my BOB. The sheet helps me quickly review the contents without completely unpacking the bag. I simply make notations on the inventory sheet with a marker for all changes that I make. I also date this sheet each time I conduct a review or make changes.

PACK STORAGE AND MAINTENANCE

I'm often asked during my Bug Out classes where is the best place to store a BOB in your home. Having lived in several apartments and homes over the past ten years, I've kept my BOB in a variety of areas. Once, when I was in an apartment with limited space, I kept my BOB inside an ottoman next to my couch. I've also kept it in an old, unplugged freezer, and under a coat in the closet. Currently, my BOB sits near my back door hidden amongst a variety of cleaning supplies. So there is no definitive answer. The general rule is that it should be out of sight yet readily available. It's not something that should be advertised to visitors.

Years ago, I lived in a small studio apartment with very little storage space. I kept my BOB and some other items in a laundry basket covered up with what appeared to be dirty clothes. One day, I came home late after work and pulled up to the outside entrance door to my apartment, like I had done so many times before. Something was different. The headlights of my truck were shining right through an *open* apartment door and into my closet. Someone had pried open the door and robbed me. They took many items—money, knives, sentimental things… it was a horrible feeling. They didn't seem too interested in my dirty laundry, though—*luckily*! There is no doubt in my mind that if I had not camouflaged my BOB with normal household items (laundry) they would have stolen it. At that time, my BOB was one of my most valuable possessions. That was a lesson I will never forget and one that I hope to pass on to you. The point of my story is to hide or camouflage your BOB. By the time you are done putting it together, you will have many hours and many dollars invested. Protect your investment.

17 MENTAL & PHYSICAL PREPAREDNESS

YOU CAN BUY GEAR. You can buy survival books like this one. You *can't* buy mental and physical readiness. You also *can't* buy the survival skills that only come from practice, repetition, and experience. That level of preparedness is reserved for those willing to train their mind and body.

Yes, survival tools are important—very important. But tools alone are insufficient and can be a false sense of security. Packing and storing a BOB is just the beginning of your preparedness journey. You must also be mentally and physically ready to follow through with your Bug Out Plan.

MENTAL PREPAREDNESS

No matter what anyone says, you can never be 100 percent mentally prepared for an emergency disaster. There's just nothing in life that trains us for that kind of "jolt" to the system. Mental readiness comes down to two basic truths:

1. having the mental fortitude to handle the stress of the situation without panicking
2. having the know-how to use the resources on hand to meet necessary survival goals

As far as the first truth goes, either you are the type of person who can keep it together when the going gets tough or you're not. Be honest with yourself. If you can't handle that kind of mental stress, I'd suggest becoming close friends with someone who can.

Truth number two is completely and wholly in your control. Knowing how to use the resources in your BOB comes down to one thing—*practice*. Survival knowledge is not an inherent talent or gift. It is the direct result of experience, repetition, trial, and error. Some of the best survival experts in the world are self-trained, and I'll take hands-on experience over classroom instruction any day of the week. You can read the best books and study under the best instructors, but until you practice the skills with your own hands, you have a slight advantage at best.

Take control of your destiny and truly understand how to use your BOB as the life-saving resource that it is. The only way to master a skill is by practice and repetition. Most important survival techniques are practiced skills—not black-and-white facts:

- fire building
- navigation
- rope work and knot tying
- food prep with few tools
- shelter building
- effective signaling

At this point, you have meticulously assembled your BOB. Now it is time to build your mental readiness. Task + Repetition = Skill. Your mind is your most valuable resource —train it.

PHYSICAL PREPAREDNESS

If your mind is your most valuable resource, then your body is your most valuable tool. Just like any piece of mechanical equipment, your body requires routine maintenance and care to be in peak condition. Have you ever let an engine just sit in the garage for a long time—a car, a lawn mower, a chain saw, or weed eater? The engine can be very difficult to start after sitting idle for so long. And when the engine does start, it doesn't run like it should. The same is true with your body. If you sit idle for a long time without proper diet and exercise, your body will not perform well when it's suddenly needed to get you through a Bug Out.

You can have the knowledge and the tools but if you don't have the endurance and strength to perform, nothing else matters. Unfortunately, the time when many people realize the importance of health is when they lose it or when they need it most. It would be a shame to go through all of the effort to assemble and prepare your BOB and not be able to physically handle a Bug Out journey. Below are some basic minimum guidelines to keep you on track physically.

Regular Exercise

A Bug Out could potentially require you to walk for many miles with a loaded pack. If you don't exercise routinely, this will be a big struggle. Being out of shape can be a real danger—slowing your progress both to your destination and away from potential threats. Don't be a liability to your group. Establish a regular exercise schedule to strengthen your muscles and boost your endurance. Join a gym or consult with a personal trainer if you need help getting started.

Diet

I'll keep this heading short and sweet. You are what you eat. Garbage in, garbage out. Make a concerted effort to eat a healthy, balanced diet. Your body will reward you for it.

Regular Medical Care

Do you have nagging medical conditions that could impede a Bug Out? Are there any debilitating physical problems that need to be addressed? For example, as I write this book I have a hernia. I've had it for a few months. During times of extreme physical exertion it bothers me. I believe it would impede my peak performance if I were ever faced with an extreme Bug Out. It's not life threatening but needs to be addressed and fixed. How about you? Do you need to schedule an appointment with your doctor to take care of an issue? Just get it over with already!

KEY PRACTICE EXERCISES

All competitive activities and sports have their own unique set of mental and physical exercises. Horse jockeys train different from long-distance track runners and tennis players. Competitive chess players have a completely difference training regimen from archers. Mentally and physically preparing for a Bug Out is no different. Although I mention more than thirty different practice exercises in chapter nineteen, there are six areas I feel are most important. Practice in these six areas will not only improve your chances of survival but will also build confidence in your abilities and tools.

Exercise 1: Fire

Practice building a fire using the fire kit in your BOB. Familiarize yourself with the different ignition devices and fire tinder.

The test of a good fire is if it can boil water. Position a metal container of water above or beside the fire and bring the water to a boil. Below is a list of fire drills to practice:

- Start a fire at night using your headlamp to help you see to prepare your materials and search for fuel.

- Start a fire after a good rain when the ground is damp and wet. Practice building a fire platform and finding dry fuel.
- Start a fire when it's cold out. You will quickly understand how the cold weather can limit the mobility in your fingers and hands.

Exercise 2: Preparing Meals

If you've decided to pack meals that require any kind of preparation, a few practice runs can work out any potential problems in your kit. Become comfortable with the following:

- Prepare a meal for yourself and your family using only your Bug Out Bag. For this meal, use whatever heating device you've decided to pack, i.e., solid fuel tablets stove or canister stove. Just have a Bug Out dinner in the backyard one night. Also practice cleaning the items with the resources in your BOB and packing everything back up. Take note of how much water is used and think of ways to make the entire process easier and smarter.
- Do exactly as listed above except heat your meal using an open fire.
- If you are really ambitious,

take a weekend camping trip and bring only the meal items in your BOB and see how realistic your food items are. Did you pack too much or not enough?

Exercise 3: Shelter

The ability to quickly and safely set up a reliable shelter system is critical. Get this wrong in a real Bug Out and it could very well be game over. The following exercises will help:

- Set up your main shelter system. Make sure you have enough cordage, stakes, etc. Take mental notes about how much space you need to set up the shelter.
- Do the same as above but do it at night with only the light from your headlamp.
- Pretend your primary shelter system has been lost, damaged, or stolen. Practice setting up a backup shelter system using a poncho, tarp, or emergency blanket. Do you have the proper materials in your BOB to get this done? Don't worry, this exercise takes practice. I've set up tarp/poncho shelters many times over the years and am still perfecting the process. Many variables can affect the set-up configuration including weather, trees or lack of trees, and soil consistency, such as rock or sand.

Exercise 4: Take a Hike!

I remember my first Bug Out Bag. I was an overzealous survivalist and got a little carried away . . . until I decided to take a ten-mile practice hike with it. I realized about one mile in that I needed to make some serious changes. First, the pack did not fit me well. It did when it was empty but not loaded to capacity. Second, it was *way* too heavy. I immediately started to refine my pack list to reduce weight and bulk.

- Hike five miles with your BOB. If you have a family, take them, too. Take the Bug Out Wagon and the dog. Do a five-mile Bug Out dry run. Don't forget to wear your Bug Out Boots. Make any necessary changes based on this experience.
- Do this at least once every two months.

Exercise 5: Water and Hydration

In any survival situation, potable water is at the top of your priority list. It is very important to be comfortable and confident with using the water purification resources you have in your BOB: boiling, filter systems, or chemical treatment. Following are some important exercises in learning and understanding your hydration equipment:

Boiling: Using your metal water container or cooking pot, bring water to a boil. Do this with both your cooking heating system and an open fire. Use your multi-tool or leather gloves to handle the hot container and manipulate it around the heat. Take note of the following:

- How long does it take to bring water to a boil?
- How close does my container need to be to the fire?
- How big does my fire need to be?
- How much fuel did I use?
- How did my container perform? Do I need a different container?

Filtering: First, practice pre-filtering water from a nearby stream or pond through a bandana into one of your water containers. Remember to always keep at least one container sanitary and untouched from contaminated water. Then, using your filter system, filter your pre-filtered water from your "contaminated" container into your sanitary container. Be sure you understand how to assemble, disassemble and store your filtration system without written directions.

Chemical Treatment: Memorize the instructions and doses of your chemical treatment tabs. This information might wear off the bottle and you need to know it by heart.

Exercise 6: Self-Defense

The average person has *zero* self-defense training. Unless your job requires some kind of close combat training (i.e., police, security, professional or amateur fighter, military), you've probably never taken any formal self-defense instruction. You should really consider enrolling in a local self-defense class to understand the basics of a few demobilizing striking techniques that may allow you to escape if ever attacked.

I'm not asking you to go get a black belt in karate. I am asking that you become familiar with the human body, it's weaknesses, and how to exploit them if necessary.

SUMMARY

Your mind and body are your two most important Bug Out resources. They both require proper and specific training to be prepared for the demands of a disaster Bug Out.

There are hundreds of ways to die and none of them require skill or repetition. Increase your chances of survival by practicing the mental and physical exercises in this book.

18 THE BUG OUT PLAN

I WISH I COULD TELL YOU that building a Bug Out Bag and being competent in using it's contents was all you needed to be prepared for a Bug Out. While you've made a *huge* stride in the right direction, the BOB is one of four Bug Out preparedness elements.

Theoretically, each element could justify it's own book like this one. For now, though, a basic understanding of each element is sufficient. I do offer a three-day Bug Out Training program at the Willow Haven Outdoor Training Facility, if you are interested.

THE BUG OUT PLAN (BOP)

A BOP is your overall action plan should a real Bug Out actually be necessary. It is a pre-thought-out play-by-play guidebook to getting out of Dodge. It can be as simple as a checklist or checklists (for families).

Preparing and storing a BOB is a part of your overall BOP. There are many facets to consider before, during, and after a Bug Out. Below are a few important questions that should be covered in a BOP.

1. Where is the family/team meeting?
2. What vehicle will we be driving?
3. What needs to be done to the house to prepare it for an evacuation?
   - install waterproof and fireproof safe
   - lock away valuables
   - turn off water and utilities
   - plug drains
   - disconnect gas lines
   - secure doorways
   - leave notes
   - get extra gas cans

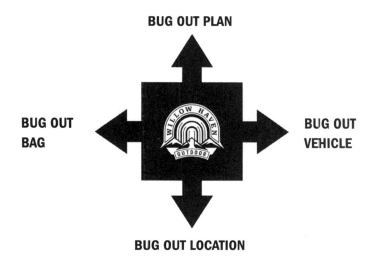

BUG OUT PLAN

BUG OUT BAG

BUG OUT VEHICLE

BUG OUT LOCATION

4. Who is responsible for each task?
5. Does each person have a checklist of responsibilities?
6. Are any pets going?
7. If we Bug Out, where is our destination?
8. How will we be getting there?

A disaster Bug Out is going to be mass chaos! Having an action plan will expedite the process as well as help to avoid costly mistakes. Don't think you can possibly remember to do everything without a clear and concise checklist and action plan. This plan is your Bug Out Plan.

Creek's 1972 Ford Bronco

Bug Out Horse

BUG OUT VEHICLE (BOV)

A Bug Out Vehicle is your preferred mode of transportation to your Bug Out Location (discussed next). It may or may not get you all the way there for a variety of reasons but ideally you need to choose a solid, capable, and reliable BOV. One of my friends swears the best BOV is a horse. He argues that it doesn't require fuel, is fairly self-sufficient, can carry plenty of gear and can travel through and across a huge variety of terrain—on and off road. He makes some great points but it certainly isn't practical for everyone to have a horse for their BOV.

I believe that all families should consider a potential Bug Out when purchasing vehicles. Here are some guidelines that I consider important when choosing a BOV:

Guideline 1: In Good Working Order/Low Maintenance

This is pretty much common sense. Your BOV must be reliable and it must be equipped with the proper tools and parts for emergency main-

Solid Spare Tire is a Must

Roof Storage Rack and Brush Guard

tenance. Below is a basic checklist of items you need to have in your BOV:

- spare tire (or 2)
- solid jack and lug wrench
- extra fluids (oil, transmission, power steering fluid, brake, coolant, etc.)
- oil filter
- new replacement belts
- spare hoses

- new battery
- maintenance tools to replace the above mentioned parts
- trickle charger
- work gloves

If you know your BOV is in good working order, you really shouldn't need a whole trunk full of spare auto parts to get you to your destination. On a side note to this first element— you should know how to work on your BOV. That may mean that you have to practice. My personal BOV is a 1972 Bronco. A big reason for this is that I can pretty much fix anything that goes wrong with the engine. Modern vehicles equipped with computers and thousands of parts can be very difficult to work on. This is definitely something to consider.

Guideline 2: Off-Road Capabilities— 4×4

Your BOV must be able to go off road. Four-wheel drive is a must. Most SUVs are probably sufficient enough to do the trick. If you are ever in a situation when you actually need to use your BOV, my guess is that it's not a far stretch to imagine that you might have to take it off road. Having a wench (or two) would be nice, but those can be pricey. You might be able to find a good used one online. At the very minimum, store a come-a-long and fifty feet of chain. Nice, solid-

Five-Gallon Refuelling Cans

Fuel Storage Rack

tread tires are a good idea for snow and mud. Keeping a set of traction devices in your vehicle is a good idea, too. A friend of mine told me that two strips of old carpet turned upside down work as good traction devices to help you get out of ditches, drifts, or mud holes.

Guideline 3: Fuel Range/Efficiency

What's the point of having a BOV unless it has the fuel range to get you to your destination? Your BOV should have a full tank of gas at all times. More than likely, your Bug Out Trip is not going to be a straight and easy uninterrupted path to your destination. You might have detours, traffic jams, and even off-road situations. It's a good idea to know exactly how much fuel you will need to get you to

your BOL. After you know that, you need four times this much stocked on your BOV—either in an aftermarket large-capacity fuel tank or separate five-gallon fuel cans. No fuel means no driving. You would be naïve to think that pulling over for a fill-up is going to be an option.

Guideline 4: Cargo Space

Clearly, you need cargo space to transport you and your loved ones. But you also need to calculate in enough space for Bug Out Bags and other essential items that should be in your BOV including shelter, food, weapons, water, maintenance tools, and gas. Roof racks and add-on cargo baskets are great solutions to storage problems. I'm not a big fan of towing a trailer with your BOV, but if

Creek's Former 4x4 Ford Van With Roof Cage Cargo Rack

Brush Guards

you have to, you will need to make sure you have a heavy-duty hitch that will take some off-road beatings. A custom roof cage provides plenty of overhead cargo storage space.

Guideline 5: Supplies

This topic is not just one item. It is a category that encompasses a variety of items that I classify as *supplies.* Your Bug Out Bag should already contain most of your 72-hour survival needs. The supplies in this category are in addition to the supplies already in your BOB. This is not necessarily a complete list. I am always changing and adapting my kits—it's what I call a "live" list. In no particular order, your BOV kit should include:

- large axe or saw for clearing brush/cutting wood
- flares/signaling devices
- shovel
- fire extinguisher
- paper maps of your local area/ region
- extra batteries for any battery-powered tools
- two flashlights
- more extensive first aid kit than what is in your BOB
- bolt cutters
- large-scale crowbar
- functional CB radio
- basic toolkit
- vehicle manual
- clean drinking water—as much as you can store
- GPS
- binoculars
- fishing gear (it packs tight and weighs almost nothing)

Bug Out ATV

Bug Out Bicycle

- blankets
- extra fuel
- one-gallon of bleach (disinfectant)

Alternative Bug Out Vehicles

Everyone's situation is different. A car might not always be the best BOV. If you live in a large city like New York, you might not even own a car or SUV. Bug Out Vehicles are only limited by your creativity. Almost any form of transportation is better than traveling by foot. Smaller BOVs, such as bicycles, scooters, motorcycles, all-terrain vehicles (ATVs), and utility terrain vehicles (UTVs) all have their own set of unique advantages.

Bicycles, for example, can be outfitted to carry a surprising amount of extra supplies in addition to the BOB on your back. They are also not dependant on fuel, which will be in limited supply during any large-scale evacuation. Bicycles, scooters, dirt-bikes, and motorcycles also have excellent maneuverability through traffic jams and congested traffic.

Three-wheelers, four-wheelers, dune buggies, and utility vehicles all make excellent BOVs for cross-country travel. They can haul tons of gear and go nearly anywhere. The big drawback is that they are not road-legal. However, if I'm running from the wake of any large-scale disaster, I don't think I will be too concerned, but it's still an issue to keep in mind.

BUG OUT LOCATION (BOL)

How can you expect to get somewhere if you don't know where you are go-

Remote Cabin

Might have to walk to BOL

ing? A BOL is your destination point. This could be your home away from home for quite a while so it needs to be chosen with thoughtful consideration. Below are my basic guidelines about a BOL:

A Realistic Distance

It is my opinion that a BOL needs to be at least one gas tank away from all large cities. Should there be a large-scale economic, infrastructure, and supply chain collapse, people will be venturing out from the cities into the surrounding area in search of resources, such as food, fuel, medicines, etc. If this happens, fuel will be scarce and very costly. Being at least one-gas tank away will drastically limit how much you encounter scavengers and population crushes.

At the same time, a BOL needs to be within a 72-hour walk from your home. If for some crazy reason you need to abandon your vehicle, you should be able to reach your BOL on foot within the survival time frame of your Bug Out Bag—72 hours. My BOL is eighty miles away from my home. I really hope I never have to walk eighty miles with my BOB. In my opinion, your BOL should be no farther than an eight-hour drive (preferably less) from your home. Theoretically, it should only be a two to three hour drive.

House, Hotel, Woods—Where?

I believe your BOL should be the home of a friend or family member who has agreed to house you and your family in the event of a Bug Out. You can of-

Two of Six Supply Shelves at Creek's BOL

fer them the same exchange. I'm not a big fan of bugging out to a hotel simply because you have no guarantees of availability. I've also heard more times than I can count from friends within the survivalist community about their plans to Bug Out into the wilderness. Typically, whoever says this hasn't spent much time in the woods. Surviving for an extended period of time in a wilderness environment is *extremely* difficult—especially after you've exhausted your immediate Bug Out supplies. Bugging out into the primitive wilderness is not practical or realistic. It sounds fun and adventurous, but the reality of it is quite the opposite—even for an experienced survivalist. My BOL is my childhood home—my parent's farm in southern Indiana. It is important to make BOL arrangements in advance.

Here are a few short-term BOL options to consider:

- Stay with friends or family (preferred option)
- Purchase and prepare a small plot of remote land with a camper, travel trailer or cabin
- Stay mobile in an RV
- Campgrounds/parks/retreat centers
- Establish relationships with local/regional preppers through clubs and meetings
- Network with co-workers, friends and church members
- Have a second home (not necessarily short-term)

Should I have supplies at my BOL?

Yes, you should. I store a three-month supply of food at my BOL as well as an extensive first aid kit. I also keep a cache of hunting supplies, ammo, and several other survival items. Without trying to sound apocalyptic, getting to your BOL might just be the first phase of survival. Your BOB covers the first 72 hours, your BOL should sustain you long-term until you are able to reestablish yourself back at home.

SUMMARY

Clearly, there is more to consider than just a Bug Out Bag. Hurricanes, floods, tornados, terrorists, wild fires, plagues

Wood Burning Stove, Solar Power Kit, Candles and Oil Lamp

and foreign invaders will show you no mercy. None of these disasters will pause while you argue about where to go or whether or not to take Freckles the Ferret with you. Survival is not about guarantees—there is always a gamble and the disaster typically has the house advantage. The only way to increase your odds of living is to plan and prepare in advance. A thorough understanding of the four facets of a Bug Out will drastically improve your chances of survival.

19 BUG OUT RESOURCES & AT-HOME EXERCISES

BUILDING A BUG OUT BAG requires three main areas of preparation: Bug Out Gear, information/knowledge and hands-on practice. I have divided this chapter into the twelve Bug Out supply categories (plus pets). Under each category I have listed the following three headings:

1. **Gear Resources:** Under this heading, I have listed many of the Bug Out Gear items mentioned in this book along with where you can purchase them.

2. **Further Study:** Under this listing, I include a variety of resources for more in-depth study of that particular category. These resources can be books, websites, organizations, schools, etc.

3. **At-Home Exercises:** Practice makes perfect. It's important that you know how to use the gear and tools in your BOB. This heading lists important At-Home Exercises to familiarize yourself and your family with key Bug Out tools and skills.

WATER & HYDRATION
Gear Resources
Nalgene Water Bottles (Resin & Stainless)

- nalgene.com
- dickssportinggoods.com
- moosejaw.com
- rei.com
- many other outdoor camping retailers and websites

Nalgene Canteen that fits inside Metal Military Canteen Cup (Resin)

- www.canteenshop.com

Collapsible Platypus Water Bottles

- cascadedesigns.com/platypus

Metal Water Bottles

- campmor.com: Search *water bottles*
- kleankanteen.com

Water Purification Tablets

- aquamira.com
- katadyn.com
- moosejaw.com
- willowhavenoutdoor.com

Water Filter Systems

- aquamira.com
- rei.com
- moosejaw.com
- dickssportinggoods.com
- forgesurvivalsupply.com

Further Study

- aquamira.com
- katadyn.com
- youtube.com: Search *survival water purification*

At-Home Exercises

- Practice pre-filtering drinking water using a variety of items in your BOB including a bandana, a feminine napkin, and an N95 dust mask.
- If you've chosen to pack a filter purification system, be sure to understand exactly how it works. Practice filtering water using the system with special attention to keeping dirty containers separate from clean containers.
- Practice bringing water to a boil in one of your metal containers. Use your modern heating system (solid fuel tablet or canister) and also a fire. Make mental notes of how much fuel is required and how long it takes.

FOOD & FOOD PREPARATION
Gear Resources
Meals Ready to Eat (MREs)

- mredepot.com
- mrestar.com
- local Army/Navy surplus stores

Camping Dehydrated Meals

- wisefoodstorage.com
- mountainhouse.com
- survivalacres.com
- moosejaw.com

- rei.com
- forgesurvivalsupply.com
- dickssportinggoods.com
- many other outdoor camping retailers and websites

Lightweight Backpack Cook Set

- gsioutdoors.com
- rei.com
- many other outdoor camping retailers and websites

Metal Mug/Cup

- gsioutdoors.com: Search *glacier cup*
- basspro.com: Search *glacier cup*

Spork

- campmor.com: Search *spork*
- industrialrev.com

P-38 Can Opener

- willowhavenoutdoor.com
- local Army/Navy surplus stores

Esbit Stove and Fuel Tablets

- campmor.com: Search *esbit*
- industrialrev.com

WetFire Solid Fuel Tablet Stove and WetFire Tablets

- campmor.com: Search *wet fire stove*

Canister Stoves

- cascadedesigns.com/msr
- snowpeak.com
- dickssportinggoods.com
- moosejaw.com
- rei.com
- campmor.com: Search *stoves*
- forgesurvivalsupply.com

Further Study

- survivalacres.com
- mreinfo.com
- youtube.com: Search *survival cooking*

At-Home Exercises

- Prepare a meal using only items in your BOB. Do this both with your BOB modern heating stove and with a fire. Clean up afterwards using only items from your BOB. Take note of any ways to improve efficiency. Have a Bug Out "meal night" once a month. This not only helps with practice and repetition but also keeps fresh meal items in your BOB.
- Practice building a tripod by which to hang a pot over a fire for warming food or boiling water. Do you need to brush up on your tripod lashing skills?

CLOTHING
Gear Resources

Clothing (Shirts, Pants, Fleeces, Underwear, Wool Socks, Gloves, Hats)

- dickssportinggoods.com
- moosejaw.com
- rei.com
- many other outdoor camping retailers and websites (buy this in person)

Further Study

- None

At-Home Exercises

- If you live in an area with cold seasons, put together a cold weather layering system. Use this system when doing outdoor work to familiarize yourself with your needs and requirements.
- Build a fire and use it to dry out wet clothes and boots. Take special note of how long this takes and how much fuel it requires to get the job done. This is a very real Bug Out task.

SHELTER & BEDDING
Gear Resources

Military-Style Poncho

- uscav.com: Search *poncho*
- local Army/Navy surplus stores

Lightweight Tarp

- moosejaw.com (awesome selection)
- equinoxltd.com
- bushcraftoutfitters.com
- bensbackwoods.com
- etowahoutfittersultralight backpackinggear.com

Backpacking Tent

- rei.com: Search *tent*
- campmor.com: Search *tent*
- dickssportinggoods.com
- moosejaw.com
- many other outdoor camping retailers and websites

Sleeping Bag

- many outdoor camping retailers and websites (buy this in person)

Ground Pad

- cascadedesigns.com/therm-a-rest
- rei.com
- many other outdoor camping retailers and websites

Emergency Blanket

- adventuremedicalkits.com
- Many other outdoor camping retailers and websites

Wool Blanket

- willowhavenoutdoor.com

Further Study

- youtube.com: Search *tarp shelter, poncho shelter, emergency blanket shelter, tarp shelter knots*
- realitysurvival.com
- animatedknots.com

At-Home Exercises

- Practice setting up your primary shelter until it becomes second nature. Use your shelter system for overnight camping at least two nights each season. This is the only way to identify flaws in your set-up and to improve processes.
- In addition to your primary shelter system, become proficient setting up an emergency shelter using a poncho, tarp, trash bag, or emergency blanket.
- Learn how to tie the following knots by memory: Taut-Line Hitch, Double Half Hitch, and Siberian Hitch. I use these knots with every shelter I build. Find an instructional video on how to tie these knots at willowhavenoutdoor.com.
- Test your sleeping bag and pad in *all* seasons. Have you chosen the right degree rating to survive a Bug Out in any season?

FIRE
Gear Resources
Weather Proof Matches
- campmor.com: Search *matches*

Ferrocerium Rods/Fire Steel
- bensbackwoods.com
- industrialrev.com
- kodiakfirestarters.com

WetFire Fire Starting Tinder
- campmor.com: Search *wetfire*
- willowhavenoutdoor.com

Further Study
- youtube.com: Search *survival fire starters, wetfire, how to build a fire*

At-Home Exercises
- Use your ignition devices (lighter, matches, fire steel) to ignite your cooking stoves. Understand what it takes to light each one.
- Practice lighting your store bought tinder (PET Balls and WetFire) using all of your ignition devices.
- Practice collecting and igniting natural found fire tinder, such as dry grasses, cattail down, and birch bark. Mix your Carmex lip balm with natural found tinder to see how it can be used as a flame extender.
- Practice building a fire large enough to cook a meal and boil water. Do this in all seasons and after it rains. Practice building a fire platform to protect your fire from the wet ground or snow.

FIRST AID
Gear Resources
Adventure Sports First Aid Kit
- adventuremedicalkits.com
- readykor.com
- rei.com
- dickssportinggoods.com
- moosejaw.com
- many other outdoor camping retailers and websites

Emergency Blanket
- adventuremedicalkits.com
- many other outdoor camping retailers and websites

Potassium Iodide Anti-Radiation Pills
- ki4u.com
- nukepills.com

Further Study
Websites
- cdc.gov
- *Wilderness Medicine* magazine: wms.org
- Wilderness Medicine Institute: nols.edu/wmi
- ki4u.com (great information

about nuclear threats and radioactive iodine)

- nukepills.com (great information about nuclear threats and radioactive iodine)

Books

- *Field Guide to Wilderness Medicine* by Paul S. Auerbach
- *Where There Is No Doctor* by David Werner, Jane Maxwell, and Carol Thuman
- *Medicine for the Outdoors: The Essential Guide to Emergency Medical Procedures and First Aid* by Paul S. Auerbach
- *Outdoor Medical Emergency Handbook* by Dr. Spike Briggs and Dr. Campbell Mackenzie

At-Home Exercises

- Take a local first aid course to learn basic first aid skills and treatment methods. Many community centers offer these classes. If yours does not, look for local class listings on americanheart.org and redcross.org.
- The Centers for Disease Control has a wealth of first aid and disaster related information on their website. Your taxes paid for it, so you might as well take advantage of the "free" information at cdc.gov.

HYGIENE
Gear Resources

Light Load Towels

- ultralighttowels.com

Personal Hygiene Items

- local markets and pharmacy stores

Further Study

The Centers for Disease Control also has some great information about disaster related hygiene issues. You can view it here: www.bt.cdc.gov/disasters

At-Home Exercises

- None

TOOLS
Gear Resources

Survival Knife

- Blackbird SK-5 Wilderness Survival Knife: hedgehogleatherworks.com
- Becker BK2 Knife: willowhavenoutdoor.com and hedgehogleatherworks.com
- Gerber Big Rock Camp Knife: gerbergear.com and dickssportinggoods.com: Search *Big Rock Camp Knife*
- Mora 840 MGKnife: willowhavenoutdoor.com and ragweedforge.com

Multi-Tool
- leatherman.com
- rei.com
- budk.com

Machete
- willowhavenoutdoor.com
- coldsteel.com
- uscav.com

Collapsible Snow Shovel (For Heavy Winter Snow)
- ebay.com: Search *ski shovel*

Further Study
- youtube.com: Search *knife batoning, feather sticks, leatherman survival, survival knife*

At-Home Exercises
- Practice "batoning" with your survival knife. Batoning is when you strike the back side of your knife with a heavy stick or rock to drive the blade into or through larger wood. This is a great method for splitting firewood or chopping down larger saplings.
- Carve a set of tent stakes and use them when setting your shelter. Make a note of how big/long they should be to work properly.
- Get in the habit of carrying a pocket knife and use it often.

LIGHTING
Gear Resources
Headlamps
- campmor.com: Search *headlamp*
- dickssportinggoods.com
- moosejaw.com
- many other outdoor camping retailers and websites

Mini Keychain Maglight
- local hardware stores

Photon Keychain LED Lights
- willowhavenoutdoor.com
- photonlight.com
- laughingrabbitinc.com

9-Hour Candles
- willowhavenoutdoor.com
- campmor.com: Search *candle*

Further Study
- None

At-Home Exercises
- Practice setting up your primary and emergency shelter at night using the light from your headlamp.
- Build a fire from scratch at night using just the light from your headlamp.
- Prepare one of your Bug Out meals at night using the light from your headlamp.

COMMUNICATIONS

Gear Resources

Hand-Crank Multi-Function Emergency Radio and Cell Phone Charger

- etoncorp.com
- campmor.com: Search *eton*
- rei.com

Heavy-Duty Document Map Case

- many outdoor camping retailers and websites: water sports section
- campmor.com: Search *map case*

Two-Way Radios

- Many outdoor camping retailers and websites

Compass

- many outdoor camping retailers and websites

Rite in the Rain All Weather Notebook

- riteintherain.com

Further Study

- Information about the National Weather Service and NOAA Weather Radio can be found at: www.nws.noaa.gov/nwr
- youtube.com: Search *how to use a compass*

At-Home Exercises

- Mark three different routes on a map to your Bug Out Location (BOL). Travel each of these routes at least once. It's a good idea to know these routes intimately with special notations made for gas stations, water sources, parking areas, camping areas, and detour options.
- Most people don't understand how to use a compass. Practice using your compass in coordination with your paper map to reach a destination. A simple Boy Scout manual will tell you everything you need to know about using a compass (called orienteering).
- Use your emergency radio to gather information. Know which stations work in your area. During bad weather, try to gather storm or weather information to make predictions. This radio is just a paperweight if you don't understand how to use it to receive valuable information.

PROTECTION & SELF-DEFENSE
Gear Resources
Pepper Spray

- coldsteel.com: Search *pepper spray*
- many other outdoor camping retailers and websites

Further Study

- local self-defense classes

At-Home Exercises

- Take a local self-defense class. Become familiar with very specific demobilizing strikes to key body parts.
- Before my first canister of pepper spray expired, I used it as a practice exercise because I had never fired a can of pepper spray. I wanted to understand exactly how it fired, how sensitive the trigger was, and what I could expect for accuracy and distance. I suggest you do the same if your canister comes to an expiration date.
- If you've decided to carry a gun, then you should know that weapon intimately. You need to know how to trouble-shoot any issues, such as clearing a jam. This knowledge will come naturally with repeated practice at a range. You should be able to disassemble and re-assemble your gun blind-folded. You should also routinely target practice with your gun. Clean your gun after every use to keep it in peak operating condition.

MISCELLANEOUS SUPPLIES
Gear Resources
Fishing Kit

- This is assembled yourself from à la carte items purchased at a local fishing shop.

550 Parachute Cord

- willowhavenoutdoor.com
- combatparacord.com
- uscav.com
- local Boy Scout shops usually carry 550 paracord

Small Sewing Kit

- local fabric store or big-box store

The following items can be purchased at pretty much any hardware store or discount department store:

- N95 Dust Masks
- contractor-grade 55-gallon garbage bags
- resealable plastic bags
- 36" length of latex tubing
- duct tape
- bandanas

Further Study

- youtube.com: Search *survival fishing kit, paracord uses, survival garbage bag*
- animatedknots.com

At-Home Exercises

- Build a makeshift rain catch in your backyard using a garbage bag.
- Using your 550 paracord, learn the following knots: Boline, Square Knot, Tripod Lashing, and Clove Hitch.
- Cut off 6" of 550 paracord and unravel the inner stands so that you understand how it's made.
- Make a quick poncho out of a 55-gallon garbage bag. Perfect the best location and size of your head and arm holes.

BUG OUT PET GEAR

Gear Resources

Dog Packs/Gear

- rei.com
- petco.com

Granite Gear Slurpin Bowl and Other Crushable Pet Bowls

- moosejaw.com

Goat Packing Supplies

- NAPgA.org
- northwestpackgoats.com
- buttheadpackgoats.com

Further Study

- NAPgA.org: pack goat information

At-Home Exercises

- If you plan on your pet carrying its own Bug Out Gear, it needs training just like you do. Start with just having your pet wear the pack or harness without any weight or gear. Over the course of a few weeks and several walks, gradually add a little weight one walk at a time.

Shopping Receipt for Majority of Bug Out Supplies

3,440 Cubic Inch Backpack

THE QUICKIE $303.80 BUG OUT BAG

For me, building a Bug Out Bag is a very fun process. I enjoy the process of sourcing and gathering all of the different kit items that go into my BOB. I am a stickler about quality, too, so most of my tools and kit items are the best of the best. I understand, though, that some people have no interest in the building process at all but still understand the importance of having a Bug Out Bag. Many people just aren't "gear junkies" and are simply looking for a quick, easy, and affordable solution to assembling a sufficient BOB to have on hand.

If this is you, I've taken the liberty of putting together a nearly complete BOB contents list that can be sourced from one trip to your local big-box store for $303.80 (at the time of this writing). And, if you already have a few key items, like a backpack, sleeping bag, or survival knife, the cost goes way down. Please note—many of the items in this list are what I would consider to be "sufficient." Big-box stores such as Wal-Mart are not a specialty outdoor retailer that carry premier camping, backpacking, and survival brands, but I have watched their camping section evolve over the years to include a very descent selection of suitable gear. If you are looking for a one-stop Bug Out shopping trip, then this is the closest you are going to get. Because of the wide degree of variables, this shopping list does not include clothing, baby/infant, or pet items. I will also note a few items that are not included in the categories below.

Water Bottles and Purification Tablets

Food for Bug Out

Big-Box Store Bug Out Bag Shopping List

Bug Out Backpack: Outdoor Products 3,440 cubic inch internal frame backpack: $59.00. Features:

- hydration reservoir compatible
- six easy-access outside pockets
- padded shoulder straps and hip belt
- bottom D-rings for strapping on sleeping pad

Water and Hydration

- Outdoor Products AluminumWater Bottle: $5.00
- .75-liter store-brand plastic water bottle: $1.50
- Outdoor Products 2.0 Liter Hydration Bladder: $9.88
- Coleman Water Purification Tablets: $5.88

NOTE: Does not include water.

Food and Food Preparation

- 2 Coleman Dehydrated Camping Meals: $4.88 each
- 3 CLIF Bar energy bars: $.98 each
- Coleman Max Micro Stove: $25.88
- Coleman Butane/Propane Fuel Canister for stove: $4.88
- Outdoor Products 4 Piece Spork Set: $3.88
- Great Value Coffee in metal can (to use as cooking pot): $2.98

NOTE: Does not include metal cup/ mug, pot scrubber, and P-38 can opener

Clothing

- Rocky Wool Hiking Socks: $7.97
- Coleman adult poncho: $6.44
- Wells Lamont Cowhide Leather Work Gloves: $2.50

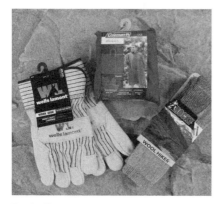

Basic Clothing Items

Sleeping Bag and Sleeping Pad

Tarp

NOTE: Does not include boots, clothing, underwear, hats, and cold weather gear.

Shelter and Bedding

- Ozark Trail 8'×10' Tarp: $6.88
- Coleman 40 Degree Sleeping Bag: $22.88
- Ozark Trail Camping Pad: $6.44

NOTE: Does not include tent or paracord.

Fire

- Generic lighter: $.97
- Coleman Magnesium Bar & Fire Striker: $7.44 (Magnesium is a form of fire tinder)
- Coleman Waterproof Matches: $1.88
- Coleman Match Case: $1.00

First Aid

- Ozark Trail Emergency Blanket: $2.88
- Coleman 15 percent DEET Insect Repellent: $2.88
- Coppertone SPF 30 Sunscreen: $.97
- Coleman Day Tripper First Aid Kit: $7.88

NOTE: Does not include any extra additions to the first aid kit.

Fire Starting Items

Basic First Aid Items

Hygiene Items

Hygiene

- Coleman Camp Soap: $3.88
- Coleman Camp Towel: $3.88
- Generic compact mirror with brush: $.97
- Purell Hand Sanitizer: $1.52
- Wet Ones Antibacterial Wipes: $.97
- Kleenex 3-pack: $.97
- Wisp 4-pack disposable toothbrushes: $1.50

NOTE: Does not include feminine items.

Lighting

- Energizer LED Headlamp: $4.88
- Rayovac Keychain LED: $2.00

NOTE: Does not include candle or glow stick.

Tools

- Remington Full Tang Fixed Blade 5³/₈" Knife With Sheath: $24.97
- Ozark Trail Multi-Tool: $9.88 (I highly recommend an upgrade)

Communications

- Ozark Trail Compass/Whistle/Thermometer/Magnifier Combo Unit: $3.88

NOTE: Does not include emergency radio, local maps or two-way radios.

Lighting Items

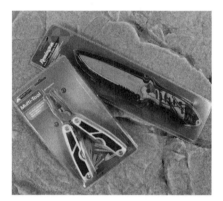

Tools

Emergency Whistle

Protection and Self-Defense
- Remington Full Tang Fixed Blade 5³/₈" Knife With Sheath: $24.97

NOTE: Does not include pepper spray, gun, or ammunition.

Miscellaneous Supplies
- 48' Secure Line Nylon Braided Rope: $2.57
- Stanley N95 Disposable Respirator: $4.97
- Great Value freezer bags—quart and gallon: $1.76 each
- Two-pack 100-percent cotton bandana: $2.00
- Duck Brand duct tape: $2.97

NOTE: Does not include garbage bags, sunglasses, sewing kit, latex tubing, fishing kit, or binoculars.

SURVIVAL BLOGS: A WEALTH OF INFORMATION

It seems a new survival blog pops up online every day. Almost all of them are unique in their own way. Some are educational and some are just entertaining, but the common thread is that the authors are all enthusiastic about survival on some level. Many of these bloggers specialize in specific survival-related topics and perspectives ranging from seed collecting to prepping tips for apartment dwellers. Every writing angle is a little

Miscellaneous Supplies

different based on the author's personal experiences and place in life—there is something for everyone. Following is a list of some survival-related blogs that you might find interesting. Some of them I read on a regular basis and some not at all. Tell them Creek sent you!

- 1800prepare.com/blog
- all-things-emergency-prepared.com/emergency-preparedness-blog.html
- amatterofpreparedness.blogspot.com

- americanpreppersnetwork.com
- apartmentprepper.com
- backdoorsurvival.com
- backwoodssurvivalblog.com
- beasurvivor.blogspot.com
- blog.iprepare.com
- bugoutsurvival.com
- canadianpreppersnetwork.com
- cardcanhelp.org/blog
- daily-survival.blogspot.com
- destinysurvival.com
- disasterpreparednessblog.com
- foodstorageandsurvival.com
- gsiep.blogspot.com
- heirloomseedswap.com
- ice-qube.com/blog
- justincasebook.wordpress.com
- modernsurvivalblog.com
- offgridsurvival.com
- pioneerliving.net
- preparednessandresponse.blogspot.com

thesurvivalmom.com

- preparednesspantry.blogspot.com
- preparednesspro.com/blog
- prepperwebsite.com
- realitysurvival.com
- saveourskills.com
- shtfamerica.blogspot.com
- shtfblog.com
- shtfplan.com
- stealthsurvival.blogspot.com
- survivalblog.com
- survivalcache.com
- survivalcommonsense.com
- survivaltopics.com
- survival-spot.com
- teotwawkiblog.blogspot.com
- texaspreppersnetwork.blogspot.com
- thereadystore.com/blog
- thesurvivalistblog.net
- thesurvivalmom.com
- thesurvivalpodcast.com
- tslrf.blogspot.com
- vikingpreparedness.blogspot.com
- wilderness-survival-skills.com

realitysurvival.com

survivalcache.com

WATER AND HYDRATION ORGANIZATIONAL SUPPLY CHECKLIST

	Primary Bug Out Bag Strongest Adult		
Contents List	**P1**	**P2**	**P3**
Fresh Drinking Water	2 liters	3 liters	3 liters
Collapsible Water Bottle	1	1	1
Nalgene Water Bottle	1	1	1
Metal Canteen (for boiling)		1	1
Water Purification Tablets (per person)	3	3	3
Purification Filter System		1	1

FOOD AND FOOD PREPARATION ORGANIZATIONAL SUPPLY CHECKLIST

	Primary Bug Out Bag Strongest Adult		
Contents List	**P1**	**P2**	**P3**
Open and Eat Bars (power, candy, granola)	6	6	6
MRE Meals or Dehydrated Meals		2	3
Baby Formula or Baby Food (infants only)			
Metal Cook Pot	1	1	1
Metal Cup	1	1	1
Spork	1	1	1
P38 Can Opener	1	1	1
Pot Scrubber		1	1
Heat System (besides fire):			
Solid Fuel Tablet Stove	1	1	1
Fuel for Solid Fuel Tablet Stove (per 2 adults)	6	6	8
Fuel for Canister Stove (per 2 adults)	1	1	1

Additional Adult Packs Ages 11+			Youth Packs Ages 6–10			Children/Infants Ages 5 & Under		
P1	P2	P3	P1	P2	P3	P1	P2	P3
2 liters	3 liters	3 liters	1 liter	2 liters	2 liters	½ liter	1 liter	1 liter
1	1	1		1	1	1	1	1
1	1	1	1	1	1			
	1	1						

Additional Adult Packs Ages 11+			Youth Packs Ages 6–10			Children/Infants Ages 5 & Under		
P1	P2	P3	P1	P2	P3	P1	P2	P3
6	6	6	6	6	6	shared	shared	shared
	2	3		1	2	shared	shared	shared
						4 days	4 days	4 days
1	1	1	shared	shared	shared	shared	shared	shared
1	1	1	shared	shared	shared	shared	shared	shared

P1 = Bare Minimum Packer, P2 = Average Packer, P3 = Extreme Packer

CLOTHING ORGANIZATIONAL SUPPLY CHECKLIST

Contents List	Primary Bug Out Bag Strongest Adult		
	P1	P2	P3
All-Weather Items (on your body out the door)			
Lightweight Long Sleeve Shirt	1	1	1
Pants	1	1	1
Underwear	1	1	1
Full-Coverage Button Onesie (infants only)			
Wool Hiking Socks	1	1	1
Ankle-High Hiking Boots (wearing these)	1	1	1
All-Weather Items (in your packs)			
Lightweight Long Sleeve Shirt	1	1	1
Pants		1	1
Underwear	1	1	1
Full-Coverage Button Onesies (infants only)			
Wool Hiking Socks	2	2	3
Mid-Weight Fleece	1	1	1
Crushable Brimmed Hat	1	1	1
Leather Work Gloves	1	1	1
Shemagh	1	1	1
Grommeted Military-Style Poncho	1	1	1
Simple Rain Poncho			
Cold-Weather Items			
Windproof/Waterproof Outer Shell	1	1	1
300-Weight Fleece or Wool Sweater (< 30°F temp)	1	1	1
Base Layer Upper Body	1	1	1
Base Layer Lower Body	1	1	1
Wool/Fleece Hat or Balaclava	1	1	1
Cold Weather Gloves/Wool Gloves	1	1	1

	Additional Adult Packs Ages 11+			Youth Packs Ages 6-10			Children/Infants Ages 5 & Under		
	P1	P2	P3	P1	P2	P3	P1	P2	P3
	1	1	1	1	1	1	1	1	1
	1	1	1	1	1	1	1	1	1
	1	1	1	1	1	1	1	1	1
							1	1	1
	1	1	1	1	1	1	1	1	1
	1	1	1	1	1	1	1	1	1
	1	1	1	1	1	1	1	1	1
		1	1		1	1	1	1	1
	1	1	1	1	1	1	1	1	1
							1	1	1
	2	2	3	2	2	3	2	2	3
	1	1	1	1	1	1	1	1	1
	1	1	1	1	1	1	1	1	1
	1	1	1						
	1	1	1						
	1	1	1						
				1	1	1	1	1	1
	1	1	1	1	1	1	1	1	1
	1	1	1	1	1	1	1	1	1
	1	1	1	1	1	1	1	1	1
	1	1	1	1	1	1	1	1	1
	1	1	1	1	1	1	1	1	1
	1	1	1	1	1	1	1	1	1

P1 = Bare Minimum Packer, P2 = Average Packer, P3 = Extreme Packer

SHELTER AND BEDDING ORGANIZATIONAL SUPPLY CHECKLIST

Contents List	Primary Bug Out Bag Strongest Adult			
	P1	P2	P3	
Tarp Shelter (sized for your group)	1	1	1	
Tent (sized for your group)		1	1	
Sleeping Bag	1	1	1	
Sleeping Ground Pad	1	1	1	
Paracord (also included in Misc. Supply Category)	50 ft	75 ft	100 ft	

FIRE ORGANIZATIONAL SUPPLY CHECKLIST

Contents List	Primary Bug Out Bag Strongest Adult			
	P1	P2	P3	
Ignition Source (lighter, matches, ferro)	2	2	3	
Fire Starting Tinder (WetFire, steel wool, magnesium bar, PET Balls)	2	2	3	
Waterproof Fire Kit Container	1	1	1	

FIRST AID ORGANIZATIONAL SUPPLY CHECKLIST

Contents List	Primary Bug Out Bag Strongest Adult			
	P1	P2	P3	
First Aid Kit in Water-Tight Container (sized for group with all items listed in chapter eight)	1	1	1	
Insect Repellant (small spray bottle)	1	1	1	
Mylar Survival Blanket	1	1	1	

Additional Adult Packs Ages 11+			Youth Packs Ages 6–10			Children/Infants Ages 5 & Under		
P1	P2	P3	P1	P2	P3	P1	P2	P3
1	1	1	1	1	1	shared	shared	shared
1	1	1	½	½	½	shared	shared	shared

Additional Adult Packs Ages 11+			Youth Packs Ages 6–10			Children/Infants Ages 5 & Under		
P1	P2	P3	P1	P2	P3	P1	P2	P3

Additional Adult Packs Ages 11+			Youth Packs Ages 6–10			Children/Infants Ages 5 & Under		
P1	P2	P3	P1	P2	P3	P1	P2	P3
1	1	1	shared	shared	shared	shared	shared	shared

P1 = Bare Minimum Packer, P2 = Average Packer, P3 = Extreme Packer

HYGIENE ORGANIZATIONAL SUPPLY CHECKLIST

Contents List	Primary Bug Out Bag Strongest Adult		
	P1	P2	P3
Disinfecting Wet Napkins (enough for group)	1	1	1
Travel Hand Sanitizer		1	1
Travel-Size All-Purposse Bar of Soap	1	1	1
Tampons/Sanitary Napkins (female only)	6	6	6
Hygiene/Signal Mirror	1	1	1
Small Pack Towel		1	1
Mini Travel Toothbrush/Pick		1	1
Toilet Paper (2 yards per person)	2	2	2
Diapers (infants only, per infant)	18	20	20
Wet Napkins (infants only, 20 pc package per infant)	2	2	2
Diaper Cream (infants only)	1	1	1

TOOLS ORGANIZATIONAL SUPPLY CHECKLIST

Contents List	Primary Bug Out Bag Strongest Adult		
	P1	P2	P3
Survival Knife with Sheath	1	1	1
Multi-Tool	1	1	1

LIGHTING ORGANIZATIONAL SUPPLY CHECKLIST

Contents List	Primary Bug Out Bag Strongest Adult		
	P1	P2	P3
LED Headlamp	1	1	1
Mini Keychain Maglite or Mini Keychain LED Light	1	1	1
Glow Stick		1	1
Candle		1	1

Additional Adult Packs Ages 11+			Youth Packs Ages 6–10			Children/Infants Ages 5 & Under		
P1	P2	P3	P1	P2	P3	P1	P2	P3
1	1	1	shared	shared	shared	shared	shared	shared
	1	1	shared	shared	shared	shared	shared	shared
			shared	shared	shared	shared	shared	shared
6	6	6						
	1	1	shared	shared	shared	shared	shared	shared
	1	1		1	1			
2	2	2	2	2	2			

Additional Adult Packs Ages 11+			Youth Packs Ages 6–10			Children/Infants Ages 5 & Under		
P1	P2	P3	P1	P2	P3	P1	P2	P3
1	1	1						

Additional Adult Packs Ages 11+			Youth Packs Ages 6–10			Children/Infants Ages 5 & Under		
P1	P2	P3	P1	P2	P3	P1	P2	P3
1	1	1						
1	1	1						

P1 = Bare Minimum Packer, P2 = Average Packer, P3 = Extreme Packer

COMMUNICATIONS ORGANIZATIONAL SUPPLY CHECKLIST

	Primary Bug Out Bag Strongest Adult			
Contents List	P1	P2	P3	
Cell Phone	1	1	1	
Alternative Power Charger (crank preferred)	1	1	1	
Emergency Radio With Batteries and Hand Crank	1	1	1	
Survival Document Portfolio in Waterproof Case	1	1	1	
$500–$1000 Cash in Small Denominations	1	1	1	
Quarters	5	5	5	
Paper Map of Local Area	1	1	1	
Compass	1	1	1	
Small Note Pad and Pencil	1	1	1	
Emergency Whistle	1	1	1	
Two-Way Radios (Optional)		1	1	

SELF-DEFENSE ORGANIZATIONAL SUPPLY CHECKLIST

	Primary Bug Out Bag Strongest Adult			
Contents List	P1	P2	P3	
Pepper Spray	1	1	1	
Survival Knife (already packed with tools supplies)	1	1	1	
Handgun (if trained properly)	1	1	1	
Rounds of Ammunition	15	20	25	

	Additional Adult Packs Ages 11+			Youth Packs Ages 6–10			Children/Infants Ages 5 & Under		
	P1	P2	P3	P1	P2	P3	P1	P2	P3
	1	1	1						
	1	1	1	1	1	1	1	1	1

	Additional Adult Packs Ages 11+			Youth Packs Ages 6–10			Children/Infants Ages 5 & Under		
	P1	P2	P3	P1	P2	P3	P1	P2	P3
	1	1	1						
	1	1	1						

P1 = Bare Minimum Packer, P2 = Average Packer, P3 = Extreme Packer

MISCELLANEOUS ORGANIZATIONAL SUPPLY CHECKLIST

Contents List	Primary Bug Out Bag Strongest Adult		
	P1	P2	P3
Feet of 550 Paracord	50	150	200
100 Percent Cotton Bandana	1	1	1
Feet of Duct Tape	15	25	25
55-Gallon Contractor-Grade Garbage Bag	1	1	2
Resealable Bags in Variety of Sizes	3	4	5
Sunglasses (double as safety glasses)	1	1	1
N95 Dust Masks	1	1	1
Sewing Kit		1	1
36" Latex Tubing	1	1	1
Fishing Kit		1	1
Binoculars/Monocular		1	1
Inspirational Item/Comfort Item	1	1	1

PETS ORGANIZATIONAL SUPPLY CHECKLIST

Contents List	Primary Bug Out Bag Strongest Adult		
	P1	P2	P3
Collapsible Water Bowl		1	1
72 Hours Worth of Water	1	1	1
72 Hours Worth of Dry Food	1	1	1
Vaccination Records	1	1	1
Leash (per animals)	1	1	1
Muzzle (if applicable)	1	1	1

Additional Adult Packs Ages 11+			Youth Packs Ages 6–10			Children/Infants Ages 5 & Under		
P1	P2	P3	P1	P2	P3	P1	P2	P3
1	1	1	1	1	1			
1	1	1	1	1	1			
1	1	1	1	1	1	1	1	1
1	1	1	1	1	1	1	1	1

Additional Adult Packs Ages 11+			Youth Packs Ages 6–10			Children/Infants Ages 5 & Under		
P1	P2	P3	P1	P2	P3	P1	P2	P3

P1 = Bare Minimum Packer, P2 = Average Packer, P3 = Extreme Packer

INDEX

ABOUT THE AUTHOR

Creek Stewart specializes in disaster preparedness and has consulted with individuals, corporations, non-profits and government agencies all over the United States about a myriad of preparedness-related subjects, projects, and initiatives.

A lifelong student of survival, preparedness, and self-reliance, Creek Stewart wrote his first survival manual at the age of twenty-one. Soon thereafter Creek began teaching survival and primitive skills courses on his family farm in Southern Indiana.

He now owns Willow Haven Outdoor, a leading survival and preparedness training facility that is 10,000 sq. ft. in size and situated on twenty-one beautiful acres in central Indiana. For information about survival clinics and training courses visit www.willowhavenoutdoor.com.

Creek is an Eagle Scout and graduate of Butler University in Indianapolis.

ACKNOWLEDGEMENTS

I am a sinner saved by grace and would like to thank my Father for His continued blessings and mercies, which I do not deserve. I would like to thank my amazing parents, Leslie and Margaret Stewart, and brother, Mike Stewart, for their continued support in my preparedness endeavors and efforts. My heartfelt thanks also go out to all of the readers, friends, and attendees of Willow Haven Outdoor and willowhavenoutdoor.com. Thank you for your continued support, readership, feedback, and instruction!

Finally, I would like to thank Brett McKay at ArtofManliness.com for allowing me to guest post on his awesome blog, Jackie Musser at F+W Media/Betterway Home Books for being the best acquisitions editor in the world, Marika Flatt and Tolly Moseley at PR by the Book for believing in this project and Dick Fetter for his abundance of rock solid advice over the years.

It's the purchaser's responsibility to read and follow all instructions and warnings on all product labels. Published by Betterway Home, an imprint of F+W Media, Inc., 10151 Carver Road, Suite 200, Blue Ash, Ohio, 45242. (800) 289-0963. First Edition.

Other fine Betterway Home books are available from your local bookstore and online suppliers. Visit our website at www.betterwaybooks.com.

20 19 18   18 17

ISBN 978-1-4403-1874-0

Distributed in the U.K. and Europe by F&W Media International, LTD
Brunel House, Newton Abbot, Forde Close, TQ12 4PU, UK
Tel: (+44) 1626 323200, Fax: (+44) 1626 323319
E-mail: enquiries@fwmedia.com

Edited by Jacqueline Musser
Designed by Clare Finney
Production Coordinated by Mark Griffin

BUG OUT BAG INVENTORY REVIEW SHEET

This five-page Bug Out Bag inventory Review Sheet will make packing and reviewing your Bug Out Bag's contents efficient and foolproof. Download it for free at **betterwaybooks.com/bobinventory**

MORE BOOKS ON SURVIVAL AND PREPAREDNESS

Build the Perfect Bug Out Vehicle
by Creek Stewart

Food Storage for Self-Sufficiency
and Survival by Angela Paskett

Living Ready Pocket Manual
First Aid by James Hubbard,
The Survival Doctor™

AVAILABLE ONLINE AND IN BOOKSTORES EVERYWHERE!

Join our mailing list at www.livingreadyonline.com.

Become a fan of our Facebook page: facebook.com/LivingReady

German

Home

Cooking

Maria M. Swearingen

German

Home

Cooking

Compiled and written by

Maria M. Swaringen
A native of Germany

Includes notes, true stories and memoirs of growing up in Germany.
Plus information regarding the "Munich Octoberfest", "Fasching"
(Mardi Gras) in Germany, etc.

ISBN: 1-4033-5293-3 (e-book)
ISBN: 1-4033-5294-1 (Paperback)
ISBN: 1-4033-5295-X (Hardcover)

This book is printed on acid free paper.

1stBooks - rev. 04/23/03

I dedicate this book to my late mother Ursula Wanderer, who taught me so patiently to learn and cook many of her recipes; to my husband Albert; my daughter Donna and family, and to my son Karlheinz, and his family.

I am very thankful to my friends and relatives for their recipes, inspiration and help, in making this a very useful German cookbook.

I am deeply indebted to:

Donna Wade, Tammy Swaringen, Marianne Keen, Edith McGowen, Ursula McHale, Heidi and Patrick McGowen, Wilma Gribble, Jonnie Kerruish, Ludwig Webel of the Tourist Information Office, Munich, Germany; to my relatives in Germany: Franziska Schuster, Karl and Renate Wanderer, Josef and Elisabeth Wanderer and Helga Wanderer; and especially to my husband Albert, who so patiently helped me with the English language.

INTRODUCTION

Born and raised in Germany, I have been living in the United States for 43 years. Naturally, most of my cooking is from the Old Country, while some of my American recipes have acquired a little touch of German taste.

Due to my husband's past career in the military, I have traveled extensively in the United States, from the tip of the north to the deep south. I have lived through record snow storms, sand storms, heat waves, and Hurricane Camille. I have met many wonderful people and sampled delicious food throughout the years; and learned how much German food is liked and appreciated by every American. Yet, one cannot find much information (if any) regarding "German cooking" in book stores.

For years I have been thinking of doing something about this, perhaps by putting only a small amount of my favorite recipes into print. However, I have discovered that to write a German cookbook, whether large or small, is quite an endeavor.

To translate a German recipe into English was not an easy task, not to mention the slight differential in measurement's, and/or weight. Most of my mother's recipes, as well as my own, were formulated without actually measuring. The recipes consisted of "a little here and a dash there", and somehow they always came out very tasty. There was no scale or a measuring cup used for most recipes, only the utilization of our sixth sense in how to accomplish it. I am also not a professional Chef; just a plain German housewife, and hope my readers realize that my English my not be perfect, since I received my education mostly in Germany.

I realized, that my choice of cookbook would have to depend upon my own personal taste. In retrospect, all of my own recipes, which are the majority of recipes found within this book, and the inclusive recipes from friends in the United States, and relatives who live back home in Germany, had to be tested before consideration of placing them in this cookbook.

Most of my recipes are southern cooking and baking; some are so old, that only a few people, and/or bakeries still make them, if at all. However, I also included a few American recipes that I have learned to love, and cook quite often for my family. While these are not bona fide German recipes, they have been, and still are prepared by a German person.

Most German foods are high in fat and calories, but one can substitute ingredients with a lesser fat content. Use fat free cream cheese for all cheese cakes, except cheese torte. Cool Whip can be used instead of whipping cream, except for cheese torte, ice coffee, etc. Use low fat sour cream, and a little less oil with vinegar and oil salad dressings. Light mayonnaise may be substituted for some of the potato and macaroni salads. Use a vegetable oil and flour spray, such as Bakers Joy, instead of the grease and flour method. For many dishes, one can use Pam for fat free cooking. Gravy mixes are also available fat free, and are found in grocery stores. However, when making butter cream, do not substitute with an off brand butter; use only the best sweet butter, such as Land O Lakes, for this butter cream is very tricky to make, but "oh", so good.

I come from the southern part of Germany, and if I may say, the most beautiful countryside in Bavaria. My home town Erding, is located within minutes from the newest airport near Munich, and within a short distance from the Bavarian Alps, as well as Austria and Switzerland. You may find my home town on the Internet at www.erding.de.

To make this a special and different "foreign" cookbook, I have included a few memoirs following some of the recipes. You will also find a few notes, and/or information regarding the Munich Octoberfest, Fasching (Mardi Gras), some little known facts about Germany, as well as, growing up in Germany during and right after World War II.

I am hoping, that these few German recipes will bring a lot of enjoyable eating into many homes. However I would like to remind my readers, that no recipe formulation is finite, and that almost every dish comes in a variety of many versions. German recipes are no exception. Not everyone has the same tastes for different foods. However, if my readers take pleasure in only one percent of these recipes, then my book was worth writing for their enjoyment.

For your convenience, I have written the Index in both German and English, so each recipe may be found easily. However, true stories and memoirs following some recipes are not listed under the Index.

Guten Appetit,

Maria M. Swaringen

CONTENTS

HERB SUGGESTIONS

BEEF AND PORK	FISH AND SEAFOOD	POULTRY
Oregano	Parsley	Bay Leaves
Rosemary	Basil	Cayenne
Basil	Tarragon	Celery Seeds
Paprika	Thyme	Chili Powder
Marjoram	Rosemary	Cloves
Caraway	Marjoram	Parsley
Parsley	Dill Weed	Dill Weed
Chives	Chives	Oregano
Cayenne	Oregano	Rosemary
Bay Leaves	Bay Leaf	Sage
Celery Seeds	Chili Powder	Marjoram
Chili Powder	Curry Powder	Tarragon
Sage	Cloves	Basil
Tarragon	Mustard	Thyme
Mustard	Paprika	Chives

SALADS	SOUPS	VEGETABLES
Bay Leaves	Allspice	Bay Leaves
Basil	Bay Leaves	Caraway
Caraway	Celery Seeds	Rosemary
Cayenne	Chives	Chives
Celery Seeds	Curry Powder	Chili Powder
Chives	Dill	Sage
Dill	Ginger	Savory
Marjoram	Marjoram	Tarragon
Mustard	Mustard	Dill
Oregano	Oregano	Marjoram
Paprika	Paprika	Mustard
Parsley	Parsley	Oregano
Sage	Sage	Paprika
Tarragon	Tarragon	Parsley

MEASUREMENTS AND WEIGHTS

3	teaspoons	=	1	tablespoon		
4	tablespoons	=	¼	cup		
5⅓	tablespoons	=	⅓	cup		
8	tablespoons	=	½	cup		
16	tablespoons	=	1	cup		
1	fluid ounce	=	2	tablespoons	or	30 ml
4	fluid ounces	=	½	cup	or	125 ml
8	fluid ounces	=	1	cup	or	250 ml
16	fluid ounces	=	2	cups or 1 pint	or	500 ml
32	fluid ounces	=	4	cups or 1 quart	or	1000 ml
					or	1 Liter.
1	ounce	=	28.125	gram		
4	ounces	=	112.5	gram		
8	ounces	=	225	gram		
10	ounces	=	281.25	gram		
12	ounces	=	337.5	gram		
16	ounces	=	450	gram	or	1 pound
17.78	ounces	=	500.06	gram		

500 gram = 1 German pound

1 cup butter or margarine	=	½ pound or 225 gram
1 cup Cheddar cheese, grated	=	¼ pound or 112.5 gram
1 cup eggs	=	4-5 whole eggs or 8 egg whites or 12 egg yolks
1 cup all-purpose flour	=	¼ pound or 112.5 gram
1 cup lard or solid vegetable fat	=	½ pound or 225 gram
1 cup chopped nut meats	=	¼ pound or 112.5 gram
1 envelope of gelatin (unflavored)	=	¼ ounce or 1 tablespoon or 7 gram
1 medium lemon (juice)	=	1½ fluid ounce (3 tablespoons)

OVEN TEMPERATURES

250 F.	=	121 C.	400 F.	=	240 C.
275 F.	=	133 C.	425 F.	=	218 C.
300 F.	=	149 C.	450 F.	=	232 C.
325 F.	=	163 C.	475 F.	=	246 C.
350 F.	=	177 C.	500 F.	=	260 C.
375 F.	=	190 C.	525 F.	=	274 C.

DEHYDRATE FRUITS, HERBS, AND VEGETABLES

In the summer, when vegetables are plentiful in the garden, a good way to save some of it is by dehydration. Of course you will need an electric dehydrator, which is available in many stores, and not really very expensive. It is a small expense in the beginning, but will pay for itself many times over.

Since I do have a vegetable garden every summer, I dry carrots, onions, beans, celery, potatoes, navy beans and many herbs. The vegetables are prepared by cleaning, slicing and/or chopping. Navy beans are cooked first, drained well and then placed on top of a cheese cloth. With some herbs, such as chopped chives or tops of spring onions, I use the same drying method as I do with navy beans, to help keep the beans from falling through the trays. I then combine the dried vegetables, including navy beans, with some dried parsley and tops of spring onions, and store in air tight jars. This combination makes a terrific vegetable soup later-on.

As for the dried chives, it comes in very handy for garnishing food during the cold winter days. I also dry many other herbs beneficial to me, such as oregano, tarragon, dill and dill weed, sweet basil, chickweed, celery leaves, savory and peppermint.

For fruit, I use my dehydrator whenever fruit is plentiful, such as strawberries or blueberries. I also utilize this method if I have too many bananas on hand and don't want them to go bad.

Realizing all this dehydrating is a little extra work during the summer, believe me, looking at all those full jars stored away for the winter will make you a PROUD DOMESTIC ENGINEER.

SAMPLE MENUS

Kartoffelsuppe
Rinderbraten
Semmelknoedel
Erbsen
Kartoffelsalat
Erdbeerkompott

Pfannkuchensuppe
Sauerbraten
Kartoffelbrei
Geduenstes Weisskraut
Kopfsalat
Pfirsichkompott

Blumenkohlsuppe
Kaesespatzen Casserole
Spargelkohl
Gemischter Salat
Gelberuebenkuchen

Huehnerjung
Hauberling
Fruchtsalat

Apfel Pfannkuchenstrudel
Pfefferminztee
Gelatin Dessert

Gulaschsuppe
Bauernfruehstueck
Salatplatte
Frucht mit Sahne

Leberknoedelsuppe
Gekochtes Rindfleisch
Blaukraut
Gebackene Roestkartoffel
Gurkensalat
Apfelkuchen

Dampfnudeln
Blaubeerenkompott
Vanillesosse
Pfefferminztee
Gelatine Dessert

Leberspatzensuppe
Sauerbraten
Kartoffelknoedel
Endiviensalat
Schokoladentorte

Zwiebelsuppe
Fisch, Gebraten
Blumenkohl, Geroestet
Deutscher Kartoffelsalat,
Fruchtsalat

Zwiebelsuppe
Sauerkraut mit Schweinefleisch
Schinkenknoedel oder
Griebenknoedel
Apfelkuechl

Spargelsuppe
Kalbsgulasch
Salzkartoffel
Gruene Bohnen
Gurkensalat mit Sahne
Zwetschgenkompott

Zwudelsuppe
Schweineschnitzel
Gebackene Roestkartoffel
Spargel mit Buttersosse
Gartensalat
Kaesetorte

Einlaufsuppe
Geroestete Leberknoedel
Blaukraut
Bratkartoffel
Kopfsalat
Punschtorte

Note: Not all of the vegetables, and/or desserts included in the above sample menus are in the cookbook. Here are the translations of unlisted vegetables, and/or desserts:

Kartoffelbrei - Mashed Potatoes
Salzkartoffel - Salt Potatoes
Gelatin - Jell-O

Spargelkohl - Broccoli
Erbsen - Peas

Menus include soup and dessert. However, even in Germany most people serve only a main dish for dinner. Soup is served sometimes with a small meal. Dessert, such as cake or torte are also served in mid-afternoon with coffee or tea. A complete menu might be served for special guests, major holidays, weddings or family gatherings.

Soups

HUEHNERSUPPE
(Chicken Soup)

Ingredients:

		bones and meat of leftover chicken
4	quarts	water
2-3	medium	carrots, cut into pieces
1	small	onion, quartered
2	tablespoons	fresh parsley, chopped
		parsley root, chopped, optional
1	slice	celeriac root
6	cubes	chicken bouillon
1	small	garlic clove
		salt and pepper to taste
		rice or egg noodles, cooked to be added to finished chicken broth.
		chopped chives, optional to garnish

Directions:

Combine first 9 ingredients (except chicken meat) in large kettle, and simmer until liquid is about half of the amount, about 2 hours.
Strain chicken broth into separate kettle.
Add chicken meat and simmer for 30 minutes.
Add cooked rice or noodles to soup.
Season to taste with salt and pepper.
Garnish chicken soup with chopped chives, optional.

Serves 6 - 8.

Note: When cooking fresh vegetables in water, most of the nutrients are left in the vegetable water, which most of us pour right down the kitchen drain. Try saving some of that water and freeze for later use. Can be used in soups and gravies later.

FLEISCHBRUEHE
(Beef Broth)

Ingredients:

1	pound	beef bones
1	pound	beef, neck, shin, etc.
2½	quarts	water
1	medium	onion, quartered
1	large	carrot, cut in pieces
1	slice	celeriac
¼	cup	fresh parsley, chopped
1		parsley root, optional
1		bay leaf
1	tablespoon	beef bouillon granules
		salt and pepper
		chopped chives to garnish

Directions:

Combine beef bones, meat and cold water in large kettle.
Bring to boil, then simmer for 1 hour.
Add onion, carrot, celeriac, chopped parsley and parsley root optional,
bay leaf, and beef bouillon granules.
Bring to boil again, then simmer for another 60 minutes, adding extra
water when needed.
Strain soup through a fine sieve.
Season with salt and pepper.
Garnish with chopped chives just before serving.

Serves 6 - 8.

Note: This broth is also used as a base for different kinds of soups,
such as eggdrop, pancake, liver-dumplings, semolina-dumplings,
liverspatzen, vegetable, noodle soup, etc. Freeze in portions for later
use. For better soup color, add a few dry outer onion skins to soup,
and cook with vegetables.

3

* During and right after World War II, my parents would raise ducks and geese, to be slaughtered and sold to people who still could afford it. However, Mother would keep the feathers each year. She would pack them in a large bed pillow, and off they went to a bakery for drying. Each day, after the baker was finished baking bread, and the oven had cooled down to warm, Mother's large feather pillow would go in the oven to dry the feathers slowly. After a few weeks the feathers would be dry, and a new bed pillow was in the making. Needless to say, all of our beds were made by mother's ingenuity and wonderful hands.

Yet, that is not the whole story. Since we had geese, there were also ganders, who at times can be pretty mean. I remember one such gander, always coming after us children, but more so after my youngest brother. My brother was only a few years old and still had a pacifier, which absolutely fascinated the gander. One day, my brother being outside playing, suddenly was screaming his head off. As we came to his rescue, we found him in the back yard, lying on his back with the gander on top of him. Within seconds, the gander took off holding the pacifier in his beak.

GEKOCHTES RINDLEISCH UND SUPPE
(Boiled Beef and Broth)

Ingredients:

1½	pounds	beef, brisket or breast
		water
1	tablespoon	salt
	few	peppercorns
2	teaspoons	beef bouillon granules
1		parsley root, optional
¼	cup	fresh parsley, chopped
1	tablespoon	dry celery leaves
1	large	carrot, sliced
1	small	onion, chopped

Directions:

Wash beef and place in enough water to cover meat.
Bring to boil and skim off foam.
Add all other ingredients, except salt.
Simmer for 2 to 2½ hours, adding salt about half way through cooking time.
Serve meat with potatoes, and/or various other vegetables and salad.
Use broth as a base for various soups, sauces, gravies, etc.

Serves 6.

Note: To increase color in broth, add a few yellow outer leaves of an onion, and discard later. I usually serve my soup with the vegetables. However, for clear soup, strain or tie vegetables together instead of chopping, and then discard vegetables when soup is done. Serve broth with liverspatzen, liver-dumplings, pancake soup or any other kind of soup one desires.

BROTSUPPE
(Bread Soup)

Ingredients:

¾	pound	tale German rye bread, sliced very thin
		salt
4	cups	water
1	large	onion, sliced thin
3	tablespoons	butter

Directions:

Place sliced rye bread in large bowl, and sprinkle with salt.
Heat water to boiling point.
Pour over rye bread, then set aside.
Fry sliced onion in butter, and pour over soup.
Season to taste with extra salt if needed.

Serves 2.

Note: This is not an ideal soup that everyone would like, but it was a very good meal during World War II. Sometimes after a pig slaughter, we would substitute fried onions with hot liver sausage and black pudding. It does not sound that good, but it sure was delicious.

EINLAUFSUPPE
(Eggdrop Soup)

Ingredients:

2		eggs
2	tablespoons	flour
2	tablespoons	water
		dash nutmeg
6	cups	Beef Broth, pg. 3 or 5
		chopped chives to garnish

Directions:

Combine flour, nutmeg, eggs and water, and beat well.
Stir batter into boiling beef broth.
Simmer for about 5 minutes.
Garnish soup with chopped chives and serve.

Serves 4.

Note: One may substitute chives with chopped parsley, or chopped green spring onion tops.

GRIESSNOCKERL-SUPPE
(Semolina-Dumpling Soup)

Ingredients:

¼	cup	soft butter
1		egg
¼	teaspoon	salt
1	dash	nutmeg
¾	cup	semolina
1	teaspoon	fresh parsley, chopped fine
6-8	cups	Beef Broth, pg. 3 or 5
		fresh chopped chives, or
		chopped greens of spring onions, optional

Directions:

Combine first 6 ingredients.

Mix well, making sure soft butter is well blended in.

Set aside in cool place for about 20 minutes.

Meanwhile, heat beef broth to boiling point.

Using a coffee spoon, scoop out and roll semolina batter in the palm of your hand, to form a small egg-shaped dumpling, and drop into boiling beef broth.

Repeat until all batter is used up. Simmer soup for 10 minutes.

Garnish with fresh chopped chives or chopped greens of spring onions, and serve.

Serves 4.

Note: Semolina is wheat grits. I use cream of wheat, which is almost the same thing and easier to find in grocery stores. However, the cooking time will be a little shorter, since cream of wheat is much finer in texture. Semolina-dumplings should be served and eaten immediately so they won't get mushy. They taste best when part of the inside of the griessnockerl is still firm and has a yellow color.

GULASCHSUPPE
(Goulash Soup)

Ingredients:

½	pound	lean beef, cut into ¼ inch pieces
3	medium	onions, chopped
2	tablespoons	oil or shortening
		salt and pepper
2	tablespoons	sweet paprika
few	dashes	cayenne pepper
¼	teaspoon	caraway seeds
⅛	teaspoon	ground marjoram
5	cups	water
5	cubes	beef bouillon
1		green pepper, chopped
1	large	tomato, peeled and diced
3	large	potatoes, peeled and diced
¼	cup	tomato ketchup
2	teaspoons	corn starch and water
2-3	tablespoons	red wine

Directions:

Brown beef in oil or shortening.
Stir in chopped onions, salt and pepper, paprika, cayenne pepper, caraway seeds and ground marjoram.
Add water and beef bouillon cubes and simmer for 30 minutes.
Add chopped green pepper, and cook for 10 minutes.
Add tomato ketchup, diced tomato and potatoes, and cook for 20 minutes.
Blend corn starch with water, and stir into goulash soup.
Remove goulash soup from stove, and add red wine.
Season to taste if still needed.

Serves 4.

Note: One may want to add a little more water during the last 20 minutes of cooking time, as some of the liquid may have boiled down too much.

LEBERSPATZENSUPPE
(Liverspatzen Soup)

Ingredients:

½	pound	liver, beef or calf
1	small	garlic clove
1	teaspoon	grated lemon rind
2	tablespoons	dry marjoram
1	dash	nutmeg
1	teaspoon	salt
¼	teaspoon	pepper
2	tablespoons	butter
¼	cup	onions, chopped fine
3	tablespoons	fresh parsley, chopped
½	cup	warm milk
1	cup	bread crumbs
2	eggs	beaten
3	quarts	water
1	tablespoon	salt for water
1	tablespoon	beef bouillon granules
6	cups	Beef Broth, pg. 3 or 5
		fresh chopped parsley or chives to garnish

Directions:

Grind liver and garlic in meat grinder.
Add grated lemon rind, nutmeg, marjoram, salt and pepper to liver and set aside.
Melt butter and sauté onions and parsley.
Combine with warm milk, bread crumbs, liver mixture, and eggs.
Mix well and set aside for 15 minutes.
In Dutch Oven, heat 3 quarts of water with 1 tablespoon of beef bouillon granules, and 1 tablespoon of salt to boiling point.

Using a spatzen grater or a large hole sieve, press liverspatzen dough through and into boiling water.
Liverspatzen are done when surfacing to the top (few minutes).
Remove liverspatzen with a skimming ladle and serve with beef broth.
Garnish with chopped parsley or chives.

Serves 6.

Note: Liverspatzen may be made in advance and frozen.

Maria Swaringen

PFANNKUCHENSUPPE
(Pancake Soup)

Ingredients:

6	cups	Beef Broth, pg. 3 or 5
9		Pancakes, sliced thin
		chopped chives to garnish, optional

Directions:

Make pancakes according to recipe, roll up and slice thin.
For each bowl of soup, use 1½ pancake and 1 cup of beef broth.
Garnish with chopped chives, optional.

Serves 6.

Note: One may use 1 beef bouillon cube per 1 cup of boiling hot water instead of beef broth. Roll up and slice leftover pancakes and freeze for soup later on. This soup is always good for a fast and tasty lunch.

ZWIEBELSUPPE
(Onion Soup)

Ingredients:

4	large	onions, peeled and sliced in rings
½	cup	oil
6	cups	water
2	tablespoons	beef bouillon granules
1	tablespoon	fresh parsley, chopped
4	slices	toast
¼	cup	grated Swiss cheese
		salt and pepper to taste

Directions:

Brown onion rings in oil.
Add water and beef bouillon granules.
Bring to boil, then simmer for 10 minutes.
Add parsley and salt and pepper to taste.
Divide onion soup into 4 oven proof soup bowls.
Place toast on top of soup and generously sprinkle with grated Swiss cheese.
Place soup bowls under broiler long enough to melt cheese.
Serve immediately.

Serves 4.

Note: One may use Parmesan or other grated cheese. This is a delightful soup for "Onion Lovers".

ZWUDELSUPPE
(Zwudle Soup)

Ingredients:

3	tablespoons	margarine
1	large	onion, sliced thin
6	cups	water
1	large	carrot, peeled and diced
1	stalk	celery, diced
2	tablespoons	fresh parsley, chopped
1	tablespoon	beef bouillon granules
1	tablespoon	salt
½	teaspoon	pepper

For Zwudle:

1	cup	flour
1		egg
¼	teaspoon	salt
	dash	pepper

Directions:

Using large sauce pan, fry onions until light brown.
Add water, carrots, celery, parsley, beef bouillon, salt and pepper.
Bring to boil, then simmer for 15 minutes.
Meanwhile, in medium size bowl, combine flour, egg, salt, and dash of pepper.
Mix well and work dough to make small crumbs.
Stir into boiling soup, and simmer for 5 minutes.
Season to taste if needed.

Serves 6.

Note: Soup can be frozen, but will get thicker when cooling or freezing. Add a little water when reheating, and season again.

* This is one of the soups, my mother made a lot of during World War II. It was cheap to make, and also filling. However, she used mainly onions and zwudle. In my family we actually call this soup "Zwullsuppe", or the "World War II Soup".

KETTLE SOUP

Ingredients:

5½	cups	water
6		beef or chicken bouillon cubes
¾	cup	pasta, uncooked
1	tablespoon	dried vegetables
⅓	cup	pre-cooked dry navy beans
¼	teaspoon	garlic powder
2	teaspoon	corn starch
⅛	teaspoon	turmeric (for color)

Directions:

Combine all ingredients in large saucepan.
Bring to a boil, then simmer for 15-20 minutes or until pasta is done.

Serves 4.

Note: For pasta, use small elbow macaroni or substitute something similar (do not use spaghetti noodles).

* During the summer months, I dehydrate many vegetables, such as onions, carrots, celery, etc., plus herbs like chives, parsley, green onions, sweet basil, oregano, dill, savory, peppermint, etc. I mix the vegetables along with chives, parsley and green onions, and store in jars to use later in soups. I also cook navy beans, then dehydrate and store them in jars for later use.

People can get discouraged caring for a vegetable garden due to the endless backbreaking work of weeding. Here is a little trick you can use that helps you to enjoy your vegetable garden. Make furrows in your garden before planting. After planting, use a regular leaf rake after a rain to rake the furrows upward, to eliminate the small weeds in the beginning. This is not hard work and takes little time to do. Then every time you cut the grass, use all your grass clippings and spread throughout the furrows and upward towards the vegetable plants. Hay may be used if grass clippings are not available.

BLUMENKOHLSUPPE
(Cauliflower Soup)

Ingredients:

1	small	cauliflower
5	cups	water
1	teaspoon	beef bouillon granules
1½	teaspoons	salt
1	tablespoon	fresh parsley, chopped
4	tablespoons	butter or margarine
4	tablespoons	flour
1		egg yolk
2	tablespoons	cold water
2	tablespoons	sour cream

Directions:

Wash cauliflower and break into small florets.
Cook in water, combined with salt, beef bouillon granules and parsley until cauliflower is done, but still firm.
Drain and save cauliflower water, by pouring into separate bowl and set both aside.
Meanwhile, in separate large sauce pan, melt butter or margarine.
Add flour and stir until pale yellow.
Add "cauliflower" water, about ¾ cup at a time, stirring constantly each time until it becomes nice and creamy before adding more water.
Simmer for 5 minutes, then add "florets".
Beat egg yolk with 2 tablespoons of water and mix with sour cream.
Stir egg mixture into cauliflower soup and serve.

Serves 4 - 6.

Note: Soup should be creamy. Depending upon how much water was left after cooking cauliflower, one may need a little more or less water to achieve a nice creamy soup. Soup can be frozen. Add a little water when reheating, and season to taste again.

Maria Swaringen

BOHNENSUPPE
(Bean Soup)

Ingredients:

16	ounces	navy beans
3	quarts	water
1		ham bone
1	cup	ham, diced
¾	cup	onions, chopped
½	cup	carrots, diced
½	cup	celery, diced
1	large	garlic clove
1	tablespoon	fresh parsley, chopped
1½	teaspoons	Jane's Krazy Mixed Up Salt
¼	teaspoon	pepper
1	teaspoon	hickory smoked salt

Directions:

Wash beans and remove all debris.
In large pot combine beans and water.
Bring to boil, then remove from stove and set aside for 1½ hours.
Add ham bone and resume cooking in same water for about 1 hour.
Add ham, onions, carrots, celery, garlic, parsley and Jane's Krazy
Mixed Up Salt, and cook for 30 minutes.
Discard ham bone, and add pepper and hickory smoked salt.
Add more seasoning if so desired.

Serves 8.

EINFACHE SPARGELSUPPE
(Simple Asparagus Soup)

Ingredients:

4	cups	asparagus water, (left over from cooking asparagus)
4	tablespoons	butter
4	tablespoons	flour
4	tablespoons	sweet cream
1	dash	nutmeg
		leftover cooked asparagus, cut into small pieces
		Homemade Croutons, pg. 160

Directions:

Melt butter in large saucepan.
Add flour, and stir until mixture is pale yellow.
Add asparagus water, about ¾ cup at a time, and stir constantly.
Continue until all water is used up and soup is creamy.
Add nutmeg, sweet cream, and leftover asparagus.
Season with salt if needed.

Serves 4.

Note: Serve homemade croutons in a separate bowl with asparagus soup. In the spring when fresh asparagus is plentiful and cheap, I freeze a lot for the winter. I always save and freeze the blanching water, measuring a few cups at a time. Then when I have some leftover asparagus from dinner, and not enough of the cooking water, I defrost a few cups of blanching water to make asparagus soup.

Maria Swaringen

KARTOFFELSUPPE
(Potato Soup)

Ingredients:

6	medium	potatoes, peeled and chopped
2	quarts	water
¼	cup	onions, chopped
2	tablespoons	fresh parsley, chopped
1	tablespoons	dry celery leaves
1	large	garlic clove, chopped
1	large	carrot, peeled and chopped
1	teaspoon	salt
¼	teaspoon	pepper
3		beef bouillon cubes
4	tablespoons	margarine or butter
4	tablespoons	flour

Directions:

Combine first 10 ingredients in stainless steel Dutch oven.
Bring to boil, and cook until vegetables are tender, about 20-30 minutes.
Set aside to cool off a little. Puree soup in blender, and set aside.
Melt margarine or butter in large saucepan.
Add flour and stir until mixture is pale yellow.
Add potato puree, about ¾ cup at a time, and stir constantly.
Continue until all potato puree is creamed.
Add a little water if soup is too thick. Season to taste.

Serves 8.

Note: A stalk of celery may be used instead of dry celery leaves. Soup can be frozen for later use. When reheating soup, add a little water and season again. For those who like potato soup a little chunky, do not puree soup. When freezing any kind of creamed vegetable soup, the fibers will separate from the liquid, and the frozen

20

soup will not look very appetizing. But it will go back to its creamy condition when reheating.

KOHLRABISUPPE
(Kohlrabi Soup)

Ingredients:

6½	cups	water
2	teaspoons	salt
4	large	kohlrabi, peeled and sliced
3	tablespoons	onions, chopped
2	tablespoons	fresh parsley, chopped
2	teaspoons	beef bouillon granules
5	tablespoons	butter or margarine
5	tablespoons	flour
⅛	teaspoon	pepper

Directions:

Combine first 6 ingredients. Bring to boil, then simmer for 15-20 minutes, or until kohlrabi is done.
In separate large sauce pan, melt butter or margarine.
Add flour, stirring until mixture is pale yellow.
Add kohlrabi soup, about ¾ cup at a time, stirring constantly until all soup has a creamy consistency.
Add pepper and season with additional salt if needed.

Serves 4 - 6.

KOHLRABI UND PORREESUPPE
(Kohlrabi and Leek Soup)

Ingredients:

4	tablespoons	margarine or butter
1	cup	leek, sliced thin
4	medium	kohlrabi, peeled, quartered, and sliced
5	cups	water
1	teaspoon	salt
1	tablespoon	beef bouillon granules
¼	teaspoon	pepper
2	tablespoons	fresh parsley, chopped
2	tablespoons	onions, chopped
3	tablespoons	flour

Directions:

Sauté leek in 1 tablespoon of margarine or butter.
Add kohlrabi, 5 cups of water, salt, pepper, bouillon granules, parsley and onions.
Cook until kohlrabi is tender but still firm, about 10-15 minutes, then set aside.
Melt 3 tablespoons of margarine or butter in large saucepan.
Add flour and stir until pale yellow.
Gradually pour in the vegetable stock, about ¾ cup at a time, stirring constantly, until all soup is creamy.
Simmer for 5 minutes, and season to taste.

Serves 6.

Note: This is a good soup for a cold winter's day. If soup is too thick, add a little more water. Can be frozen for later use. Creamed soups will get thicker when refrigerated, and/or frozen. Add a little water when reheating. In the summer, when vegetables are plentiful, freeze leek and sliced kohlrabi for soup in the winter.

LEBERKNOEDELSUPPPE
(Liver-Dumpling Soup)

Ingredients:

1	recipe	for Beef Broth, pg. 3 or 5
1	recipe	for Liver-Dumplings, pg. 156
		fresh chives to garnish soup

Directions:

Prepare beef broth and liver-dumplings according to recipes.
Combine per serving 1 liver dumpling with ¾ cup of beef broth, and
garnish with fresh chopped chives.

Serves 6 - 8.

Note: Beef broth can be made earlier and frozen for later use.
Leftover Liver-dumplings may be frozen as well for later use.

* Dinner in Germany is served at noon. My mother would always
make liver-dumplings on Saturday. So while Mother was preparing
dinner, my little brother was busy with his talented occupation as a
mouse catcher. His little white dog called "Spitz" was also well
trained for the job, not to mention his two friends. These four would
walk right behind the farmer who was out in the field plowing, to
watch for the mice jumping out. The dog would hold the mice down
for my brother to pick up and bring home in his pants pockets. My
brother had a little bird cage for the mice to enjoy themselves. When
he got tired of the mice, he would give them to the cat.

One day, my brother stepped on a rusty nail, and had to stay off of
his foot for a while. But that did not stop him from catching mice.
There he was, his two little friends pulling a small wooden wagon, my
brother sitting in the wagon, holding the leash for his dog "Spitz",
who was walking behind the wagon. It was a perfect Norman
Rockwell picture.

LINSENSUPPE
(Lentil Soup)

Ingredients:

16	ounces	dry lentils
3½	quarts	water
2½	tablespoons	beef bouillon granules
¾	cup	onions, chopped
1	large	bay leaf
2	teaspoons	salt
¼	teaspoon	pepper
½	cup	vinegar
2	medium	carrots, chopped
¾	cup	celery, chopped
2	tablespoons	margarine
2	tablespoons	flour

Directions:

Wash lentils and soak in 1½ quarts of water overnight.
The next day, add beef bouillon granules, bay leaf, ¼ cup, vinegar, and salt and pepper.
Cook for 30 minutes.
Add 2 quarts of water, onions, carrots, and celery.
Cook for 20 minutes.
Melt margarine in 3 quart saucepan.
Add flour and stir until pale yellow.
Add lentil soup, about ¾ cup at a time, stirring constantly.
Add remaining ¼ cup vinegar. Season with salt and pepper if still needed.

Serves 6 - 8.

SCHWAMMERLSUPPE MIT SEMMELKNOEDELN
(Mushroom Soup with Bread Dumplings)

Ingredients:

½	pound	fresh mushrooms, cleaned and sliced
1	small	onions, chopped fine
¼	cup	butter or margarine
¼	cup	flour
4	cups	hot water
4	teaspoons	beef bouillon granules
¼	teaspoon	caraway seeds
2	tablespoon	fresh chopped parsley
½	teaspoon	grated lemon peel
½	cup	sour cream
		salt and pepper to taste
1	recipe	for Bread-Dumplings, pg. 158

Directions:

Sauté mushrooms and onions together in butter or margarine for 10 minutes.
Stir in flour.
Stir in 4 cups of hot water and bring to a boil.
Add beef bouillon granules, caraway seeds, grated lemon peel and simmer for a few minutes.
Stir in sour cream and fresh chopped parsley. Season with salt and pepper.
Serve with freshly prepared bread-dumplings.

Serves 4.

Note: While one can use a variety of edible mushrooms, the most common mushroom used is the Champignon, which is a white edible mushroom, and the "Steinpilz, Boletus edulis" (Bot.), a large brown mushroom found in the woods.

* I remember back in Germany as a child, we would go mushroom picking early in the morning, and found most of them in the nearby cow pastures. After arriving back home with the mushrooms, it was our (children's) job to clean the mushrooms; actually peel the mushroom caps and scrape the stems. Mother would then prepare the mushroom soup and bread dumplings for lunch.

Many years later, after I moved to the United States and lived in a subdivision out in the country, I noticed all the mushrooms growing in my yard. I went out to pick some, and one of my neighbors inquired what I was doing. I told her that these were the same mushrooms one finds in the grocery store, and that I will have steak with mushrooms for dinner. As we parted, my neighbor smiled and said, 'See you tomorrow, if you are still alive". As you can see, I have lived to tell about it. However, I do want to caution you, DO NOT pick and eat mushrooms, unless you are familiar with them.

Bread Dumplings, pg. 158

SPARGELSUPPE
(Asparagus Soup)

Ingredients:

⅓	cup	onions, sliced
1	tablespoon	butter
1	pound	asparagus
4	cups	chicken broth
1	tablespoon	butter
1	tablespoon	flour
1		egg yolk
¼	cup	heavy cream
		salt and pepper
		fresh chopped parsley or
		chives to garnish

Directions:

Clean asparagus, cut into 1 inch pieces, then set aside.
Sauté onions in 1 tablespoon of butter.
Add chicken broth and asparagus, and cook until tender, about 25 minutes.
Puree asparagus soup in blender and set aside.
In large sauce pan, melt 1 tablespoon of butter.
Add flour, and stir until mixture is pale yellow.
Add asparagus soup, about ½ cup at a time, stirring constantly.
Beat egg yolk, blend with heavy cream, and stir into asparagus soup.
Season with salt and pepper.
Garnish with fresh chopped parsley or chives and serve.

Serves 4.

Note: For instant chicken broth, use 1 chicken bouillon cube or 1 teaspoon of chicken bouillon granules per cup of water. This is really a superb soup for asparagus lovers, and should be served with Homemade Croutons, pg. 160

Maria Swaringen

SPARGELKOHLSUPPE
(Broccoli Soup)

Ingredients:

3-4	cups	broccoli (small rosettes and sliced stems)
6	cups	water
2	teaspoons	beef bouillon granules
½	teaspoon	salt
2	dashes	pepper
6	tablespoons	butter
6	tablespoons	flour
2	slices	american cheese
3	tablespoons	sour cream
		Homemade Croutons, pg. 160

Directions:

Combine clean and prepared broccoli with water, beef bouillon granules, salt and pepper.
Cook until broccoli is done, but still firm.
Drain broccoli, setting both liquid and broccoli aside.
Heat butter.
Add flour and stir until pale yellow in color.
Add ¾ cup of liquid at a time, stirring constantly each time until soup is creamy.
Add broccoli and simmer for a few minutes.
Stir in sour cream and American cheese.
Serve with Homemade Croutons, pg. 160

Serves 4.

Note: This is a delicious soup and very easy to make. It can also be made with leftover broccoli. Just use water and spices with cooked broccoli and then proceed with heating the butter, etc.

* My mother was an old fashioned cook. She used to say, "What the farmer doesn't know, he won't eat". She never grew tomatoes or

28

string beans in her vegetable garden, and never used them in her meals, but my father would use a slice of tomato in the pork gravy off and on during the later years. My mother was a good cook; she could make a perfectly good meal out of almost nothing. During World War II, that was a miracle by itself. In those days, cooking would also take a lot longer, for there was only a wood and coal stove, and no amenities. The average meal would take about 2 hours to cook in a very hot kitchen in the summer and without an air conditioner.

Goulash Soup, pg. 9

Maria Swaringen

Appetizers

and

Sauces

Maria Swaringen

AVOCADO DIP

Ingredients:

2	ripe	avocados
1	clove	garlic, minced
2	tablespoons	onions, grated
¾	teaspoon	salt
1	medium	tomato, ripe and peeled
1¼	teaspoons	chili powder
		cayenne pepper

Directions:

Cut avocados in half lengthwise.
Remove seeds and scoop out pulp.
Mash avocado pulp and tomato.
Add garlic, onions, salt, and chili powder, and mix well.
Add cayenne pepper to your taste.
Chill before serving.
Serve with your favorite chips, and/or crackers.

Note: Amount of ingredients may vary a little, depending on the size of the avocados. One can use a food processor to mix ingredients.

FONDUE MIT CHAMPIONS
(Mushroom Fondue)

Ingredients:

4	tablespoons	butter
1	pound	white mushrooms (Champions) sliced
2	slices	white American cheese, melted
2	cups	sour cream
4	tablespoons	flour
2	tablespoons	onion, grated
¼	teaspoon	pepper
		salt to taste
1	dash	nutmeg
1	teaspoon	fresh chives, chopped
		French bread cubes, about 1" size

Directions:

Sauté mushrooms in butter until tender.
In separate saucepan, combine sour cream, melted cheese, flour, onions and pepper, and cook over low heat until thickened, stirring occasionally.
Stir in sautéed mushrooms.
Add a dash of nutmeg and season with salt if needed.
Sprinkle with chopped chives just before serving.
Serve warm in fondue dish with French bread cubes.
An ideal holiday party dish.

Note: The Swiss are known for their fondues. It is said, they have dozens of fondue recipes. It is called a friendship food, and everyone helps themselves at a gathering or party, using a long fondue fork.

OBATZTER
(Cheese Spread)

Ingredients:

8	ounces	camembert cheese, (room temperature)
⅓	cup	sour cream
¼	cup	soft butter
¼	cup	onion, chopped very fine
		salt and pepper to taste
		paprika to garnish

Directions:

Slice Camembert cheese (room temperature) very thin.
Squeeze cheese through fork and cream or use small food processor.
Add sour cream, butter, onions, and salt and pepper.
Mix together with fork, and continue to cream cheese spread, to achieve a thick, creamy and somewhat lumpy spread.
Divide cheese spread into 2 servings, and place onto dessert plates.
Garnish with paprika, and serve with 2 slices of German rye bread per serving.
Can also be used as a party dip, by adding more sour cream.

Note: Most Bavarian people use a little leftover, or so-called stale beer and less sour cream in the cheese spread. Paprika may also be mixed into the cheese spread, instead of garnish. If using paprika method, use a little fresh chopped chives to garnish.

SALSA

Ingredients:

2	cups	green peppers, chopped
2	large	onions, chopped
1	small	whole garlic, minced
1	tablespoon	dry sweet basil
1	tablespoon	dry thyme
2½	quarts	canned tomatoes
1	cup	canned or fresh hot banana peppers, chopped
1½	tablespoons	salt
½	cup	vinegar
		cayenne pepper
3	tablespoons	corn starch
5	tablespoons	water

Directions:

Using a large stainless steel pot, combine first 5 ingredients plus 1 cup of canned tomatoes.
Cook for 10 minutes.
Add remaining canned tomatoes, hot banana peppers, and salt and vinegar.
Add cayenne pepper to your taste.
Bring to a boil, then simmer for 5 minutes.
Blend corn starch with water and stir into salsa. Ladle salsa into clean hot pint jars.
Adjust hot lid and process in water bath.

Makes 6 pints.

Note: If fresh tomatoes and hot peppers are used instead of canned goods, use a few more tomatoes, and cook both with the first 5 ingredients, before adding salt and pepper.

* I have a vegetable garden every year, so I do a lot of canning and freezing. However, I don't have much time in the summer to make sauces, dips, etc. The winter months are just perfect for that, keeps the kitchen warm, and me very busy. All peppers can be chopped and frozen for use in the winter.

BARBECUESOSSE
(Barbecue Sauce)

Ingredients:

2	medium	onions, chopped
2	tablespoons	oil
2	tablespoons	vinegar
2	tablespoons	brown sugar
1	tablespoon	honey
4	tablespoons	lemon juice
1½	cups	ketchup
3	tablespoons	Worcestershire sauce
½	teaspoon	prepared mustard
½	teaspoon	salt
½	teaspoon	garlic powder
1	tablespoon	chili powder
½	cup	water
¼	teaspoon	ginger
		cayenne, optional

Directions:

Heat oil and brown onions.
Add remaining ingredients, and simmer for 5 minutes, stirring occasionally.

Makes about 2½ cups.

Note: An ideal sauce for leftover chicken, turkey, beef, or pork. Add some sauce to leftover meat, and simmer for 15 minutes. Cool a little, and serve on Ritz crackers as a snack or Hors d'oeuvres. Can be frozen with or without meat for later use.

HOT SAUCE

Ingredients:

6	tablespoons	ketchup
2	tablespoons	water
1½	teaspoons	vinegar
¼	teaspoon	salt
	dash	cayenne pepper

Directions:

Combine all ingredients and chill.
Serve with oriental dishes in a separate bowl.
More cayenne pepper may be used, if so desired.

PAPRIKASCHOTENSOSSE
(Green Pepper Sauce)
(for filled Green Peppers)

Ingredients:

1	quart	tomatoes, peeled and sliced
½	cup	onions, chopped
½	cup	green peppers, chopped
½	teaspoon	dry sweet basil
1	teaspoon	salt
1	tablespoon	sugar

Directions:

Combine all ingredients and cook for about 15 minutes, stirring occasionally.
Pour into clean and hot canning jars, adjust hot lids and process in water bath.

Makes 1 quart or 2 pints.

Note: Use one quart of sauce for 4 servings. Pour over four filled green peppers, and cook until done. This sauce is ideal for canning during the summer, while vegetables are plentiful and cheap, for use in the winter. Sauce may also be frozen.

SPAGHETTISOSSE
(Spaghetti Sauce)

Ingredients:

5	quarts	tomatoes, peeled and quartered
1½	cups	onions, chopped
2	large	green peppers, chopped
½	cup	fresh sweet basil, chopped
2	tablespoons	dry oregano
1	tablespoons	dry savory
1	tablespoon	dry Italian seasoning
2½	tablespoons	garlic, minced
1	teaspoon	Season All seasoned salt
2	teaspoons	salt
1	teaspoon	pepper
1	can	mushrooms 6.5 oz., chopped

Directions:

Combine all ingredients, except mushrooms.
Bring to a boil, then simmer for about 3 hours, stirring occasionally, or until tomato mixture has boiled down about ⅓ of the amount.
Cool and liquefy mixture in blender.
Add chopped mushrooms, and season with additional salt and pepper if still needed.
Pour into clean and hot canning jars.
Adjust hot lids, and process in water bath.

Makes about 3 quarts.

Note: Use with meatballs or fried hamburger meat and serve over spaghetti. Spaghetti sauce may also be frozen. If fresh sweet basil is not available, substitute with 2 teaspoons of dry sweet basil. Should the sauce be too spicy, add a cup of tomato juice.

VANILLESOSSE
(Vanilla Sauce)

Ingredients:

1	box	vanilla pudding, 3 oz. (cook and serve)
3	cups	milk
2	tablespoons	sugar

Directions:

Cook pudding according to directions, but use 3 cups of milk, instead of 2 cups.
Pour into bowl and add sugar.
Cool and serve with main dish or dessert.

Serves 4.

Note: Vanilla sauce will thicken a little more as it cools. This sauce is so easy to make and can be used with many desserts, such as baked apple crisp, various fruit short cakes, etc. My family loves vanilla sauce with dampfnudeln, pg. 127

Salad

Dressings

And

Salads

ESSIG & OEL SALATSOSSE # 1
(Vinegar & Oil Salad Dressing # 1)

Ingredients:

2	tablespoons	oil
1	tablespoon	vinegar, wine or distilled
		salt
1	dash	garlic powder
		fresh chives, chopped, optional

Directions:

Combine all ingredients and mix well.
Pour over salad and toss gently just before serving.

Note: Above salad dressing is used for Boston lettuce salad, Boston lettuce and tomato salad, tossed or Chef's salad, and mixed salad. More than one recipe of vinegar & oil salad dressing # 1 may be needed, depending on the amount of salad. This is a basic recipe. If vinegar is too strong, add a few drops of water. Cider vinegar may be used instead of wine or distilled vinegar. If health, conscious, use olive or canola oil. For any kind of leaf lettuce, one may substitute vinegar with lemon juice, and oil with a small amount of fried bacon (crumbled) and hot bacon grease.

ESSIG & OEL SALATSOSSE # 2
(Vinegar & Oil Salad Dressing # 2)

Ingredients:

2	tablespoons	oil
1	tablespoon	vinegar, wine or distilled
		salt
		pepper
3	tablespoons	onions, sliced or chopped
		fresh chives, chopped, optional

Directions:

Combine all ingredients and mix well.
Pour over salad and toss gently just before serving.

Note: This dressing is used for tomato salad, cucumber salad, and garden salad. More than one recipe of vinegar & oil salad dressing # 2 may be needed, depending on the amount of salad. This is a basic recipe. If the vinegar is too strong, add a few drops of water. Cider vinegar may be used instead of wine or distilled vinegar. Other herbs may be added. If health conscious, use olive or canola oil.

ESTRAGON SALATSOSSE
(Tarragon Salad Dressing)

Ingredients:

1	tablespoon	onions, chopped fine
¼	teaspoon	garlic powder
1	tablespoon	tarragon vinegar
2	tablespoons	canola oil
¼	teaspoon	spicy mustard
		salt and pepper to taste
		chopped chives

Directions:

Combine all ingredients and mix well.
Pour over mixed salad and toss gently before serving.
Makes about ¼ cup of salad dressing.

Note: If one wishes to use less oil, substitute half with water. How do you make your own tarragon vinegar? Heat vinegar to boiling point. Add a slice or two of onion, little garlic, peppercorns, and/or few mustard seeds. Pour vinegar and herbs into clean bottle. Add a few sprigs of fresh tarragon after vinegar has cooled off somewhat, so fresh herb won't turn dark. May be used after 24 hours, leaving herbs in the bottle.

ITALIENISCHE SALATSOSSE
(Italian Salad Dressing)

Ingredients:

¼	cup	wine vinegar
¼	cup	water
¼	teaspoon	sugar
1	teaspoon	salt
¼	teaspoon	garlic powder
¼	teaspoon	lemon & pepper
¼	teaspoon	dry sweet basil
1	teaspoon	fresh parsley, chopped
½	teaspoon	fresh chives, chopped
1	tablespoon	onions, chopped very fine
½	cup	canola oil

Directions:

Combine all ingredients and mix well.
Pour over salad and toss gently just before serving.

Makes 1 cup.

Note: Use for most tossed salads. Keep refrigerated only for a few days. One may use less oil and a little more water.

BLAUKRAUTSALAT
(Red Cabbage Salad)

Ingredients:

1	pound	red cabbage
1	teaspoon	salt
1	tablespoon	sugar or honey
2½	tablespoons	vinegar
1½	tablespoons	oil
1	small	apple, grated

Directions:

Slice red cabbage very fine.
In separate bowl, combine and blend together all other ingredients.
Add red cabbage, and blend well.
Set aside for a few hours, or overnight before serving.

Serves 6.

Note: One may add orange, and/or apple slices, bananas or walnuts to red cabbage. The cabbage may be shredded. It is also an ideal salad to use on a salad plate with a variety of salads.

BOHNENSALAT
(String Bean Salad)

Ingredients:

1	quart	canned green string beans
½	cup	liquid from canned beans
⅓	cup	onions, chopped
¼	teaspoon	liquid bouillon, (Maggi seasoning)
½	teaspoon	salt
¼	teaspoon	pepper
2	tablespoons	oil
2	tablespoons	vinegar

Directions:

Combine and mix all ingredients in bowl, breaking up beans slightly with a spoon.
Set aside for about 10-15 minutes. Serve with your favorite dinner.

Serves 4.

Note: Plain water may be used instead of liquid from canned beans. I use the liquid from beans, because it contains most of the nutrients. Ideal salad, when the price of lettuce is very high. Can be made ahead of time and refrigerated.

Maria Swaringen

ENDIVIENSALAT
(Endive Salad)

Ingredients:

4	medium	potatoes
2	cups	endive, sliced thin
1	teaspoon	salt
2	tablespoons	vinegar, wine or distilled
3	tablespoons	oil
½	teaspoon	liquid bouillon (Maggi seasoning), optional

Directions:

Boil potatoes in their skins until tender.
Meanwhile, clean endive (discard outer leaves, wilted and/or spoiled, and cut off root).
Slice thin and soak in cold water for 15-30 minutes, then drain well.
Peel potatoes and slice thin while still warm.
Add to drained endive.
Add salt, vinegar, oil and liquid bouillon (Maggi seasoning), optional.
Mix well and serve.

Serves 4.

Note: If endive tastes bitter, soak in warm water for a few minutes, drain and soak for about 15 minutes in cold water. Restaurants usually serve this salad separate from German potato salad. However, I learned to mix it with the potatoes, and find it tastes a lot better.

FELDSALAT
(Lamb's Lettuce Salad)

Ingredients:

4	medium	potatoes
2	cups	lamb's lettuce
½	teaspoon	salt
1	tablespoon	vinegar, wine or distilled
2	tablespoons	oil
¼	teaspoon	liquid bouillon (Maggi seasoning), optional

Directions:

Boil potatoes in their skins until tender.
Meanwhile, clean lamb's lettuce (cutting off roots and removing wilted outer leaves), wash and drain.
Peel and slice potatoes thin while still warm.
Add drained lamb's lettuce, salt, vinegar, oil and liquid bouillon (Maggi seasoning), optional.
Mix and serve.

Serves 4.

* Living in Germany after World War II, I used to pick this lettuce out in the fields, before the farmers would plow in the Spring. It was free and it was the first fresh lettuce of the season. Now I have to get the seeds from Germany if I want to plant this lettuce in my vegetable garden. Planting time is early Fall through Spring.

GARTENSALAT
(Garden Salad)

Ingredients:

		salad bowl lettuce from the garden
		fresh spinach leaves
few		spring onions, sliced
2		tomatoes, sliced
1	stalk	celery, sliced
few		radishes, sliced
½		cucumber, peeled and sliced
½	medium	green pepper, sliced
		Vinegar and Oil Salad Dressing # 2, pg. 43

Directions:

Clean and wash lettuce and spinach, draining well.
Prepare all other vegetables and add to lettuce and spinach.
Add vinegar and oil salad dressing #2, toss and serve.

Serves 6.

Note: Most of the vegetables, lettuce and spinach come directly from my garden. This type of salad makes a good and nutritious lunch during the summer time. More than 1 recipe of vinegar and oil salad dressing #2 may be needed, depending on the amount of salad.

GELBERUEBENSALAT
(Carrot Salad)

Ingredients:

5	large	carrots
2½	tablespoons	oil
2	tablespoons	vinegar or lemon juice
2	tablespoons	honey
½	teaspoon	salt

Directions:

Clean and shred carrots.
Add remaining ingredients and mix well.
Set aside for 30 minutes before serving.

Serves 2 - 4.

Note: The amount of ingredients for the salad dressing may vary a little, depending on the size of carrots.

Mixed Salad, pg. 65

GURKEN & KRABBENSALAT
(Cucumber & Crab Salad)

Ingredients:

few		leaves of lettuce
1	small	cucumber
8	ounces	crab meat

Dressing:

2	tablespoons	onions, chopped fine
½	teaspoon	garlic powder
2	tablespoons	Tarragon Vinegar
3	tablespoons	canola oil
½	teaspoon	spicy mustard
		salt and pepper to taste
		chopped chives

To garnish:

1	medium	tomato, sliced
1		boiled egg, sliced
1	tablespoon	fresh chopped chives

Directions:

Peel cucumber, cut lengthwise, remove seeds and slice.
Blend cucumber with crab meat and place on top of salad leaves.
Mix all ingredients for dressing together, and pour over cucumber and crab meat.
Garnish with sliced tomatoes and sliced boiled egg.
Sprinkle with fresh chopped chives, and serve with crackers.

Serves 2.

GURKEN UND KARTOFFELSALAT
(Cucumber and Potato Salad)

Ingredients:

4	medium	potatoes
1	medium	cucumber
2	teaspoons	salt for sliced cucumber
¼	teaspoon	liquid bouillon (Maggi seasoning), optional
¼	teaspoon	salt
¼	teaspoon	pepper
1	tablespoon	vinegar
1	tablespoon	oil
		chives, chopped, optional

Directions:

Boil potatoes in their skins until tender.
Meanwhile, peel and slice cucumber very thin.
Add 2 teaspoons of salt, mix, and set aside for 15 minutes.
Peel and slice potatoes while still warm.
Squeeze most of the water out of cucumber and discard.
Add cucumber to sliced potatoes.
Add salt, pepper, vinegar, oil, and liquid bouillon (Maggi seasoning) optional, and mix well.
Garnish with chopped chives and serve.

Serves 4.

Note: This is a salad that my family, in-laws, and friends are crazy about. No matter whom I visit for dinner, I have to prepare this salad. So try it, it might become your favorite too.

GURKENSALAT
(Cucumber Salad)

Ingredients:

2	medium	cucumbers
1	tablespoon	salt
		Vinegar and Oil Salad Dressing # 2, pg. 43
		chives, chopped, optional

Directions:

Peel cucumber and slice paper-thin.
Add salt and mix well, then set aside for 15 minutes.
Drain off water, squeezing sliced cucumbers gently.
Add vinegar and oil salad dressing # 2 to cucumber.
Garnish with chopped chives, optional, and serve.

Serves 4.

Note: Cucumbers contain a lot of water. The salt will draw out the water, which need to be discarded before adding the vinegar and oil salad dressing # 2.

GURKENSALAT MIT SAHNE
(Cucumber Salad with Sour Cream)

Ingredients:

1	large	cucumber
2	teaspoons	salt
¼	teaspoon	pepper
1½	tablespoons	vinegar
2	tablespoons	onions, chopped fine
¼	cup	sour cream
1	teaspoon	chives, chopped

Directions:

Peel cucumber and slice very thin.
Add 2 teaspoons of salt, mix and set aside for 15 minutes.
Drain off water, squeezing cucumber slices slightly.
Blend vinegar, onions, and sour cream with cucumber.
Sprinkle with pepper and chopped chives before serving.

Serves 4.

Note: This cucumber salad should be served at once. It cannot be stored as a leftover in the refrigerator. One may want to use a little less vinegar, and/or more sour cream depending on the size of the cucumber.

DEUTSCHER KARTOFFELSALAT
(German Potato Salad)

Ingredients:

5	medium	potatoes
3	tablespoons	onions, chopped very fine
¾	teaspoon	salt
¼	teaspoon	pepper
1	teaspoon	liquid bouillon (Maggi seasoning), optional
3	tablespoons	oil
2	tablespoons	vinegar
		chives, chopped

Directions:

Boil potatoes in their skins until tender.
Peel and slice potatoes very thin while still warm.
Add onions, salt, pepper, liquid bouillon optional, oil and vinegar.
Mix well and garnish with chopped chives.
Serve with main dish or Cole-cut sandwiches.

Serves 4.

Note: This is a basic recipe for German potato salad. However, if potatoes are larger or smaller, change the amount of salt, pepper, oil and vinegar slightly.

AMERIKANISCHER KARTOFFELSALAT
(American Potato Salad)

Ingredients:

5	medium	potatoes, boiled in their jackets, peeled, and sliced
⅓	cup	onions, chopped fine
¼	cup	dill pickles, chopped fine
⅓	cup	celery, diced
3		eggs, hard boiled and diced
2	tablespoons	fresh parsley, chopped
¾	teaspoon	salt
½	teaspoon	pepper
½	teaspoon	liquid bouillon (Maggi seasoning), optional
¾	cup	mayonnaise
2	teaspoons	mustard
1	tablespoon	oil
2	tablespoons	vinegar

Directions:

Combine all ingredients and mix well.
Perhaps a little more seasoning may be needed, depending on the size of the potatoes.

Serves 4.

Note: Salad tastes best freshly made. However, do refrigerate leftover salad.

KOPFSALAT
(Boston Lettuce Salad)

Ingredients:

1	large	Boston lettuce
		Vinegar & Oil Salad Dressing # 1, pg. 42
		fresh chives, chopped, optional

Directions:

Clean and wash Boston lettuce.
Drain well.
Add vinegar & oil salad dressing # 1 just before serving, and toss lightly.
Sprinkle with chopped chives, optional.

Serves 4.

Note: More than 1 recipe of vinegar & oil salad dressing # 1 may be needed, depending on the size of the Boston lettuce. One may alternate this salad by adding a dash of sugar, or substitute fresh lemon juice for vinegar. Another choice may be to prepare Boston lettuce with fresh lemon juice, and add hot bacon grease along with crumbled fried bacon just before serving. Boston lettuce is the most commonly used lettuce in Germany. I had never even seen Iceberg lettuce until I moved to the United States.

KRAUTSALAT
(Cole Slaw)

Ingredients:

4	cups	white cabbage, sliced thin or shredded
2	large	carrots, peeled and grated
1	cup	mayonnaise
2	tablespoons	oil
½	teaspoon	salt
3	tablespoons	sugar
2	tablespoons	vinegar, wine or distilled

Directions:

Mix all ingredients in large bowl, and set aside for 15 minutes.
Serve with your favored meat entrée.

Serves 6.

Note: This Cole slaw yields better results when sliced very thin instead of shredded. One may substitute the sugar and vinegar with sweet pickle juice. Leftover Cole slaw can be stored in refrigerator, but should be eaten within 24 hours.

MAKKARONISALAT
(Macaroni Salad)

Ingredients:

4	cups	macaroni, cooked
½	cup	onions, chopped
¾	cup	celery, diced
⅓	cup	dill pickles, chopped fine
⅓	cup	green peppers, chopped
4		eggs, hard boiled and diced
1½	tablespoons	parsley, chopped
½	teaspoon	salt
¼	teaspoon	pepper
½	teaspoon	liquid bouillon (Maggi seasoning), optional
¾	cup	mayonnaise
2½	teaspoons	mustard
2	teaspoons	oil
2	tablespoons	vinegar

Directions:

Combine and mix all ingredients.
Chill before serving.

Serves 6 - 8.

Note: Do refrigerate leftover macaroni salad.

SALATPLATTE
(Salad Plate)

Ingredients:

½	cup	string been salad
⅓	cup	white cabbage salad
¾	cup	German potato salad
2	cups	Boston salad
½	cup	cucumber salad
½	cup	tomato salad
¼	cup	celeriac salad
¼	cup	carrot salad
½	cup	pasta salad
		crackers, or hot bread and butter

Directions:

Arrange salads on large platter.
Serve with crackers, or hot bread and butter.

Serves 2 - 4.

Note: Salads are so popular, especially in the summer. Above salad plate is German-made. Each salad has been prepared with the dressing before placing salad on a platter. You may want to use different kinds of salads; the choice is yours.

SELLERIESALAT # 1
(Celeriac Salad # 1)

Ingredients:

2	medium	celeriac
2	pints	water
1	teaspoon	salt
2½	tablespoons	vinegar

Marinade:

1	teaspoon	salt
⅓	cup	vinegar
2	cups	water
¼	cup	honey
1	tablespoon	onions, chopped fine
1		bay leaf
3		pepper corns
3		juniper seeds
1	teaspoon	mustard seed
1	tablespoon	oil, optional

Directions:

Remove roots and scrub celeriac under running water.
Combine water, salt and vinegar, and bring to boil.
Add celeriac, and cook until tender, about 60-90 minutes, depending on the size of celeriac.
Meanwhile, combine all ingredients for marinade except oil.
Bring to boil, then simmer for 10 minutes.
Drain off marinade and discard spices.
Season marinade if still needed.
When celeriac is done, drain off hot water, then rinse with cold water to make peeling easier.
Peel and slice celeriac while still warm.
Pour marinade over sliced celeriac and let cool together.
Just before serving, drain off some liquid and add oil, optional.

Serve with any main dish.

Serves 4 - 6.

Note: This celeriac salad should be made ahead of time. It can also be made a day before. This type of salad is usually served on a salad plate with a variety of salads. However, celeriac lovers prefer this salad by itself.

* My parents grew celeriac in the garden every year, but the salad was not made very often. Mother used celeriac mainly in soups. When I first came to the United States, I didn't know that there were two kinds of celery, for we only grew the celery for the root, which is called celeriac in the United States.

I remember back in the old days people did not measure very much. It was a little here and a dash there, and somehow the meal came out just fine. My mother was no exception to that practice. The only time I ever saw her do some measuring was when she baked Christmas cookies and/or some cakes.

Macaroni Salad, pg. 60

Maria Swaringen

SELLERIESALAT # 2
(Celeriac Salad # 2)

Ingredients:

1	medium	celeriac
1	pint	water
½	teaspoon	salt
1½	tablespoons	vinegar

Vinegar and Oil Dressing:

2	tablespoons	vinegar
		salt
		pepper
⅛	teaspoon	dry tarragon
1	tablespoon	onions, chopped very fine
2½	tablespoons	oil
		fresh chives, chopped to garnish, optional

Directions:

Remove roots and scrub celeriac under running water.
Combine water, salt and vinegar, and bring to boil.
Add celeriac and cook until tender, about 60-90 minutes, depending on the size of celeriac.
When celeriac is done, drain off hot water, then rinse with cold water to make peeling easier.
Peel and slice celeriac.
Blend ingredients together for vinegar and oil dressing, and pour over sliced celeriac.
Garnish with fresh chopped chives, optional.
Serve when cool with main dish or on a salad plate with a variety of salads.

Serves 2 - 4.

Note: As I mentioned before, celeriac is also used to flavor beef broth, or other soup. A slice of celeriac is tied together in a small bundle with a slice of onion, parsley, parsley root and a small carrot. It is called "Suppengruen", and discarded when the soup is done.

GEMISCHTER SALAT
(Mixed Salad)

Ingredients:

1	medium	cucumber
2	teaspoons	salt
1	small	Boston lettuce
2	medium	tomatoes
½	small	onion, sliced
		Vinegar & Oil Salad Dressing # 1, pg. 42
		fresh chives, chopped, optional

Directions:

Peel cucumber and slice very thin.
Add salt, mix well, and set aside for 10-15 minutes.
Meanwhile, clean and wash Boston lettuce and drain well.
Wash and slice tomatoes.
Drain off water from cucumber by gently squeezing
Combine Boston lettuce, tomatoes, cucumber and onions.
Add vinegar & oil salad dressing # 1 and toss.
Garnish with fresh shopped chives, optional, and serve.

Serves 4.

Note: More than 1 recipe of vinegar & oil salad dressing may be needed, depending on the amount of salad. Cucumber should be sliced paper thin. Discard water drawn from cucumber before adding to lettuce and tomatoes.

TOMATEN UND KOPFSALAT
(Tomato and Boston Salad)

Ingredients:

1	large	Boston lettuce
2	large	tomatoes
		Vinegar & Oil Salad Dressing # 1, pg. 42
		fresh chives, chopped, optional

Directions:

Clean and wash Boston lettuce, and drain well.
Wash and slice tomatoes, and add to Boston lettuce.
Add vinegar & oil salad dressing # 1 just before serving, and toss lightly.
Sprinkle with fresh chopped chives, optional.

Serves 4.

Note: More than 1 recipe of vinegar & oil salad dressing # 1 may be needed, depending on the amount of salad.

TOMATENSALAT
(Tomato Salad)

Ingredients:

4	large	tomatoes
		Vinegar & Oil Salad Dressing # 2, pg. 43
		fresh sweet basil, chopped, optional
		fresh chives, chopped, optional

Directions:

Wash and slice tomatoes.
Add vinegar and oil salad dressing #2 and a little fresh chopped sweet basil, optional.
Toss before serving. Sprinkle with fresh chopped chives, optional.

Serves 4.

Note: More than one recipe of vinegar and oil salad dressing #2 may be needed, depending on the amount of tomatoes. Onion lovers may want to add a little more onions. Use vine ripened tomatoes only.

WEISSKRAUTSALAT
(White Cabbage Salad)

Ingredients:

1	pound	white cabbage
1	teaspoon	salt
1	teaspoon	sugar
3	tablespoons	vinegar, distilled
1½	tablespoons	oil
1	teaspoon	caraway seeds

Directions:

Slice cleaned cabbage very fine.
Combine all other ingredients and mix well.
Add sliced cabbage and blend well.
Set aside for at least for 30 minutes before serving.

Serves 6.

Note: If available, fill tomatoes or green peppers with cabbage salad and serve. This is also an ideal salad to serve on a salad platter with various kinds of salads.

Meats

From

The

Land

And

Sea

BEANBURGER

Ingredients:

2	tablespoons	oil or shortening
¾	cup	chopped onions
¾	cup	diced celery stalk
1	pound	ground beef
1	teaspoon	salt
¼	teaspoon	pepper
1	can	tomatoes, 14 oz.
1	can	kidney beans, 14 oz.
1½	teaspoons	corn starch
2	tablespoons	water
1	teaspoon	chili powder

Directions:

Heat oil or shortening in large skillet.
Sauté onions and celery until onions are pale yellow.
Add ground beef, salt and pepper.
Fry meat until done, about 10 minutes.
Add tomatoes, kidney beans and chili powder.
Simmer for 15 to 20 minutes.
Mix corn starch with water and stir into beanburger.

Serves 6.

Note: A pint of home canned tomatoes may be used instead of a 14 oz. can of tomatoes. All of the corn starch may not be needed, depending on how much liquid has boiled off. If ground beef contains too much fat, drain off some before adding vegetables. For those who like "hot" food, add a dash of cayenne pepper.

BEEF CUBE STEAKS

Ingredients:

		Teriyaki sauce to marinade meat
2		cube steaks
2	tablespoons	oil
½	cup	flour
		salt and pepper
3	tablespoons	chopped onions
1	small	carrot
1	tablespoon	fresh chopped parsley
1	teaspoon	beef bouillon granules
1	can	sliced mushrooms, 4 oz.
		corn starch
		water
2	tablespoons	sour cream

Directions:

Marinade cube steaks in teriyaki sauce for about 15-30 min.
Sprinkle marinated cube steaks with salt and pepper.
Dip into flour, and brown one side in hot oil.
Turn cube steaks and add chopped onions.
When onions are light brown, add carrot, parsley, mushrooms, beef bouillon and small amount of water.
Simmer for 1¼ hours, adding water from time to time.
Blend corn starch with water and thicken gravy.
Stir in sour cream, and add salt and pepper if needed.

Serves 2.

Note: If time permitting, marinade meat longer.

Maria Swaringen

BEEF STEAK, PORTERHOUSE OR T/BONE

Ingredients:

4   steaks, Porterhouse or T/bone
                          Teriyaki sauce
                          Mrs. Dash's Herbs
                          Lemon & Pepper seasoning

Directions:

Tenderize steaks in Teriyaki sauce for 20-30 minutes.
Sprinkle steaks with Mrs. Dash's Herbs, and Lemon & Pepper seasoning.
Broil on each side for about 5-10 minutes, depending on the thickness of steaks.
Serve with steak sauce, your favorite vegetables and salad.

Serves 4.

FLEISCHPFLAENZCHEN
(Hamburger Patties)

Ingredients:

3	slices	bread, white or wheat
¼	cup	milk
1	teaspoon	salt
1		egg
1	pound	hamburger meat
¼	teaspoon	pepper
3	tablespoons	onions, chopped
¼	cup	fresh parsley, chopped
¼	cup	flour
2	tablespoons	margarine

Directions:

Combine bread and salt.
Add milk and egg, and mix well.
Add hamburger meat, pepper, onions, parsley and flour.
Mix all ingredients together and shape into patties.
Heat margarine and brown patties slowly on both sides.

Serves 6.

Note: Serve with mashed potatoes, green vegetables, and tossed salad. Just before serving mashed potatoes, pour hot leftover margarine with crumbs from frying pan over mashed potatoes. It is very tasty. One can also mix hamburger meat with ground pork. Fleischpflaenzchen, also known in the Bavarian dialect as "Fleischpflanzl" can also be made from leftover cooked meat, or mixed with leftover meat. I learned that from my mother right after World War II. However, to me they taste best with fresh meat.

GEBACKENE LEBER
(Fried and Baked Liver)

Ingredients:

1	pound	liver, beef or calf
½	cup	flour
¼	teaspoon	garlic salt
½	teaspoon	oregano
3	tablespoons	oil
1	large	onion, sliced
4	tablespoons	oil
3	cups	warm water
1	small	carrot
3	tablespoons	fresh parsley, chopped
2	teaspoons	beef bouillon granules
1½	teaspoons	corn starch
		salt and pepper

Directions:

Preheat oven to 350 degrees.
Combine flour, garlic salt and oregano.
Set aside.
Fry onions in 3 tablespoons of oil, then set aside on plate.
Dust and pat liver with flour mix.
Heat 4 tablespoons of oil and brown liver quickly on both sides.
Transfer liver to roasting pan or casserole dish.
Top with fried onions.
Carefully add 1-2 cups of warm water to frying pan and heat, then pour over liver and onions.
Add carrot, parsley, beef bouillon granules, and salt and pepper.
Bake at 350 degrees in oven for 45-60 minutes, adding some remaining water from time to time.
Thicken gravy with corn starch blended with water.
Season to taste.

Serves 4.

Note: This is a recipe for those who don't like liver because it usually is tough, or so they say. Serve with mashed potatoes, green vegetable and salad.

Maria Swaringen

GEFUELLTE PAPRIKASCHOTEN
(Filled Green Peppers)

Ingredients:

4	large	green bell peppers, cleaned
2	slices	white or wheat bread
2	tablespoons	milk
1		egg
½	pound	hamburger meat
¾	teaspoon	salt
¼	teaspoon	pepper
4	tablespoons	onions, chopped
2	tablespoons	fresh parsley, chopped
2	tablespoons	oil or shortening
¾	cup	cooked rice
3	tablespoons	flour
1	quart	Green Pepper Sauce, pg. 38
		corn starch and water
2	tablespoons	sour cream, optional

Directions:

Combine bread with milk and mix.
Add egg, hamburger meat, 2 tablespoons chopped onions, parsley, cooked rice, flour, salt and pepper, and mix well.
Fill green bell peppers.
In a large 3 quart saucepan, heat oil or shortening, and brown 2 tablespoons of chopped onions.
Add filled green peppers, (standing up in saucepan).
Pour 1 quart of green pepper sauce over filled peppers.
Bring to boil, then simmer for 1 hour, lifting peppers with a spoon occasionally, to avoid burning.
Blend corn starch with water, and thicken sauce.
Stir in sour cream optional, and season to taste.

Serves 4.

GEMISCHTE RINDSROULADE
(Mixed Beef Roll)

Ingredients:

1½	pounds	beef, top round steak, butter-flied
1	pound	pork tenderloin, boneless, butter-flied
		salt and pepper
¼	cup	onions, chopped
2	tablespoons	bacon grease
1	small	bay leaf
1	cup	tomato juice
		corn starch
		water
1	tablespoon	sour cream, optional

Filling:

2		Kaiser rolls, sliced thin
	dash	salt
⅓	cup	hot milk
1	tablespoon	butter, melted
1		egg
1	tablespoon	grated onion
1	tablespoon	fresh parsley, chopped
1	teaspoon	Lemon & Pepper seasoning

Directions:

Pound beef and pork lightly so both slices will get larger and thinner.
Season both with salt and pepper.
Place pork on top of beef, and set aside.
Sprinkle sliced Kaiser rolls with salt.
Pour over hot milk and melted butter, and set aside for 30 minutes.
Add egg, grated onion, parsley, Lemon & Pepper seasoning, and mix well.
Spread filling evenly on top of pork.
Roll meat together with sides tucked in.

Tie a string around beef roll several times, plus once lengthwise.
Heat bacon grease in Dutch oven, and quickly brown beef roll, adding onions toward end of browning.
Add ⅔ cup of tomato juice and bay leaf.
Bring to boil, then simmer for 90 minutes, or until done, adding remaining tomato juice towards the end.
Add a small amount of water when done to make more gravy.
Thicken gravy by adding corn starch blended with water.
Stir in sour cream, optional.

Serves 6.

Note: One may use other ingredients and herbs for mixed beef roll filling. Sage, onion and parsley is always a good combination for a bread filling and/or stuffing. One tablespoon of corn starch will thicken 1 cup of gravy. If more gravy is needed, use packaged beef onion gravy, which will make 1 cup of gravy. One may also use 1 teaspoon of beef bouillon granules to 1 cup of water to add to original gravy. Use additional corn starch, and sour cream, optional. Serve mixed beef roll with pasta, spaetzle or bread-dumplings and salad.

HACKBRATEN
(Meat Loaf)

Ingredients:

1		Kaiser roll, sliced thin
1	teaspoon	salt
¼	cup	hot milk
1		egg
1	pound	hamburger meat
¼	teaspoon	pepper
⅓	cup	chopped onions
3	tablespoons	fresh chopped parsley
¼	cup	flour
		salt and pepper to sprinkle over meat loaf

For roasting:

2	tablespoons	margarine
3	tablespoons	chopped onions
1	small	carrot, peeled
1	tablespoon	fresh chopped parsley
		water
1	teaspoon	beef bouillon granules
		corn starch and water

Directions:

Preheat oven to 350 degrees.
Melt margarine in small roasting pan or casserole dish, and set aside.
Combine sliced Kaiser roll with salt and hot milk.
Add egg, hamburger meat, pepper, chopped onions, fresh parsley, flour and mix well.
Form meat loaf, sprinkle with salt and pepper, and place in roasting pan or casserole dish.
Add 3 tablespoons of chopped onions to roasting pan or casserole dish and brown.

Add carrot, 1 tablespoon fresh chopped parsley, beef bouillon granules, and ½ to ¾ cup of water after onions have browned.
Roast at 350 degrees for one hour, adding water and basting occasionally.
Add extra water for gravy when meat loaf is done.
Mix corn starch with a small amount of water, and add to gravy to thicken.
Season to taste.

Serves 6.

Note: Meatloaf is actually roasted in a roasting pan just like any other meat roast and will have gravy. However, meatloaf gravy contains a lot of fat due to the hamburger meat. One may want to spoon off some of the fat before finishing the gravy. One my also add some onion gravy mix, if more gravy is needed. Some may also want to add a small amount of sour cream to gravy.

Dry parsley may be used in a lesser amount. Fresh parsley gives it a much better flavor. I freeze fresh chopped parsley to have it available throughout the year.

One may want to serve meatloaf and gravy with noodles, a vegetable and German potato salad. A small amount of gravy on top of the German potato salad is very tasty.

Refrigerated German potato salad will taste better when reheated in the microwave oven for just a few seconds.

KRAUTWICKEL
(Cabbage Rolls)

Ingredients:

2	slices	bread, white or whole wheat
2	tablespoons	milk
1		egg
½	pound	hamburger meat
2	tablespoons	onions, chopped
1	tablespoon	fresh parsley, chopped
½	teaspoon	salt
¼	teaspoon	pepper
¼	teaspoon	liquid bouillon (Maggi seasoning), optional
½	head	white cabbage leaves
		salt water
		shortening or oil for frying
1	cup	beef broth
1	tablespoon	sour cream
1	package	onion gravy mix

Directions:

Preheat oven to 350 degrees.
Soak bread in milk, and mix with egg.
Add hamburger meat, onions, parsley, salt, pepper and liquid bouillon (Maggi seasoning), optional.
Mix well and set aside.
Clean white cabbage and use the larger cabbage leaves.
Boil in salted water just long enough for leaves to become slightly wilted.
On each cabbage leaf, place about 2 tablespoons of hamburger mixture.
Roll up cabbage leaf with filling, turning ends under to secure each roll.
Fry cabbage rolls on all sides.
Place in casserole dish and sprinkle with salt.
Add beef broth.

Cover and bake at 350 degrees for 30-40 minutes.
Prepare onion gravy, add sour cream, and pour over baked cabbage rolls.

Serves 4.

Note: Use only 1 tablespoon of hamburger mixture if leaves are small. It is best to use outer leaves of cabbage. To make instant beef broth, heat 1 cup of water with 1 teaspoon of beef bouillon granules.

* Many people were hungry and homeless toward the end and right after the war. It was not uncommon to hear that someone in the neighborhood was killed by a person breaking into a home, looking for food.

I remember my father warning my mother on several occasions, not to let a stranger into the house while he was at work. Mother certainly agreed to my father's strict rules, for as long as she did not see a hungry person, that is.

I remember one day a man came to the house begging Mother for a few coins. Mother said to the man, "I have no money, for I have six children and only one provider, but if you are hungry, I do have some soup on the stove and you are welcome to have some. Would you like to come into the house?" The man went into the kitchen, and all of us children looked at mother very surprised, to say the least. "Children," she said, "it's OK, go and play and I will talk to you later." After the man had left, Mother called us children together, asking us to make this our little secret. She said, "This man was hungry, and so I fed him. Now watch; in a few days the Lord will send someone to bring me some food I need to have for the family." A few days later, one of the neighboring farmers came for a short visit to bring us some much needed butter on his way to town. After the farmer had left, Mother reminded us children again of what she said earlier, "Give and the Lord will provide" she said. What a wonderful lesson my mother gave to all of us children. As for my father, he never found out.

ORIENTAL BEEF AND BROCCOLI

Ingredients:

1	pound	lean and boneless beef
⅓	cup	Teriyaki marinade sauce
4	cups	broccoli-florets & stem pieces
1	cup	onions, cut into chunks
1	package	Adolph's Stir Fry Mix
¾	cup	water
		oil for frying

Directions:

Cut lean beef into thin strips, removing any fat.
Add Teriyaki marinade sauce to tenderize, setting aside for at least 15 minutes.
Meanwhile, clean broccoli-florets and stems, cut into bite size pieces, and set aside.
Stir fry beef strips in oil for about 2-3 minutes.
Add broccoli and onions, and sauté together with beef strips for about 8 minutes.
Blend together Adolph's Stir Fry Mix with water, and stir into beef and broccoli.
Cook for 1-2 minutes, or until liquid has thickened.
Serve with rice, and/or Chow Mein Noodles, and hot sauce if desired.

Serves 6.

Note: Disregard directions on Adolph's Stir Fry Mix envelope. One may substitute Adolph's Stir Fry Mix with onion gravy mix. Add a little more water if gravy should get too thick. Freeze leftover beef and broccoli for later use.

PAPRIKA STEAK
(Green Pepper Steak)

Ingredients:

1	pound	lean beef
		Teriyaki sauce
5	tablespoons	oil
2	medium	onions, cut into large pieces
3	medium	green peppers, cut up in large pieces
3	stalks	celery, sliced thick
1	can	mushroom pieces, drained, 4 oz.
½	teaspoon	salt
½	teaspoon	garlic powder
¼	teaspoon	pepper
1	cup	water
1	package	onion gravy mix

Directions:

Remove fat and slice meat into thin strips.
Add Teriyaki sauce, cover and refrigerate for 30-60 minutes.
Meanwhile, prepare all vegetables.
Heat 3 tablespoons of oil in wok or large frying pan.
Stir fry vegetables for about 6 minutes, adding mushrooms last, and season with ¼ teaspoon of salt and ½ teaspoon of garlic.
Place vegetables in bowl and set aside.
Heat remaining oil in wok or large frying pan.
Add marinated meat and remaining salt and pepper.
Fry meat until done, about 6-8 minutes.
Add stir fried vegetables and onion gravy mix combined with 1 cup of water.
Heat and simmer for 1 minute.
Season to taste if needed.

Serves 4 - 6.

Note: Vegetables and meat can be stir-fried with a Non Stick Cooking Spray by adding a small amount of bouillon broth from time to time. Serve with rice and/or Chow Mein noodles.

Author's Vegetable Garden

Maria Swaringen

RINDSGULASCH
(Beef Goulash)

Ingredients:

1-1½	pounds	lean beef cubes
		Teriyaki sauce to marinade
2	tablespoons	shortening or oil
2	medium	onions, sliced
2	large	garlic cloves, minced
1	teaspoon	salt
¼	teaspoon	pepper
2	tablespoons	paprika
2	cups	water
1	tablespoon	corn starch and small amount of water
1	tablespoon	sour cream, optional

Directions:

Marinade beef cubes in Teriyaki sauce for 30 minutes.
In large saucepan, heat shortening or oil.
Add marinated beef cubes and brown quickly.
Add salt, pepper, onions, garlic, paprika and 1 cup of water.
Stir together well and bring to boil.
Simmer for 1½ hours, stirring occasionally, and adding water from time to time.
Blend corn starch with water and add to beef goulash to thicken gravy.
Stir in sour cream, optional.
Season to taste with pepper and salt.

Serves 4.

Note: Add more water for gravy if needed. Beef goulash can be made earlier, and it also freezes well. The onions will make the beef goulash a little spicy. However, one can still add some extra hot pepper. Bread-dumplings go well with beef goulash.

RINDERROULADEN
(Beef Rolls)

Ingredients:

4	slices	of beef (sliced thin)
½	cup	flour
4	slices	bacon, cut in half
4	thin	spears of dill pickles, cut in half
		mustard
8		toothpicks
		salt and pepper
		shortening or oil for browning
3	tablespoons	onions, chopped
		hot water
1	tablespoon	fresh parsley, chopped
1	small	carrot, peeled and cut in half
1	teaspoon	beef bouillon granules
1	tablespoon	corn starch
1	tablespoon	sour cream

Directions:

Cut beef slices in half and pound lightly.

Spread mustard on beef and sprinkle with salt and pepper.

Place half slice of bacon and dill pickle on top.

Roll up slices and secure with toothpick.

Roll beef rolls in flour and brown all sides in shortening or oil, adding chopped onions toward end of browning.

Slowly add about 1 cup of hot water, parsley, carrot, and beef bouillon granules.

Cover and simmer for about 90 minutes or until done, adding small amounts of water from time to time.

To thicken gravy, blend corn starch with water and stir into liquid.

Stir in sour cream and season with salt and pepper.

Serves 4.

Note: When liquid is too low, beef rolls will stick to pan. Add still small amount of water when beef rolls are done to make gravy.

SAUERBRATEN
(Beef in Marinade)

Ingredients:

2	pounds	beef, (boneless rump roast, bottom round)

For marinade:

2	cups	distilled vinegar
3	cups	cold water
6		peppercorns
		whole cloves
1	large	bay-leaf
1	small	onion, sliced
2	teaspoons	salt

For braising:

2	tablespoons	oil or shortening
2	tablespoons	chopped onions
2	cups	warm water
1	small	carrot
		salt and pepper
3	tablespoons	sour cream
		corn starch and water

Directions:

Wash meat and place in large bowl.
Add all ingredients needed to marinade.
Cover bowl and place in refrigerator for four days, turning meat over once a day.
To braise: Remove meat from marinade and pat dry.

Quickly brown in oil or shortening on all sides, adding chopped onions toward end of browning.

Carefully add one cup of warm water and carrot to meat.

Add salt and pepper, cover and simmer for 1½ to 2 hours, adding water occasionally.

Prepare gravy, adding extra water if needed.

Stir in corn starch mixed with water to thicken gravy.

Add sour cream, and season with salt and pepper if needed.

Serves 6.

Note: One may use some of the marinade instead of plain water, and add a bay-leaf, a few whole cloves and peppercorns. But do remember, the marinade will make the gravy very vinegar-strong, so use only a small amount according to your own taste. Serve with potato-dumplings or spaetzle, and sweet and sour red cabbage.

Sauerbraten and spaetzle (homemade noodles) is as well known to the Schwaebisch region as pork roast and potato dumplings to southern Bavaria. The people in southern Germany are pork eaters.

SCHMORBRATEN
(Braised Roast Beef)

Ingredients:

2	pounds	beef, round rump roast
		salt and pepper
3	tablespoons	shortening or oil
½	cup	onions, chopped
		warm water
1	medium	bay leaf
2	medium	garlic cloves, chopped
2	tablespoons	fresh parsley, chopped
1	medium	carrot, peeled and quartered
1½	teaspoons	beef bouillon granules
2	tablespoons	sour cream
		corn starch and water

Directions:

Season meat with salt and pepper.
Heat shortening or oil in Dutch oven.
Brown roast quickly, adding onions toward end of browning.
When onions are light brown, add 1 cup of warm water, bay leaf, garlic, parsley, carrot and beef bouillon granules.
Cover and simmer for 2 hours, or until meat is done, adding water occasionally when needed.
Add corn starch mixed with water to thicken gravy.
Stir in 2 tablespoons of sour cream, and season gravy with salt and pepper.

Serves 6.

Note: Add a little more water if more gravy is needed, and season to taste. Serve with bread-dumplings or noodles, vegetables and salad.

SPAGHETTI AND MEAT # 1

Ingredients:

1	pound	hamburger meat
1	tablespoon	shortening
1	small	onion, chopped
1	quart	Homemade Spaghetti Sauce, pg. 39
1	pound	spaghetti noodles, cooked
		salt and pepper
		Parmesan cheese

Directions:

Heat shortening and brown onions.

Add hamburger meat, salt and pepper and cook until done.

Meanwhile, heat Homemade Spaghetti Sauce.

Add fried hamburger meat to homemade spaghetti sauce and simmer for 15-20 minutes.

Serve with cooked spaghetti noodles, and sprinkle with Parmesan cheese per serving.

Serves 4 - 6.

Note: One may make and brown meatballs, then simmer in homemade spaghetti sauce as above. If spaghetti sauce is too spicy, add 1-2 cups of canned tomatoes, or tomato juice, and simmer 15 minutes longer.

Maria Swaringen

SPAGHETTI AND MEAT # 2

Ingredients:

1	pound	hamburger meat
1	tablespoon	shortening
1	small	onion, chopped
2	cups	tomato juice
2	cups	canned tomatoes
2	small	cloves of garlic, minced
1		bay leaf
1	tablespoon	dry oregano
		salt and pepper
		Parmesan cheese
1	pound	spaghetti noodles, cooked

Directions:

Heat shortening in pressure cooker and brown onions.
Add hamburger meat, salt and pepper and cook until done.
Add tomato juice, canned tomatoes, garlic, bay leaf and oregano.
Cook for 10 minutes in pressure cooker.
Serve with spaghetti noodles.
Sprinkle with Parmesan cheese per serving.

Serves 4 - 6.

Note: If a pressure cooker is not available, cook and simmer spaghetti sauce with meat for 1 hour. Meatballs can be used in place of plain hamburger meat. Brown meatballs before adding remaining ingredients.

UNGARISCHES GULASCH
(Hungarian Goulash)

Ingredients:

¼	cup	oil or shortening
4	large	onions, sliced
2	pounds	beef, cut in cubes
2½	cups	water
1	teaspoon	salt
1		hot pepperoni, sliced
1	tablespoon	paprika
1	dash	cayenne pepper, optional
		corn starch and water, if needed

Directions:

Sauté onions in oil or shortening.
Add beef cubes and brown together with onions.
Add 1 cup of water and salt.
Bring to a boil, then simmer for 1½ - 2 hours, adding water when needed.
Add sliced pepperoni within last 15 minutes of cooking time.
Add paprika, cayenne pepper, optional and season to taste.

Serves 8.

Note: Thicken gravy with corn starch blended with a small amount of water, if needed.

Maria Swaringen

KALBSGULASCH
(Veal Goulash)

Ingredients:

1½	pounds	veal, cut in cubes
¼	cup	oil or shortening
3	medium	onions, chopped fine
¼	teaspoon	garlic powder
½	teaspoon	salt
1	teaspoon	paprika
1	tablespoon	fresh chopped parsley
2	cups	water
2	teaspoons	beef bouillon granules
½	cup	sour cream
		corn starch and water

Directions:

Brown veal cubes in oil or shortening with onions.
Add salt, paprika, and garlic powder.
Add 1 cup of water, 1 teaspoon of beef bouillon granules, and parsley.
Cover and simmer until done, about 1 hour.
Blend together remaining water and beef bouillon granules, and add to veal goulash as needed.
Blend corn starch with small amount of water.
Add to veal goulash to thicken gravy.
Stir in sour cream, and season with more salt if needed.

Serves 4 - 6.

KRAEUTERSCHNITZEL
(Herb Schnitzel)

Ingredients:

4	small	fillet of veal or pork, or pork tenderloin
		salt and pepper
⅓	cup	flour
1	tablespoon	chopped onions
2	tablespoons	margarine for frying

Herb sauce:

3	tablespoons	butter
3	tablespoons	flour
2	tablespoons	onions, chopped very fine
2	tablespoons	fresh parsley, chopped
⅛	teaspoon	dry rosemary
⅜	teaspoon	dry oregano
¼	teaspoon	caraway seeds
¼	cup	canned mushroom, chopped
2¼	cups	water
2	teaspoons	beef bouillon granules
2	tablespoons	sour cream
½	teaspoon	fresh lemon juice
		salt and pepper to taste
1	teaspoon	fresh chives, chopped to garnish

Directions:

Blend beef bouillon with water and set aside.
Make herb sauce first.
Sauté onions in butter.
Add flour, stirring constantly until mixture is light brown.
Add beef bouillon water, a little at a time, and stir constantly until all liquid is used up.
Add parsley, rosemary, oregano, caraway seeds and chopped mushrooms.

Simmer for 10 minutes, then set aside.
Meanwhile, pound each fillet of veal or pork.
Season with salt and pepper, then dust with flour.
Fry fillets on both sides, adding onions toward end of frying.
Pour herb sauce over fillets, and simmer for 10-15 minutes.
Blend in sour cream and lemon juice.
Season to taste with salt and pepper.
Garnish with chopped chives.

Serves 4.

Note: If sauce should get too thick, add a small amount of water.

WIENERSCHNITZEL
(Veal Schnitzel)

Ingredients:

6	slices	of veal loin, boneless
1	large	egg, well beaten
1	cup	bread crumbs
		salt and pepper
		butter for frying
6		lemon slices
		cranberry sauce

Directions:

Remove fat and skin from veal.
Pound veal slices very thin and season with salt and pepper.
Dip into beaten egg, then roll in bread crumbs.
Fry in hot butter about 3-4 minutes on each side, or until done.
Serve each wiener schnitzel with a slice of lemon and a tablespoon of cranberry sauce.

Serves 6.

Note: Frying time depends on the thickness of veal slices. Veal has very little taste, so it is best to use fresh veal instead of frozen. In Germany, veal is the most expensive meat, so most people use pork for schnitzel. One may use margarine or shortening for frying. However, butter does give the best taste.

BRAISED PORK CHOPS

Ingredients:

4		pork chops
3	tablespoons	margarine or oil
2	tablespoons	chopped onions
		salt and pepper
1	tablespoon	chopped parsley
1	small	carrot, peeled and quartered
¼	teaspoon	caraway seeds
		water
		corn starch and water

Directions:

Sprinkle pork chops with salt and pepper.
Add to heated margarine or oil, and brown quickly on one side.
Turn pork chops over and add chopped onions.
When onions are brown, carefully add ½ cup of water, parsley, carrot and caraway seeds.
Cover and simmer pork chops for about 1 hour or until done, basting often, and adding water when needed.
When pork chops are done, add more water to make gravy.
Thicken with corn starch and water.
Season with salt and pepper if needed.

Serves 4.

Note: Braised pork chops is an ideal way for someone who does not want to use a big pork roast. It is cheaper, but just as good. Strain gravy through sieve if one does not like to see the vegetables in the gravy. Thicken with corn starch mixed with water. Pork chops will become a lot more tender by basting often.

*   I grew up in Germany during World War II. There were 6 children in the family and my father was the sole provider. It was a frightening time, and food was also hard to come by. So during World War II and for sometime after, my parents would raise two pigs every year for extra meat.

This was also the time when every family was given food stamps, and if one slaughtered a pig, the food stamps for meat would be taken away for 6 months. All livestock for slaughtering had to be registered. However, my father chose to register only one pig per year. The second pig was slaughtered in the middle of the night. I remember as children we would sometimes walk with my mother and father in the middle of the night to a farmer to get a trough that was needed for slaughtering. It was usually in the winter, with lots of snow, and very cold. As we walked through the cow pastures, every step of the way one could hear the crunching of the snow.

I also remember my first experience watching the butcher slaughter a pig and preparing different kinds of sausages. I could not eat any meat or sausage for months.

After everything was over, we would carry the trough back to the farmer again during the night. My father would salt down the meat, place it in a big barrel, and ten days later the meat was taken to the farmers smoke-room. Everyday, as I walked to school and passing by the farm, I could smell the aroma of the smoked meat coming from the chimney.

Most people would think of a "Smoke-house", but this smoke-room was upstairs in the farmer's house. A little room with the chimney going through. Come to think of it, it must have been a specially constructed brick room, to have this sort of thing in the house. To my knowledge, most of the farmers in Germany had a smoke-room in those days, for they all smoked their own meat.

The German smoked meat looks very black on the outside from all of the smoke, but the flavor is out of this world! Smoked meat is very expensive at the butcher shop. Besides using it for lunch meat, it will cook just as fast as any other meat. It is quite different from smoked Virginia ham.

Years ago I had a neighbor whose family loved Virginia ham. I liked smoked meat, so I thought I would try the Virginia ham with my sauerkraut. Not knowing any better, I cooked the ham the same way as I would the German smoked meat in my sauerkraut, for dinner was supposed to be sauerkraut with bread-dumplings and smoked meat. Well, after two hours dinner was served. The bread-dumplings were fine. But the sauerkraut was so salty and full of pepper, it was impossible to eat. The so-called Virginia ham was nothing but salt, and as hard as a rock. Needless to say, my dinner went to the dogs. The next day, I talked to my neighbor about my delicious dinner and to my surprise, I found out that one needs to cook Virginia ham for many hours, changing the water several times. Needless to say, I have never tried Virginia ham since. I guess my mother was right when she said, "Woas da Bauer net kennt, des frisst da net", which means in English, "What the farmer doesn't know, he won't eat".

PINEAPPLE GLAZED BAKED HAM

Ingredients:

5	pounds	smoked, cooked ham, semi boneless (Smithfield or Dietz & Watson, etc.)
1	can	apple juice, 32 oz
		whole cloves
1	can	pineapple slices, 8 oz
few		maraschino cherries
½	cup	orange juice
⅓	cup	brown sugar
1	tablespoon	butter

Directions:

Soak ham in apple juice overnight.
Preheat oven to 350 degrees.
Make shallow cuts of squares across top of ham.
Insert 1 clove into edge of every second or third square.
Drain pineapple slices, setting juice aside.
Arrange pineapple slices on top of ham.
Place a maraschino cherry in the middle of each pineapple slice, and secure with a half toothpick.
Place ham in preheated oven.
Bake at 350 degrees for about 1½ hours, basting with pineapple glaze every 15-20 minutes.

Serves 8 - 10.

Pineapple Glaze:

Combine pineapple juice, orange juice, brown sugar and butter.
Bring to boiling point and simmer for 10 to 15 minutes.

*   My father used to work at the German Air Force Base in my home town. Whenever there was an air raid, the civilian workers were not allowed to leave the Base to come home. So Mother would be alone with us children, praying our house would not get hit, for there were many attacks on the Base.

Toward the end of the war during an air raid, we always had some prisoners taking cover under the pine trees on our hillside. Mother often wondered if those people were hungry and if they would help us in case of a direct hit. So one day Mother went out to inquire, and to her surprise, the prisoners not only assured Mother that they would rescue us in case of a hit, but offered Mother a ham, telling her that they had no need for food, for they were working at a farm and were allowed to leave the farm with food during an air raid. I do remember these prisoners were all foreigners, very polite, and were actually looking out for us.

Pineapple Glazed Ham, pg. 101

PORK CHOPS 'N STUFFING

Ingredients:

4		pork chops
		salt and pepper
2	tablespoons	shortening
2	tablespoons	onions, chopped
1	tablespoon	fresh parsley, chopped
1	small	carrot, cut in half
½	teaspoon	caraway seeds
		water
		corn starch

Stuffing:

6	slices	bread, white or wheat
⅓	cup	milk
1		egg
		salt and pepper
1	teaspoon	dry sage
2	teaspoons	fresh parsley, chopped
2	teaspoons	onions, chopped

Directions:

Combine and mix all ingredients for stuffing and set aside.
Sprinkle pork chops with salt and pepper, and brown in shortening on one side.
Turn pork chops, add onions, and top pork chops with stuffing.
When onions are lightly browned, add about ½ cup of water, parsley, carrot and caraway seeds.
Cover and simmer for about 1 hour or until pork chops are done, adding small amounts of water when needed.
Blend together corn starch and water, and thicken gravy.
Season with salt and pepper.

Serves 4.

RAHMSCHNITZEL
(Cream Schnitzel)

Ingredients:

4	slices	of pork tenderloins
		salt and pepper
½	cup	flour
6	tablespoons	butter or margarine
2	tablespoons	onions, chopped fine
½	cup	sour cream
1½	cups	water
few		drops of lemon juice or
		a little white wine
		fresh chopped parsley to garnish

Directions:

Remove fat, if any from pork tenderloins.
Pound each slice of pork well and season with salt and pepper.
Set aside for 30 minutes, then dust with flour.
Using 2 frying pans, heat 3 tablespoons of butter or margarine per pan.
In each pan, fry 2 cream schnitzel on both sides, adding 1 tablespoon of chopped onions toward end of frying.
In each frying pan stir ¼ cup of sour cream and ¾ cup of water.
Cover and simmer for a few minutes.
Add a little white wine or a few drops of lemon juice.
Season with salt and pepper if needed.
Garnish with fresh chopped parsley.

Serves 4.

Note: One may use beef stock instead of water. Not all of the liquid may be needed, depending on how fast it will boil down. Veal can be used instead of pork. Serve with noodles, spaetzle, or rice.

SCHWEINEBRATEN
(Pork Roast)

Ingredients:

2-3	pounds	pork (tenderloin, loin center cut, rib or loin end cut)
4	tablespoons	margarine or oil
1	small	onion, chopped
1	small	carrot, peeled
3	tablespoons	fresh parsley, chopped
½	teaspoon	caraway seeds
		water
		salt and pepper
		corn starch and water

Directions:

Preheat oven to 350 degrees.
Season pork with salt and pepper.
Melt margarine or oil in medium roasting pan.
Add onions and pork.
After onions have browned, add about one cup of water, carrot, parsley, and caraway seeds.
Roast pork at 350 degrees for 2 - 2¾ hours, depending on the size of the roast) adding water from time to time, and basting pork about every 20 minutes.
More water may be needed to make gravy.
Thicken gravy with corn starch blended with water.
Season to taste with salt and pepper.

Serves 4 - 6.

Note: There are two ways to serve the gravy. One may serve it as is with the vegetables or strain the gravy through a sieve. Tenderloin and center cut will take about 40 minutes per pound to roast, while loin end will take about 55 minutes per pound to roast. Serve with German potato-dumplings and salad.

* People in Southern Germany are pork eaters. In most homes, Sunday dinner consists of pork roast with potato-dumplings and salad. I still remember smelling the delightful aroma of pork roast every Sunday as I walked home from Church through the narrow side roads and passed one house after another. By the time I got home it was 12:00 P.M. and I was ready for Sunday dinner.

There were six children in our family, and on Sunday no one complained about dinner. In fact, one of my brothers, a tall and skinny teenager then, fixed his dinner plate one Sunday with a slice of pork roast, 9 potato-dumplings topped with a broken up Kaiser roll and a few spoons of salad and gravy. By the time my brother started to eat, the rest of the family was done eating. But that was not all; after my brother was finish eating his Sunday dinner, Mother still fixed him a butter and jelly sandwich upon request, because he still was hungry. This brother of mine is now the proud owner of my parents restaurant.

People in Germany love potato-dumplings to go with their pork roast. When I grew up, most of the dumplings were made from scratch. The shredded potato-dumpling has a somewhat grayish color, and is not as light in texture as the now store-bought package for shredded potato- dumplings. Homemade leftover potato-dumplings also get a little harder in texture, and during my time had been used in one instance for another reason. Many years ago at the old Munich airport, there seemed to be a strange problem with the planes. Some of the flight personnel were reporting hearing a "thump" every so often during take-off's, and/or landings. Upon investigation they found a person (obviously disgruntled about the air planes coming and going) using some kind of homemade catapult and shooting potato-dumplings at the air planes.

SCHWEINEGULASCH
(Pork Goulash)

Ingredients:

3	tablespoons	oil or shortening
2	large	onions, sliced
1½	pounds	pork, cut in cubes
2-3	cups	water
1	teaspoon	salt
2	cloves	garlic, minced
1½	tablespoons	paprika
		corn starch & water
1	dash	cayenne pepper, optional

Directions:

Brown pork in oil or shortening.
Add sliced onions and sauté together with pork for 5-10 minutes, stirring occasionally.
Add ¾ cup of water, salt and garlic.
Cover and simmer for 1 hour stirring occasionally, and adding more water as needed.
Add paprika and cayenne pepper, optional.
Add remaining water.
Thicken gravy with corn starch blended in water.
Season to taste.

Serves 4.

SCHWEINESCHNITZEL
(Pork Schnitzel)

Ingredients:

4	slices	of pork tenderloins or boneless chops
1	large	egg, well beaten
1	cup	bread crumbs
		salt and pepper
		butter for frying
4		lemon slices
		cranberry sauce

Directions:

Remove fat from pork tenderloins or boneless chops.
Pound each slice well, and season with salt and pepper.
Dip pork into beaten egg, then roll in bread crumbs.
Fry slowly in butter till golden brown on each side.
Serve each pork schnitzel with a slice of lemon and 1 tablespoon of cranberry sauce.

Serves 4.

Note: This is a very easy recipe to prepare, and so delicious. Use only butter for frying to achieve good flavor. Serve with mashed potatoes (sprinkled with butter dripping), a green vegetable and salad.

* I do remember an incident regarding my parents raising two pigs every year for food during and right after World War II. One day after the war, I was home having dinner with my parents. Naturally, my job was washing the dishes afterwards while Mother was taking care of feeding the pigs. Well, I was long done with the dishes, and still there was no sight of mother. I was just getting ready to look for mother, when she came stomping through the door, disgusted and mumbling something about the pigs. Upon asking what was wrong, Mother told me she had fed the pigs, then went into the pig sty with her fork. As she was trying to clean out the pig sty while they were eating, one of the pigs turned around, caught Mother off guard, went between her legs, and lifted her up from the floor. So here was Mother in the middle of the pig sty, riding a pig with no place to reach out or over to get off the pig until the pig moved to the side of the wall. Needless to say, the pig took Mother for a nice long ride.

Pork Roast and Potato Dumplings, pgs. 105 and 154

SCHWEINSKOTELETTS
(Breaded Pork Chops)

Ingredients:

4		pork chops
1		egg, well beaten
¾	cup	bread crumbs
		salt and pepper
		butter for frying
4		lemon slices

Directions:

Remove most fat from pork chops.
Pound meat of chops slightly.
Season with salt and pepper.
Dip pork chops into egg, then into bread crumbs.
Fry slowly in butter on both sides, about 5-7 minutes on each side, depending on the thickness of the meat.
Serve each pork chop with a slice of lemon (to sprinkle juice on meat).

Serves 4.

Note: Pour leftover brown butter and crumbs over mashed potatoes, and serve with pork chops.

* My mother loved animals. People knew it, and more so all the neighboring farmers. It was not unusual for a farmer to show up in the middle of the night at my parents house asking Mother to please help with a sick animal, or a calf that was on the way being born. My mother was not a Veterinarian, but did have a lot of knowledge about animals, and I guess love helped a great deal too. No farmer was ever turned down, nor did they forget mother's kindness.

Whenever it was time for Mother to find two piglets she would raise every year, she would visit farms until she found a farmer who had just been blessed with a litter of piglets. Every litter has one or two piglets kind of sickly, and most of them would not make it beyond a few weeks. So Mother would bring them home at no charge, empty the wood and coal box underneath the stove, put some straw in it so the piglets would have a warm place to stay. Mother would nurse them back to good health with a baby bottle, and never lost one of them. After the piglets were well and gained a few pounds, their new home would be out in the barn.

We needed two pigs every year for food. One pig would be registered and slaughtered with the Government's knowledge, and we would loose all the food stamps for meat for 6 months, while the second pig was not registered and was slaughtered during the night to keep the meat stamps.

BAKED CREAMED CHICKEN BREAST

Ingredients:

4		chicken breast
		salt and pepper
3	tablespoons	shortening or oil
2	tablespoons	onions, chopped
2	cans	cream of mushroom soup, 10 ¾ oz.
1	can	cream of celery soup, 10 ¾ oz.
2	tablespoons	sour cream
1	large	carrot, diced
⅓	cup	peas, fresh or frozen
½	cup	water

Directions:

Preheat oven to 350 degrees.
Cut through thickness of chicken breast when still half frozen.
Sprinkle thawed chicken breast with salt and pepper.
Brown lightly on both sides in shortening or oil, adding onions toward end of browning.
Place chicken breast in casserole dish.
Add cream of mushroom soup, cream of celery soup, sour cream, diced carrots and peas.
Heat water in frying pan, then add to casserole making sure chicken is covered with liquid.
Cover casserole dish with foil.
Bake at 350 degrees for 60 to 90 minutes.
Serve with potatoes or rice and salad.

Serves 4 - 6.

HUENERSCHNITZEL
(Chicken Schnitzel)

Ingredients:

3		chicken breast, frozen
1		egg, well beaten
1	cup	bread crumbs
		salt and pepper
		butter or margarine for frying
6		lemon slices
6	tablespoons	cranberry sauce

Directions:

Remove fat and skin from chicken breast and cut through thickness of meat to have 6 portions.
Pound each portion of chicken breast and season with salt and pepper.
Dip into beaten egg, then roll in bread crumbs.
Fry slowly in butter or margarine on both sides.
Serve each chicken schnitzel with a slice of lemon and 1 tablespoon of cranberry sauce.

Serves 6.

Note: I prefer butter for frying, because it gives a better flavor. Pour hot leftover butter and crumbs over mashed potatoes before serving for an extra treat.

Maria Swaringen

HUEHNERJUNG
(Creamy Sour Chicken)

Ingredients:

8		chicken drumstick
8	cups	water
1	cup	distilled vinegar
1	tablespoon	salt
¼	teaspoon	pepper
1	large	bay leaf
8		whole cloves
½		lemon
8	tablespoons	margarine or butter
8	tablespoons	flour

Directions:

Combine first 8 ingredients in large pot and cook for about 40 minutes, or until chicken drumsticks are tender.
Discard chicken skin, bones and lemon.
Heat margarine or butter in 3 quart sauce pan.
Add flour and stir until light brown.
Add sour chicken broth, about 1 cup at a time, stirring constantly until nice and creamy.
Add chicken meat.
Season with additional vinegar, salt and pepper if needed.

Serves 4 - 6.

Note: Huehnerjung should be like a medium thick creamy soup. Instead of chicken drumsticks, one may use a whole chicken cut up in pieces, including the giblets, and serve without discarding the bones. My mother used to make it that way. Serve with hauberling, pg. or if not available, serve with boiled potatoes. This is an unusual dish for Americans, but my family would never want to miss that dinner.

114

UNGARISCHES GEFLUEGELGULASCH
(Hungarian Poultry Goulash)

Ingredients:

¼	cup	oil or shortening
4	large	onions, sliced
2	pounds	chicken or turkey, cut in cubes
2½	cups	water
½	teaspoon	salt
1		hot pepperoni, sliced
1	tablespoon	paprika
1	dash	cayenne pepper, optional

Directions:

Sauté onions in oil or shortening.
Add chicken or turkey cubes, and fry together with onions, about 10 minutes.
Add 1 cup of water and salt.
Bring to boil, then simmer for 30-45 minutes, adding water when needed.
Add hot pepperoni slices within last 15 minutes of cooking time.
Add paprika, cayenne pepper, optional, and season to taste.

Serves 6 - 8.

Note: If too much liquid, or gravy is too thin, add a little corn starch blended with water.

*   My parents also raised turkeys during the bad times, but we never ate a turkey; they were only for sale. One day my mother cut off a turkey's head. We children looked at it, then picked up the dead turkey, threw it into a pail and poured cold water over it. To our surprise, the turkey jumped out of the pail and ran through the entire back yard without its head until it collapsed.

CRAB CAKES

Ingredients:

1	pound	crabmeat
1½		Kaiser rolls, sliced thin
½	cup	hot milk
2	small	eggs, slightly beaten
⅓	cup	mayonnaise
¼	teaspoon	salt
½	teaspoon	seafood seasoning
1	teaspoon	Worcestershire sauce
½	teaspoon	prepared mustard
2	tablespoons	fresh parsley, chopped fine
¼	cup	bread crumbs
		butter or margarine for frying

Directions:

Pour hot milk over sliced Kaiser rolls, then set aside for 30-60 minutes.

Add eggs, mayonnaise, salt, seafood seasoning, Worcestershire sauce, prepared mustard and mix well.

Gently but thoroughly mix in crabmeat, fresh parsley and bread crumbs.

Shape into 10 crab cakes.

Fry in butter or margarine until brown, about 5 minutes on each side.

Serves 4 - 6.

Note: When frying, use only enough butter or margarine to prevent crab cakes from sticking.

CRAB IMPERIAL

Ingredients:

½		Kaiser roll, sliced thin
3	tablespoons	hot milk, to soak Kaiser roll
3	tablespoons	butter
2	teaspoons	onions, chopped very fine
1	tablespoon	flour
½	cup	milk
1¼	teaspoons	Worcestershire sauce
½	cup	mayonnaise
1	tablespoon	lemon juice
¼	teaspoon	salt
½	teaspoon	seafood seasoning
1	tablespoon	fresh parsley, chopped fine
1	pound	crabmeat
		paprika

Directions:

Preheat oven to 450 degrees.
Pour 3 tablespoons of hot milk over sliced Kaiser roll and set aside.
Meanwhile, melt 1 tablespoon of butter and sauté onions.
Stir in flour.
Slowly add milk, stirring constantly to keep mixture smooth.
Heat and stir until mixture comes to a boil and thickens.
Press soft Kaiser roll through fork to smooth out lumps.
Add Worcestershire sauce and Kaiser roll to mixture.
Mix well, then set aside to cool.
Blend together mayonnaise, lemon juice, salt and seafood seasoning, and stir into first mixture.
Heat remaining butter in separate pan until lightly browned.
Add crabmeat, chopped parsley and toss lightly.
Combine crabmeat with first mixture.
Spread into 4 to 5 greased shells or small heat-proof bowls.
Sprinkle with paprika.

Bake at 450 degrees for 10-15 minutes or until lightly browned on top.
Serves 4 - 5.

* I absolutely love any kind of crab meat. However, that is not the way it started out. I had never seen a crab until I came to the United States. I remember, shortly after my arrival from Germany, my sister-in-law talked my husband into going to Pop's Creek, Maryland for a crab feast. I was wondering why my sister-in-law thought I was dressed to well to go out to eat. After all it was Sunday, and from where I came from, one dresses up on Sunday for a dinner occasion. I was soon to find out.

Upon arrival in Pop's Creek, I thought I would gag from the smell outside the restaurant. As I walked into the restaurant I could not believe what I saw. All of those red creatures lying on top of everyone's table, and the people banging away with pieces of the crab shells flying all over the place.

We found our table, my sister-in-law ordered the crabs, and suggested I try an order of crab cakes since I am not used to eating crabs. I remember when the waitress dropped the crabs on our table I backed up on my bench as far as I could. I could not touch one of those creatures. I could not even eat my order of crab cakes. All I wanted was to get out of that restaurant. As for my Sunday dinner out, I realized that I was overdressed for this occasion, and I came back home with no dinner, and hungry.

FISCH, GEBRATEN
(Fried Fish)

Ingredients:

1	cup	flour
1		egg
¾	teaspoon	salt
¼	teaspoon	pepper
1	cup	milk
1	teaspoon	fresh chopped parsley
½	teaspoon	dry oregano
1	pound	fish fillets, haddock, cod, etc.
		salt and pepper to sprinkle fish
½	cup	oil
4	slices	of lemon
		tartar sauce

Directions:

To make batter, blend together first 7 ingredients and mix well.
Sprinkle fish fillets with salt and pepper.
Heat oil in frying pan.
Dip fish fillets into batter, then fry 2-4 minutes on each side, depending on the thickness of fillets.
Serve with sliced lemon and tartar sauce.

Serves 4.

*   Years ago, I used to work in Munich, Germany. I remember going to a "Fish-Fry Restaurant" every so often with my friends. The fish would be served with German potato salad. But instead of using regular oil when preparing the salad, they would use the hot oil and crumbs from the fish fry. It was delicious. Try it some time.

GEGRILLTER SCHWERTFISCH
(Grilled Swordfish)

Ingredients:

| 4 | | swordfish steaks |
| | | salt and pepper |

For marinade:

¼	cup	wine vinegar
½	cup	water
3	tablespoons	canola oil
¼	teaspoon	sugar
¾	teaspoon	salt
¼	teaspoon	garlic powder
¼	teaspoon	Lemon & Pepper seasoning salt
1	tablespoon	onions, chopped very fine
1	teaspoon	fresh chopped parsley
¼	teaspoon	dry sweet basil
½	teaspoon	fresh chopped chives

Directions:

Combine all ingredients for marinade and mix well.
Marinade swordfish steaks for 1- 2 hours, turning over steaks several times.
Place on hot grill and sprinkle with salt and pepper.
Grill for about 4-6 minutes on each side or until pink inside, basting often with marinade.

Serves 4.

SHRIMP WITH HOT SAUCE

Ingredients:

| 2 | pounds | shrimp, boiled, peeled and cleaned |

Hot sauce:

1	cup	mayonnaise
½	cup	tomato sauce
⅓	cup	onions, finely chopped
⅓	cup	green peppers, finely chopped
1	teaspoon	garlic, minced
1	tablespoon	horseradish
1	tablespoon	mustard
2	teaspoons	sugar
	dash	cayenne pepper
		salt and pepper to taste

Directions:

Arrange boiled shrimp on platter and chill, leaving space in the middle of the platter to place a small bowl with hot sauce.
To make hot sauce, combine and stir together ingredients and chill.
Just before serving, fill small bowl with hot sauce and place in the center of shrimp platter.
Refill small bowl with remaining hot sauce when needed.

Serves 6.

Maria Swaringen

Meatless

Dishes

APFEL PFANNKUCHENSTRUDEL
(Apple Pancake Strudel)

Ingredients:

18		German Pancakes, pg. 134
4	large	apples, peeled, cored and sliced thin
¾	cup	raisins
6	tablespoons	butter
3	cups	milk, or half & half
		cinnamon
		sugar

Directions:

Preheat oven to 350 degrees.
Use two 7 x 11 inch casserole dishes.
Melt 3 tablespoons of butter in each dish, and add ½ cup of milk, or half & half.
Place on top of pancake a small amount of sliced apples, a few raisins, about a teaspoon of sugar, and a generous dash of cinnamon.
Roll up pancake and place in casserole dish crosswise.
Repeat until each casserole dish is full (9 apple pancake strudels per casserole dish).
Sprinkle top of apple pancake strudels with sugar.
Bake in oven at 350 degrees for 25-30 minutes, adding milk, or half & half often so apple pancake strudel won't burn or dry out.

Serves 4 - 6.

Note: If larger casserole dishes are used, additional milk may be needed and apples may take longer to bake. Rolled up pancakes should be snug in casserole dish. Mother also used to make rhubarb pancake strudel. It is made the same way without raisins, but extra sugar needs to be added to sliced rhubarb. In Germany, this is a main dish. However, in the United States, one might serve this dish as a dessert.

APFELSTRUDEL
(Applestrudel)

Ingredients:

2	cups	flour
1		egg
2	tablespoons	soft butter
2	teaspoons	Vanilla Sugar, pg. 262
½	teaspoon	salt
½	cup	warm water
3	tablespoons	melted butter to brush on dough
½	cup	sour cream to spread on dough
⅓	cup	bread crumbs to sprinkle on dough

Apple filling:

2-3	pounds	apples, peeled, cored and sliced thin
½	cup	raisins
3	ounces	blanched almonds, chopped
½	cup	sour cream
⅔	cup	sugar
1½	teaspoons	cinnamon
1	dash	nutmeg
		melted butter to brush on rolled-up applestrudel

Directions:

Preheat oven to 375 degrees.
Combine flour, salt and vanilla sugar.
Add egg, soft butter and small amounts of water at a time.
Work dough, then knead until nice and smooth.
Place dough in warm bowl, cover and set aside in warm place for 20-30 minutes.
Meanwhile, combine all ingredients for apple filling and set aside.
Divide dough in half.

Roll out first half of dough on floured surface, then place on large floured cloth.

Stretch dough from all sides to achieve a very thin sheet of dough.

Cut off uneven edges, then brush with half of melted butter, spread half of sour cream over butter and sprinkle with half of bread crumbs.

Spread half of apple filling over bread crumbs and fold in side ends.

Roll up applestrudel by lifting the cloth, and moving slightly forward.

Place applestrudel in generously greased deep 10 x 14 inch baking pan

Repeat with second half of dough, and place with first applestrudel in baking pan.

Generously brush both applestrudel with melted butter, and bake at 375 degrees for 50-55 minutes.

Serve hot or cold.

Serves 10.

Note: Applestrudel will practically roll up by itself when lifting cloth, and moving forward. Serve slices sprinkled with sugar. In Germany this is a main dish; however, it can be served as a dessert. Other fruits can be used such as cherries or damson plums. One can also make the applestrudel by just rolling out the dough very thin. However, by stretching one can achieve a much thinner and twice as much dough. See recipe and note for Vanilla Sugar.

Apple Pancake Strudel, pg. 124

DAMPFNUDELN
(Steamnoodles)

Ingredients:

1		Yeast Dough # 1, pg. 188
1¼	cups	milk
2	tablespoons	sugar
6	tablespoons	butter
2	tablespoons	flour

Directions:

Prepare yeast dough # 1.
Form 12 - 14 round balls, about 2½ inch in diameter, and place on floured surface.
Cover and let rise in warm place (20-30 minutes).
Melt butter in large Dutch oven.
Add milk and sugar, and heat until warm.
Place dampfnudeln (round balls) into warm milk mixture (milk cannot cover top of dough. Milk should be about ¾ inch below the top of round balls).
Dust with 2 tablespoons of flour.
Cover Dutch Oven tightly, bring to boil, then simmer damfnudeln for 20 - 25 minutes until done.

Serves 4.

Note: DO NOT OPEN LID DURING COOKING TIME. It is the steam inside that makes the dumpfnudeln rise. When done, open lid briefly a few times before leaving lid off. If the heat is too high, dampfnudeln will burn. One may need two pots if Dutch oven is not big enough. A "Heat Master Plate" is highly recommended to avoid burning dampfnudeln on a gas and/or electric stove. Serve with vanilla sauce and canned blueberries, apple sauce, plum compote, etc.

* Again, in Germany, dampfnudeln is a main dish. It used to be a Friday dinner during the time when Catholic's were not aloud to eat meat (except for fish) on Friday's. Now we eat it anytime.

Since dampfnudeln are made mostly of flour, it reminds me of the time when there was not much flour or bread for that matter. People were hungry during and right after the War, and were looking for ways to find food.

The farmers would almost clean their fields with a fine toothcomb one might say. But that did not stop my mother as well as many other people, from going to the fields to glean wheat.

Looking back, I don't know how we did that. There we were out in the fields with mother, most of the time barefoot, walking on the wheat stubs picking up one stem at a time during terrible heat all afternoon. Mother would always plan a little picnic for us that consisted of a sandwich and a cold drink to keep us going.

In the fall when the threshing machine would come around to a neighboring farmer, Mother would take our wagon-load of wheat there, and then off it went to the mill. One year our gleaning produced one hundred pounds of flour.

KAESENUDELN
(Cheese Noodles)

Ingredients:

8	ounces	wide, or elbow noodles, cooked
2-3	ounces	grated Swiss cheese
1	small	onion, sliced
⅓	cup	butter
		fresh chives, optional

Directions:

Heat butter and fry onion slices until light brown.
Remove onion slices and set aside.
Add half of cooked noodles to remaining hot butter in pan.
Top with half of grated Swiss cheese.
Repeat, then top with fried onion slices.
Cover and heat well on low heat shaking pan a few times, so noodles won't stick.
Just before serving garnish with fresh chopped chives, optional
Serve hot with Boston or tossed salad.

Serves 4.

Note: Above recipe makes a nice lunch. This dish is also well known in the German Alps. One may use spaetzle instead of noodles.

KAISERSCHMARRN
(Emperor's Schmarrn)

Ingredients:

4		eggs, separated
⅓	cup	sugar
½	teaspoon	vanilla extract
2	cups	flour
2	cups	milk
3	tablespoons	butter, melted
	dash	salt
⅓	cup	raisins
		butter for frying

To sprinkle Kaiserschmarrn:

⅓	cup	sugar
1	tablespoon	Vanilla Sugar, pg. 262

Directions:

Beat egg yolks together with ⅓ cup of sugar.
Add vanilla extract and melted butter.
Stir in flour, salt, milk and raisins, and beat well.
Beat egg whites until stiff, and fold into batter.
Heat 2 tablespoons of butter in large frying pan.
Pour 1 cup of batter into frying pan (enough to cover bottom of frying pan).
When batter is light brown on bottom, break up batter to small pieces with pancake turner and fork, and finish frying.
Repeat until all batter is used up.
Blend ⅓ cup of sugar with vanilla sugar and sprinkle finished kaiserschmarrn.
Serve while still hot with apple sauce or compote.

Serves 4.

* My mother use to make this meal with plain German pancake batter. I believe this recipe originated in the Alps many, many years ago. At that time it was and perhaps still is a meal made by the Alpine dairy maids, and since has been improved upon. A "Schmarrn" is a broken-up omelet or pancake. An Alpine dairy maid is called a "Sennerin".

LEBERKNOEDEL, GEROESTET
(Fried Liver-Dumpling)

Ingredients:

6		Liver-Dumplings, pg. 156 (leftover)
2-3		eggs, beaten
4	tablespoons	margarine
		salt and pepper to taste

Directions:

Slice leftover liver-dumplings very thin.
Melt margarine in large frying pan.
Add sliced liver-dumplings and fry until well heated.
Add beaten eggs and finish frying.
Season with salt and pepper.

Serves 4.

Note: This is a very good leftover dish. Serve with sweet and sour red cabbage, and/or home fried potatoes.

* It seemed we always had liver-dumplings on Saturday for dinner which is served at noon in Germany, called "Mittagessen". My father would also be home on that day, helping mother around the house.

One Saturday there was an air raid. I remember it was very quiet outside. All of us children were in the cellar with mother while my father would finish cooking dinner upstairs. After a while my father came down to the cellar to tell us that dinner was done and that it was okay for us to come upstairs and eat. No sooner had we all sat around the table when all hell broke loose. It sounded like an explosion and in seconds, it was pitch black during only mid-day. My father yelled, "Lay down!", and mother kept yelling, "Let me open the door!", until finally daylight appeared again and we all headed for the door. Mother just started to open the door when there was another explosion, the door shut again and daylight once again became pitch black, except for the flickering of fire, not to mention the glass breaking all around us. Then there was silence, daylight was back again, and we all rushed back down to the cellar.

Not knowing what really happened my father went up to the attic and looked out of the roof, which had lost most of its terracotta shingles, to see what had happened. To his horror, he learned that a German plane had crashed about fifty yards in front of our house. It had just taken off at the air base with a full tank of fuel. The German pilot was killed (too awful to go into details). The soil had not only piled itself two feet deep around our house, it had also blown two feet of soil into every upstairs bedroom with broken windows facing the crash site.

I don't think, we ate too much of our liver-dumpling dinner on that Saturday. Needless to say, the Lord was with us on that day.

MACARONI AND CHEESE DINNER

Ingredients:

16	ounces	elbow macaroni, cooked and drained
16	ounces	Kraft Velveeta cheese, cut in small chunks
2	tablespoons	margarine or butter cut up
8	tablespoons	onions, chopped
1½	cups	milk
8-10	strips	bacon, cut in half
		salt and pepper

Directions:

Preheat oven to 375 degrees.
Place 1 tablespoon of margarine or butter in large casserole dish.
Cover with one-third of cooked elbow noodles.
Top elbow noodles with half of Kraft Velveeta cheese.
Sprinkle with half of chopped onions.
Sprinkle with salt and pepper.
Repeat, starting with remaining tablespoon of margarine or butter.
Cover casserole with remaining third of elbow noodles.
Add milk to casserole.
Arrange bacon strips on top of elbow noodles.
Bake at 375 degrees for 40-45 minutes, or until bacon is crisp.

Serves 8.

Note: Leftover hot dogs or fried breakfast sausage can be added and is quite tasty. One may fry the bacon strips first and spread crumbled bacon over macaroni and cheese before baking. Depending on the size of casserole dish, a little less milk may be used. Place casserole dish on top of cookie sheet in case milk spills over. Serve with a green vegetable and tossed salad.

PFANNKUCHEN
(Pancakes)

Ingredients:

2	cups	flour
3		eggs
1¾	cups	milk
¼	teaspoon	salt
		shortening for frying
		sugar
		marmalade

Directions:

Stir flour and milk together until smooth.
Add eggs and salt, and beat batter until well mixed.
Heat 1 tablespoon of shortening in average size frying pan.
Add ⅓ cup of pancake batter, tilting frying pan carefully so batter will spread throughout frying pan.
Fry on both sides until light brown.
Repeat until all batter is used up.
Spread each pancake with marmalade, roll up, and sprinkle with sugar.
Serve while still hot.

Serves 4.

Note: Pancakes are served with coffee or tea for lunch or dinner in Germany. Omit marmalade and sugar and use pancakes to make pancake soup or apple pancake strudel. See recipes.

*   As I was growing up in Germany, having pancakes on Sunday evenings, was quite a treat for us children. There were six of us standing in line holding our plate for the next pancake out of the frying pan. Sometime my father added a few cooked potatoes to stretch the batter.

Vegetables

BAKED POTATO WEDGES

Ingredients:

4	large	potatoes
2	tablespoons	oil
		Season All seasoned salt
		none stick cooking spray

Directions:

Preheat oven to 400 degrees.
Scrub potatoes, cut out blemishes and cut into wedges.
Soak in cold water for 15 minutes.
Drain off water and pat-dry potato wedges.
Spray baking sheet with none-stick cooking spray.
Place potato wedges on baking sheet.
Brush with oil, then sprinkle lightly with Season All seasoned salt.
Bake at 400 degrees for 20 minutes.
Turn over potato wedges, sprinkle again with Season All seasoned salt, and finish baking for 20 minutes or until potato wedges are done.

Serves 4.

Note: One may use Old Bay seasoning instead of Season All seasoned salt.

BLAUKRAUT
(Sweet and Sour Red Cabbage)

Ingredients:

1	head	red cabbage
3	tablespoons	shortening or oil
1	small	onion, chopped fine
1	large	apple, peeled and sliced
1	teaspoon	caraway seeds
½	tablespoon	salt
1	cup	water
1		beef bouillon cube
2	tablespoons	vinegar
1	tablespoon	sugar
1	tablespoon	corn starch

Directions:

Remove coarse outer leaves from red cabbage.
Cut into four sections and remove the core.
Wash cabbage and slice very fine.
Heat shortening or oil and fry onions until pale yellow.
Add sliced cabbage, apple, caraway seeds, salt, water and beef bouillon cube.
Cook for about 45 minutes or until tender, adding more water if needed.
Season to taste with sugar and vinegar.
Thicken cabbage with corn starch blended with a small amount of water.

Serves 6.

Note: More salt, vinegar, and/or sugar may be needed, depending on the size of red cabbage. The Bavarians call red cabbage "blue cabbage"; why, I don't know. It looks blue to us, but then turns red when vinegar is added. "Blaukraut" (blue cabbage) is also called

"Rotkohl" and "Rotkraut" (red cabbage) in other parts of Germany. It just goes to show, that Bavarians have a language of their own.

BLUMENKOHLDATSCHI
(Cauliflower Patties)

Ingredients:

2	cups	cooked cauliflower
1		egg
1	cup	dry bread crumbs
½	cup	flour
¼	teaspoon	salt
		butter or margarine for frying

Directions:

Mash cooked cauliflower and mix with egg, bread crumbs, flour and salt.
With floured hands, form patties and brown on both sides in butter or margarine.

Serves 4.

Note: This is a good way to use up leftover cooked cauliflower.

BLUMENKOHL, GEROESTET
(Fried Cauliflower)

Ingredients:

3	cups	cooked, but firm cauliflower florets
1		egg, beaten
¾	cup	bread crumbs
		salt
		butter for frying

Directions:

Dip cauliflower florets into egg, roll in bread crumbs, and sprinkle lightly with salt.
Fry in butter on all sides.

Serves 4.

Note: Do not overcook cauliflower. It still needs to be very firm before frying. This is a very tasty side-dish.

BRATKARTOFFELN
(Fresh Fried Potatoes)

Ingredients:

4	large	raw potatoes, peeled and sliced thin
1	medium	onion, peeled and sliced thin
		salt and pepper to taste
		shortening or oil for frying

Directions:

Heat shortening or oil in large frying pan.
Add a layer of sliced potatoes and onions.
Sprinkle with salt and pepper, then repeat.
Cover and fry over medium to low heat, turning potatoes and onions from time to time so they won't burn.
Fry for about 20 minutes or until potatoes are done.
Serve as a side-dish with dinner.

Serves 4.

* My parents did have a vegetable garden, and grew potatoes in the Spring. Needless to say, there were never enough potatoes for the family throughout the year, plus we needed some for the animals. So every year, after the farmers were finished with their potato fields, we would walk through the fields with a hoe to look for leftover potatoes. The nice potatoes would be for the family to eat during the winter while the green and cut-up potatoes were set aside for the animals. I remember one year we (6 children and Mother) picked a ton of potatoes, which were stored in the potato cellar. As Spring would come around and we still had some potatoes in the cellar, our job was to take off all the new sprouts from the potatoes.

In those days during and after World War II, everyone was out in the fields looking for potatoes.

GEBACKENE ROESTKARTOFFEL
(Baked Home Fries)

Ingredients:

6	medium	potatoes
1	small	onion, chopped
½	teaspoon	salt
1	teaspoon	caraway seeds
¼	cup	butter or margarine

Directions:

Preheat oven to 350 degrees.
Wash and boil potatoes in their skins.
Cool potatoes, then peel and slice thin.
Heat butter or margarine in small roasting pan or casserole dish.
Add onions, sliced potatoes, salt and caraway seeds.
Bake in oven at 350 degrees for about 45 minutes, turning potatoes occasionally.

Serves 4.

Note: My father used to make this dish. For better flavor, let onions brown a little before turning potatoes for the first time.

* At age nine I already had a job picking potatoes after school hours during the Fall season. In fact, most of us children were out in the fields. In those days the potatoes had to be hand-picked, for there were no fancy machines to do it and most of the men were away at war, or never came back from the war. Besides earning a little money, most of the earnings were in the form of extra potatoes for the family, to last through the winter. It was not an easy job but there were no complaints. In fact, all of us children would revel on who would pick the most bushels of potatoes.

Maria Swaringen

Toward the end of World War II, I remember one frightening day. We had an air raid one afternoon while picking potatoes out on the field. A plane was shooting at us. Fortunately, no one was hit. Today, this would be called child labor and/or abuse, which was unheard of during my time and over fifty years ago.

GEDUENSTETES WEISSKRAUT
(Steamed Cabbage)

Ingredients:

6	strips	bacon, sliced
1	small	onion, chopped
1	small	head of white cabbage
1	teaspoon	caraway seeds
½	teaspoon	salt
¾	cup	water
½	teaspoon	beef bouillon granules
1	teaspoon	corn starch
1	tablespoon	water

Directions:

Discard outer leaves of cabbage, cut into quarters, and remove core.
Wash and slice cabbage and set aside to drain.
In large saucepan, fry sliced bacon, adding onions toward end of frying to brown slightly.
Add cabbage, caraway seeds, salt, water and beef bouillon granules.
Stir, cover and simmer until cabbage is done, stirring occasionally so cabbage won't stick or burn.
Mix corn starch with water and stir into cabbage.
Season to taste, if needed.

Serves 4.

GRUENE BOHNEN
(String Beans)

Ingredients:

2	pounds	fresh string beans
few	sprigs	fresh savory
2	tablespoons	onions, chopped very fine
1	tablespoon	parsley, chopped
2	tablespoons	butter
2	tablespoons	flour
1½	cups	bean water
1	teaspoon	beef bouillon granules
		salt and pepper to taste

Directions:

Clean and wash fresh string beans.
Add a few sprigs of fresh savory.
Cook string beans in lightly salted water until tender, removing savory after 10 minutes of cooking.
Drain string beans when done, saving 1½ cups of bean water.
Mix beef bouillon granules with bean water and set aside.
Melt butter in large saucepan.
Add flour and onions, stirring until mixture is pale yellow.
Add bean water, blended with beef bouillon granules, about a ½ cup at a time, and stirring constantly until all bean water is used.
Simmer for 5-10 minutes, then add cooked string beans.
Add chopped parsley and season to taste.

Serves 4 - 6.

Note: A small amount of dry savory may be used if fresh savory is not available.

KARTOFFELDATSCHI
(Potato Patties)

Ingredients:

8	medium	potatoes, boiled in their skins
1		egg
¾	cup	flour
		salt to taste
		sour butter to fry

Directions:

Peel and rice cool boiled potatoes.
Add egg, flour, and salt and mix well.
Form thick round potato patties.
Brown in sour butter on both sides.
Serve with meat and/or sauerkraut.

Serves 6.

Note: If potato dough is too sticky, add a little more flour. Potatoes cooked a day earlier work better for this recipe. Sour butter is the foam of melted butter.

* My mother would always make her own shortening called "Butter Schmalz". She would heat the butter and skim off the foam to get pure shortening. She would then use the foam which is sour butter for special recipes such as this one, or sour fried noodles (made from yeast dough). It gives it a much better flavor. However, one may use butter or margarine.

KOHLRABIGEMUESE
(Kohlrabi Vegetable)

Ingredients:

4	large	kohlrabi
1	large	potato
		water
		salt
1	tablespoon	fresh parley, chopped
2	tablespoons	butter
2	tablespoons	flour
1⅓	cups	vegetable water
		salt and pepper to taste

Directions:

Peel kohlrabi and potato, and cut into thin slices.
Cook in lightly salted water until done (about 10 minutes).
Drain kohlrabi and potato, saving 1⅓ cups of vegetable water.
Melt butter in large saucepan.
Add flour, stirring until mixture is pale yellow.
Add vegetable water, about a ½ cup at a time and stirring constantly until all vegetable water is used.
Simmer for 5-10 minutes.
Add cooked kohlrabi and potato, chopped parsley and season to taste.
Serve with main dish.

Serves 4.

Note: The kohlrabi is a member of the cabbage family. It almost looks like a turnip, but the bulb grows above the ground and has a milder taste compared to a turnip. It tastes delicious raw.

REIBERDATSCHI
(Potato Pancakes)

Ingredients:

8	medium	raw potatoes
2		eggs
1	small	onion, grated
1	tablespoon	sour cream
		salt
⅓	cup	flour or breadcrumbs
		shortening or oil to fry potato pancakes

Directions:

Wash, peel and grate potatoes.
Discard potato liquid by squeezing grated potatoes lightly.
Add eggs, grated onion, sour cream, salt, flour or breadcrumbs, and mix well.
Spread small amounts onto hot greased griddle or frying pan to make small potato pancakes.
Fry on both sides until crispy and golden color.

Serves 4.

Note: If potato mixture is too soft, add a little more flour or breadcrumbs. Place peeled potatoes in water so they won't get dark. Grated potatoes should be drained and mixed with other ingredients immediately to keep a nice color. Serve with meat, sauerkraut or compote.

* "Reiberdatschi" is the Bavarian dialect word for "Kartoffelpuffer". Our dialect is almost like a different language within the same Country. It also changes in different areas of Bavaria. One can travel 10-20 miles and find a completely different dialect. I would learn the written German in school, but then at home I would speak the dialect. It is not easy to master the writing of our dialect, and as for understanding, well some words have a different meaning in other parts of Germany and can be insulting to those who don't understand the dialect.

SAUERKRAUT

Ingredients:

1¾	pounds	sauerkraut, or 27 oz. can
3	tablespoons	shortening, or bacon grease
1	small	onion, chopped
8	dried	juniper berries
1	teaspoon	caraway seeds
2		pork chops, end cut
1½	cups	water
		corn starch and water
		hickory smoked salt

Directions:

Squeeze most liquid out of sauerkraut, then add cold water, drain and set aside.
Using a pressure cooker, fry onions in shortening or bacon grease.
Add sauerkraut, juniper berries, caraway seeds, pork chops, 1½ cups of water, and cook for 10 minutes in closed pressure cooker.
When done, take out pork chops, discard fat and bones and add pork back into sauerkraut.
Thicken sauerkraut with corn starch and water.
Season with hickory smoked salt to your taste.
Serve with bread-dumplings, fried polish sausage or bratwurst, and home fried potatoes.

Serves 4.

Note: If pressure cooker is not available, cook sauerkraut for about 1 ½ hours, adding more water occasionally. **If wine sauerkraut is used, only rinse lightly.** In Germany, when available, we use natural smoked pork instead of fresh pork in the sauerkraut. If so, no hickory smoked salt is needed. The smoked pork will give the sauerkraut a wonderful flavor, and will cook as fast as the sauerkraut. DO NOT use Virginia ham.

SPARGEL
(Asparagus)

Ingredients:

2	pounds	asparagus
		lightly salted water to cook asparagus
½	cup	bread crumbs
¾	cup	butter

Directions:

Clean asparagus and cut stalks into equal length.
Tie asparagus into bundles of about 8-10 each.
Add to lightly salted water and cook until done.
Meanwhile, brown ¼ cup of butter.
Add bread crumbs and stir for 1 minute, then set aside.
When asparagus is done, remove bundles from water.
Untie and serve with side dishes of fried bread crumbs and remaining ½ cup of hot butter.
At the table, per servings pour hot butter over asparagus, then sprinkle with fried bread crumbs.

Serves 6.

Note: Save leftover asparagus and cooking water for asparagus soup.

SWEET POTATO CASSEROLE

Ingredients:

3	cups	sweet potatoes, mashed
1	cup	sugar
½	teaspoon	salt
2		eggs
3	tablespoons	butter, melted
1	cup	milk
2½	teaspoons	vanilla extract

Topping:

1¼	cups	brown sugar
1¼	cups	pecans or walnuts, chopped
½	cup	flour
½	cup	soft butter
		mini marshmallows, optional

Directions:

Preheat oven to 350 degrees.
Combine first 7 ingredients and mix well.
Spoon into baking or casserole dish.
Mix together all ingredients for topping.
Sprinkle over sweet potato mixture.
Bake at 350 degrees for 40 minutes.
Top with mini marshmallows, optional during last 10 minutes of baking or when re-heating frozen casserole.

Serves 6.

WEISSKRAUT MIT MAKKARONI
(White Cabbage with Macaroni)

Ingredients:

2	pounds	white cabbage, (med. size)
⅓	cup	butter
1	small	onion, chopped fine
¾	teaspoon	salt
⅔	cup	water
3	cups	elbow macaroni, cooked

Directions:

Wash cabbage, cut into quarters and remove core.
Slice cabbage, and set aside to drain.
Meanwhile, melt butter and sauté chopped onions.
Add sliced cabbage, salt and small amount of water.
Simmer cabbage until done, stirring occasionally, and add small amounts of water when needed.
Stir cooked elbow macaroni into finished cabbage and heat together.
Season to taste if needed.

Serves 4.

Note: One may add a small amount of liquid bouillon (Maggi seasoning).

Dumplings

And Other

Side Dishes

Maria Swaringen

FRIED RICE

Ingredients:

1	cup	rice, uncooked
2¼	cups	water
½	teaspoon	salt
2	teaspoons	butter
6	strips	bacon, sliced
3	tablespoons	onions, chopped
2		eggs
		salt & pepper to taste

Directions:

Add salt and butter to water and cook rice as directed on box.
Fry sliced bacon until crisp, adding onions toward end of frying to brown.
Add cooked rice and mix well.
Beat eggs and fry scrambled in separate pan.
Stir into rice during last minute of frying.
Season with salt and pepper to taste.
Serve with creamed chicken or vegetables.

Serves 4.

GRIEBENKNOEDEL
(Bread Dumpling with Bacon)

Ingredients:

1	loaf	French bread, 12 oz. or 6 Kaiser rolls
½	teaspoon	salt
1⅜	cups	hot milk
1	teaspoon	baking powder
2		eggs
3	tablespoons	flour
6	slices	bacon, fried and crumbled
1	small	onion, chopped

Directions:

Cut French bread or Kaiser rolls into thin slices.
Add salt.
Pour hot milk over bread mixture.
Cover and set aside for 30-45 minutes.
Meanwhile, fry bacon and onions (crumble bacon).
Add to softened bread mixture fried bacon crumbs, onions, eggs, baking powder and flour and mix well.
With wet hands, form dumplings and add to lightly salted boiling water.
Bring to boil again and simmer uncovered 15-20 minutes, or until done.

Serves 4.

Note: Dumplings should be about 2½ inches in diameter, and will swell during cooking time. Serve with goulash, and/or sauerkraut.

* My mother used to make these dumplings after a pig slaughter. She would melt the pig fat to get the lard for cooking, and the "Grieben", known as cracklings, would be used for the dumplings. Since I don't slaughter a pig, I use fried bacon.

KARTOFFELKNOEDEL
(Potato Dumpling)

Ingredients:

8	large	raw potatoes
3	medium	boiled potatoes, cold
1		Kaiser roll, sliced thin, or equal amount of French bread
¼	cup	hot milk
1		egg
1	teaspoon	salt
3	tablespoons	flour

Directions:

In large bowl, combine sliced Kaiser roll or French bread and salt.
Pour over hot milk, and set aside to cool.
Add egg and mix well.
Peel cold boiled potatoes, rice and add to bread mixture.
Peel and grate raw potatoes.
Squeeze out as much water as possible from grated potatoes, see Note.
Discard water and add squeezed grated potatoes to bread, and/or dumpling mixture.
Add 3 tablespoons of flour and mix well.
With wet hands, form round dumplings, about 2½ inches in diameter, and drop into salted boiling water.
Bring to boil again and simmer for 20 minutes.

Serves 4.

Note: Use a fine grater for raw potatoes. To squeeze water out of grated potatoes, use the following method. Place a strainer on top of bowl or pot. Line with a thin cotton cloth. Pour a portion of grated potatoes into lined cotton cloth, close and squeeze out as much liquid as possible. Repeat until done. Serve potato - dumplings with beef or pork roast and lots of gravy. It is the gravy, that will season the potato-dumpling.

* This is an old recipe my mother used, to make potato-dumplings every Sunday. She used to peel a standard size bucket of potatoes and grate them. Mother worked about three hours every Sunday on this meal, but there were never any complaints at the dinner table. Now these dumplings can be made a lot easier by just purchasing a "Potato Dumpling Mix" in major grocery stores, located in the foreign food section, or in foreign food stores. Above recipe is for raw potato-dumplings, known in stores as "Shredded Potato Dumpling Mix".

However, most stores carry the "Panni Bavarian Potato Dumpling Mix", made of half cooked and half raw potatoes. Another company is "Dr. Willy Knoll." Either one of the potato dumpling mixes, shredded or half and half, are an excellent product, but I think, most American people would favor the "Bavarian Potato Dumpling Mix" or "Dr. Willy Knoll"s halb & halb."

My children grew up with grandmother's recipe. So now when my own children come home to visit, I use the "Shredded Potato Dumpling Mix" for them, and the "Bavarian Potato Dumpling Mix" for my husband, and all other American visitors.

There are several other companies who make the potato dumpling mix, but the dumplings taste the same.

LEBERKNOEDEL
(Liver Dumpling)

Ingredients:

1	loaf	French bread 16 oz. or 8 Kaiser rolls
¾	teaspoon	salt
1⅔	cups	hot milk
2		eggs
1	teaspoon	baking powder
⅓	cup	flour
½	pound	liver, beef or calf
¼	cup	hot melted butter
2	medium	garlic cloves
1	small	onion, quartered
¼	teaspoon	pepper
½	teaspoon	salt
1	tablespoon	marjoram
2	teaspoons	lemon rind, grated
¼	cup	fresh parsley, chopped

Directions.

Cut French bread or Kaiser rolls into thin slices.
Add ¾ teaspoon of salt.
Pour hot melted butter and milk over bread slices and salt.
Cover and set aside for 30-45 minutes.
Meanwhile, remove skin from liver (if any), and grind liver together with garlic and onion in meat grinder.
Add ground liver along with pepper, salt, marjoram, grated lemon rind, chopped parsley, eggs, flour and baking powder to softened bread, and mix well.
With wet hands, form round dumplings and add to lightly salted boiling water.
Bring to boil again and simmer uncovered for 15-20 minutes, or until done.

Serves 6.

Note: Dumplings should be about 2½ inches in diameter, and will swell during cooking time. Serve with beef broth and/or boiled beef, sweet and sour cabbage, and home fried potatoes. One may add a few beef bouillon cubes to boiling water instead of salt.

I know for many people liver-dumplings sounds just awful, let alone would they eat them; but believe me, they are absolutely delicious.

Liver-dumplings are a little extra work, so I usually make a larger amount and freeze half of them for later use. I can use them with soup and/or as a whole meal. Leftover liver-dumplings are also very good when fried.

* My parents used to scrape the liver instead of using a meat grinder. They also added a small amount of kidney fat, chopped very fine, to the liver.

Kaiser rolls are not as good anymore as they used to be for making dumplings. So I use mostly French bread for my dumpling bread.

In Bavaria, one may go to the bakery and just ask for sliced rolls. The bakeries have a slicing machine to slice the day old rolls paper thin for dumpling bread. Well, years ago I lived in Ramstein, Germany. I knew this was not Bavaria, and the people were not like Bavarians either, but to me the bakeries were and looked the same. So one day I went to the bakery and asked for 10 rolls sliced. The sales clerk looked then went into another room, came back and said, "the rolls will be done in a minute," and went on serving the next customer. I waited, walked and looked around in the bakery, when I seen an elderly lady out in the hallway slicing my rolls by hand. Upon asking the sales clerk, why this lady is slicing my rolls, I was told they don't have a machine for slicing rolls in that part of Germany.

SEMMELKNOEDEL
(Bread Dumpling)

Ingredients:

1	loaf	French bread, 12 oz. or 6 Kaiser rolls
½	teaspoon	salt
3	tablespoons	hot melted butter
1⅜	cups	hot milk
2		eggs
1	teaspoon	baking powder
3	tablespoons	flour
2	tablespoons	parsley, chopped

Directions:

Cut French bread or Kaiser rolls into very thin slices.
Add salt.
Pour hot melted butter and hot milk over bread slices.
Cover bowl and set aside for 30-45 minutes.
Add eggs, baking powder, flour and parsley, and mix well.
With wet hands, form round dumplings and add to salted boiling water.
Bring to boil again, and simmer uncovered until done, about 15-20 minutes.

Serves 4.

Note: Dumplings should be about 2½ inches in diameter and will swell during cooking time. Serve with any meat dish and gravy, or with German sauerkraut. The dumpling is served as a side dish to the Bavarian, like the spaetzle is to the Schwaebisch people.

SCHINKENKNOEDEL
(Ham Dumpling)

Ingredients:

1	loaf	French bread, 12 oz. or 6 Kaiser rolls
½	teaspoon	salt
1⅜	cups	hot milk
1	teaspoon	baking powder
2		eggs
3	tablespoons	oil or margarine
¼	cup	onions, chopped
¼	cup	fresh parsley, chopped
¾	cup	ham, chopped
3	tablespoons	flour

Directions:

Cut French bread or Kaiser rolls into very thin slices.
Add salt.
Pour hot milk over bread slices.
Cover and set aside for 30 - 45 minutes.
Sauté onions, parsley and ham in oil or margarine, and pour over softened bread.
Add eggs, baking powder and flour, and mix well.
Form round dumplings, and add to slightly salted boiling water.
Bring to boil again, and simmer uncovered for 15-20 minutes, or until done.

Serves 4.

Note: Dumplings should be about 2½ inches in diameter, and will swell during cooking time. Serve with any meat dish and/or German cooked sauerkraut.

Maria Swaringen

HOMEMADE CROUTONS

Ingredients:

2		Kaiser rolls
		butter flavored no stick cooking spray
¼	cup	melted butter

Directions:

Preheat oven to 325 degrees.
Cut Kaiser rolls into small cubes, about ¾ inch in diameter.
Generously spray cookie sheet with butter flavored non-stick cooking spray.
Place bread cubes onto cookie sheet, and dab with melted butter.
Bake at 325 degrees for 12 minutes.
Serve with various soups and salads.

Serves 2 - 4.

Note: Use day-old Kaiser rolls, French bread or Italian bread to make croutons. There is no comparison between store bought and homemade croutons. Homemade croutons can be frozen for later use.

SPAETZLE
(Schwaebisch Homemade Noodles)

Ingredients:

2	cups	flour
2-3	large	eggs
¾	cup	water
½	teaspoon	salt
1	tablespoon	oil for cooking water

Directions:

Combine and stir together first 4 ingredients.
Using a cooking spoon, beat dough thoroughly for 8-10 minutes until dough forms bubbles.
Using a large pot, fill ⅔ full with slightly salted water.
Add oil and bring to a boil.
Place small portion of dough into large-holed colander, then place colander on top of large pot, and press dough through holes into boiling water.
When spaetzle rise to the top, simmer for about 1 minute.
Remove from water with a skimming ladle, and place in warm bowl.
Place bowl in warm oven and repeat until all dough is used up.

Serves 4.

Note: Spaetzle dough need to be worked thoroughly before cooking. DO NOT place colander on top of hot boiling water while filling with dough.

* Spaetzle is nothing more then homemade noodles. They are however, very popular in the Schwaebisch region of Germany, and the people there do make the best spaetzle, while the Bavarians make the best dumplings.

Above recipe is for people who do not have a spaetzle grater. If one has a spaetzle grater, use only ½ cup of water.

There are some 400 spaetzle recipes, according to my Schwaebisch friends. While the real spaetzle is prepared with water only, some use mineral water for a lighter spaetzle. Another variation is to use milk instead of water, but to the Schwaebisch, that is unacceptable.

As for the tools, one can use a colander or a spaetzle grater to press the dough through, and into the boiling slightly salted water. In the old days, people would use a small thin cutting board, place a small amount of spaetzle dough on top, and scrape the dough, a little at a time into the slightly salted water. One of my Schwaebisch friends still does it.

One may serve spaetzle with any main dish, meat and gravy, etc. Spaetzle can also be tossed in browned butter or served with browned breadcrumbs. They are also used in casseroles.

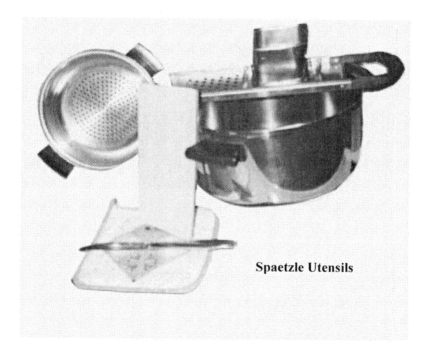

Spaetzle Utensils

HAUBERLING
(Deep Fried Noodles for Creamy Sour Chicken)

Ingredients:

2	cups	warm milk
1	package	dry yeast
3½	cups	all purpose flour
1	cup	rye flour
1		egg
1¾	teaspoons	salt
3	teaspoons	caraway seeds
⅓	cup	fresh parsley, chopped
½	cup	beer, room temperature
		shortening or oil for deep frying

Directions:

Soften dry yeast in 1 cup of warm milk.

In large bowl, combine 1½ cups of all purpose flour, egg, caraway seeds and parsley.

Add softened yeast, mix well, then set aside for 20 minutes.

Stir in remaining all purpose flour, rye flour and salt, alternating with remaining milk and beer.

Mix together well, then beat dough for 3-5 minutes, until bubbles appear.

Cover and let dough rise in warm place until double (about 1-1½ hours).

Use a large stainless steel pot, or Dutch oven to deep fry hauberling.

Use enough shortening or oil to obtain ½ inch depth in pot.

Heat shortening or oil for deep frying.

With a stainless steel soup spoon, add ½ spoon full of dough to hot grease, connecting three ½ spoon fulls to make a 5 inch row.

Use a large stainless steel cooking spoon, to ladle hot grease over hauberling, until hauberling have risen to about double in size.

When hauberling are brown on bottom side, turn over to finish.

Repeat until all dough is used up.

Serves 6.

Note: Dip spoon into hot grease before spooning out dough, so that dough will come off easier from spoon. More shortening or oil may be needed during frying but do not add too much, for hauberling should not float in grease. If grease is too hot, hauberling won't bake through, and if not hot enough, hauberling will soak up all the grease. Serve hot with sour chicken stew (huehnerjung pg.   ). Leftover hauberling may be re-heated. For best results, use oven. Heat oven to 350 degrees, sprinkle hauberling with cold water, then bake for 6-8 minutes. If frozen, heat a little longer. White flour and milk may be used instead of rye flour and beer.

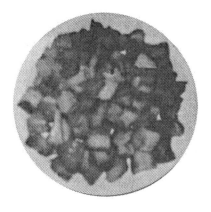

Homemade Croutons, pg. 160

HOLLERKUECHEL
(Fried Elderberry Blossoms)

Ingredients:

1	recipe	for Pancakes, pg. 134
12		elderberry blossoms
		shortening or oil for deep frying
		sugar and cinnamon to sprinkle fried
		elderberry blossoms

Directions:

Shake and rinse elderberry blossoms, then drain in colander.
Prepare pancake batter as directed.
Holding stem of elderberry blossom, dip blossom into pancake batter.
Deep fry in shortening or oil until golden color.
Combine sugar and cinnamon, then sprinkle over hot fried elderberry blossoms.
Serve while still hot with apple sauce or compote.

Serves 2 - 4.

Note: The reason for shaking the elderberry blossoms is to remove bugs, if any. After all, this is a meatless meal. Elderberry bushes grow wild in Bavaria, and they grow very easy. So there is plenty to pick for elderberry juice, wine, compote and jelly.

Maria Swaringen

TOPFEN - PFANNLING
(Fried Cheese Noodles)

Ingredients:

1	package	dry yeast
¾	cup	warm milk
2	teaspoons	sugar
4½	cups	flour
¾	teaspoon	salt
⅔	cup	small curd cottage cheese
2	large	day old boiled potatoes, peeled and riced
1		egg
2	tablespoons	milk
		shortening or canola oil for deep frying

Directions:

Soften dry yeast in ¾ cup of warm milk and 2 teaspoons of sugar.
Using large bowl, stir softened yeast into 1 cup of flour and mix well.
Set aside for 20-30 minutes.
Meanwhile, combine 3½ cups of flour and salt. Set aside.
Add egg, cottage cheese, riced potatoes, milk and 3 cups of flour to soft yeast dough (large bowl) and mix well.
Knead 3-5 minutes, adding remaining ½ cup of flour.
Cover and allow to rise in warm place for 30 minutes.
Form 3" balls.
On floured surface, roll out each ball about ½ inch thick, then cut rolled out dough into four pieces.
Deep fry in hot shortening or canola oil until done, turning once.
Serve as a side-dish to soup, vegetables, salad, or braised meat meal.

Serves 6 - 8.

Note: Fried cheese noodles may be frozen and re-heated in oven. May also be used as a dessert. Sprinkle with sugar and cinnamon when hot, and serve with coffee.

Beverages

Hot and Cold

GLUEHWEIN
(Gluehwine)

Ingredients:

4	cups	red wine
1	cup	water
¼	cup	sugar
2		cinnamon stick
4		cloves
		lemon peel of ½ lemon

Directions:

Combine water, sugar, spices and lemon peel and bring to boil.
Add wine and steep over low heat for 20-30 minutes.
Do not boil, but heat slowly to allow wine to absorb flavors.
Strain hot gluehwein into heat-proof glasses and serve while still hot.

Serves 4.

Note: In Germany, gluehwein is a holiday beverage (Christmas and New Year). One may also find it during the winter season in the Alpine area restaurants.

*   The Christmas season was always a joyous time for all of us children at home. The preparations and expectations were wonderful, in spite of the war and right after, when there was not much to give or to buy in the stores.

Then there was the anxiety, wondering if we get the gift we wished for so much, or what kind of gift will it really be under the Christmas tree. At the end, it did not matter what the Christkindl (Christ child instead of Santa Claus) brought for each of us; no matter how poor, we were, we were happy.

I remember some Christmas gifts were nothing but a plate of goodies, such as an apple, orange, a few walnuts, candy, and some cookies my mother had baked for the holiday. That was still a nice Christmas, for there were many children, who did not even receive that much.

In Bavaria, and during my childhood, the Christmas celebration would be on Christmas Eve. Parents would decorate the tree secretly behind locked doors, and in a room where all the gift-giving would take place, about 7:00 P.M.

After the gift-giving and eating some of our goodies, it was time to see what the neighborhood children received for Christmas. So for hours we would run from one house to another, and likewise, the neighboring children would come to our house to visit and play together.

As it got closer to midnight, all the neighborhood children were back in their own homes again and Mother would get us ready to walk with her along the snow covered streets to the Midnight Mass.

As for Christmas day, Mother would prepare a good dinner, usually pork roast and potato-dumplings, and all of us children would play or at times argue who had the largest piece of candy.

Germany has two Christmas holidays. The second day is usually for visiting or just a plain day for resting after all the hustle and bustle of holiday preparations is over.

Maria Swaringen

GROG

Ingredients:

1	cup	water
1	tablespoon	sugar
½	cup	rum or cognac
1	slice	lemon

Directions:

Bring water to a boiling point.
Pour over sugar in heat-proof glass and stir.
Add rum or cognac and serve immediately with slice of lemon

Serves 2.

Note: This beverage is good after an outdoor winter recreation. It is an ideal drink in the mountains, after a day of skiing or a long cold walk. It also makes a good tonic for a cold. DO NOT serve to children or alcoholics.

KAMILLENTEE
(Chamomile Tea)

Ingredients:

1		chamomile tea bag
1	cup	water
1	teaspoon	sugar or honey to sweeten

Directions:

Prepare using direction for Peppermint Tea.

Serves 1.

*   Used as a table beverage, chamomile is known throughout Germany and is one of the old fashioned healing herbs. It is used for mild stomach problems, and can also be used externally to cleanse and heal wounds, or to inhale for sinus problems etc.; the list is long. I have used chamomile tea for all of the above and more with great results. I do believe no family, and/or home in Germany is without this tea. As a child I used to pick chamomile along the roadside, and dried the strong smelling daisy-like flowers to be used later as a tea. Chamomile also has a calming effect and is a nice beverage just before bedtime.

Maria Swaringen

KUEMMELTEE
(Caraway Tea)

Ingredients:

1	pint	water
4	teaspoons	caraway seeds
		sugar to taste

Directions:

Combine water and caraway seeds.
Bring to boiling point, then simmer for 15-20 minutes.
Strain tea and discard caraway seeds.
Sweeten with sugar to taste.

Serves 2.

* Caraway tea is excellent for digestion. Also an excellent tea for babies with gas problems. It is known throughout Germany with great results, and has been used in my family throughout generations. In the United States, catnip is used for the same purpose. Doctors refer to as an "Old Wives Tale". Well, I used it with my children, and it is a wonderful "Old Wives Tale" for a young mothers.

LINDENBLUETENTEE
(Lime Flowers Tea)

Ingredients:

4	tablespoons	lime flowers tea or tea bags
4	cups	water
		sugar or honey to sweeten

Directions:

Using a tea pot, steep lime flowers tea or tea bags in boiling hot water for about 10 minutes.
Strain tea and sweeten each cup with sugar or honey.

Serves 4.

*   I remember gathering lime flowers along the roadside every year. Mother would clean and dry the lime flowers, and then store them for the winter to make tea.

Sleigh-riding was always our main occupational sport during the winter. Sunday was the best time for it; no homework and no chores around the house.

It seemed Mother would just work continually for all of us children on that day. As she dried clothes, the lime flower tea would be on the woodstove, ready for all of us as we came into the house, one by one, wet and half frozen, to change into dry clothes and warm up with a cup of hot lime flower tea, just to be ready in 30 minutes for sleigh riding again.

Lime flowers are well known in Germany. Not far from my hometown and along the very road where I use to pick the lime flowers, there is a small town called "Aufhausen", which to this day still has a lime flowers festival every year called "Lindenbluetenfest".

Maria Swaringen

In the United States lime flowers are also called "Basswood Blossoms" and/or "Tilia Blossoms".

PFEFFERMINZTEE
(Peppermint Tea)

Ingredients:

1		peppermint tea bag
1	cup	water
1	teaspoon	sugar or honey to sweeten

Directions:

Heat water to a boiling point and pour into cup with tea bag.
Let steep for a few minutes, then discard tea bag and sweeten tea.

Serves 1.

Note: This tea is excellent for colds or as an after dinner drink to help with digestion. No family should be without it. I grow my own peppermint and dry it for use throughout the year. Instead of a tea bag in a cup, I use loose peppermint tea in a tea pot, strain it and drink it hot or cold. The only teas I grew up with were peppermint, lime flower or linden, chamomile and caraway tea. They were and still are a household beverage. Peppermint tea can also be mixed with other teas.

Peppermint plants can also be used as a ground cover in the yard, in hard to grow areas and in or around flower beds. It has a wonderful fragrance, grows almost anywhere and the roots travel fast.

WEIHNACHTSPUNSCH
(Christmas Punch)

Ingredients:

1	bottle	red wine
2	cups	ready made hibiscus tea
2-3	shots	cognac
1		cinnamon stick
	dash	nutmeg
8		whole cloves
⅓	cup	sugar

Directions:

Combine all ingredients and heat slowly (do not boil).
Let steep for 10 minutes.
Discard spices.
Serve hot with Christmas cookies.

Serves 4 - 6.

Note: Use a Pyrex or stainless steel pot to heat punch. DO NOT serve this punch to children or alcoholic's.

* In Germany, hibiscus tea, known as "Malventee" is available in grocery stores. However, in the United States, one can find the hibiscus tea only in herb places, health food or natural food stores. One may substitute with other herb spice teas such as orange cinnamon tea. The flavor will be somewhat different and the color of the punch won't be quite as red, for the hibiscus tea has a very deep red color, and is ideal for Christmas.

ZWIEBELTEE
(Onion Tea)

Ingredients:

3	large	onions
1	quart	water
4-8	ounces	sugar candy, or rock sugar (brown or clear)

Directions:

Peel and slice onions.
Boil in water for about 20 minutes, adding sugar candy or rock sugar during last 5 minutes of boiling.
Strain tea and discard onions.
Serve hot.

Serves 2 - 4.

Note: This tea is very helpful for a sore throat, chest cold, etc. My mother always made this tea if someone in the family had a cold.

ALL OCCASION PUNCH

Ingredients:

3	tablespoons	sugar sweetened Kool-Aid, (strawberry or cherry flavor)
2	cups	hot water
2¼	cups	sugar
1	can	pineapple juice, 32 oz.
1	tablespoon	rum extract
2	quarts	Sprite or 7-Up
3	cups	sherbet
		ice cubes

Directions:

Dissolve Kool-Aid in 2 cups of hot water.
Add sugar and stir until dissolved.
Add pineapple juice and rum extract.
Pour into punch bowl.
Just before serving, add Sprite or 7-Up, ice cubes and sherbet.
Serve immediately.

Serves 15 - 20.

Note: Add color and/or flavor, of sherbet to go with Kool-Aid flavor. For a superb punch, substitute the sherbet with ice cream.

FRUIT SHAKE

Ingredients:

8	scoops	vanilla ice cream
1		banana
1	cup	strawberries, fresh or frozen
2	cups	milk
		Cool Whip or whipping cream

Directions:

Combine first four ingredients in blender and blend until smooth.
Pour into tall glasses and top with Cool Whip or whipping cream.
Place fresh whole strawberry on top of Cool Whip or whipping cream
if available.

Serves 2 - 4.

Beverages, pgs. 174, 179, and 183

EISKAFFEE
(Ice Coffee)

Ingredients:

1	cup	cold coffee
3	scoops	ice cream, vanilla or coffee flavor
1		Maraschino cherry
2		sugar wafers
		whipping cream or Cool Whip

Directions:

Place 3 round scoops of ice cream in tall drinking glass.
Pour cold and lightly sweetened coffee over ice cream.
Top with whipping cream or Cool Whip.
Garnish with Maraschino cherry and 2 sugar wafers.
Serve with straw and small spoon.

Serves 1.

Note: Coffee should be made from ground coffee. I usually make more coffee in the morning and keep the leftover coffee in the refrigerator. Try this beverage on your guests on a hot summer afternoon, and you will be the talk of the town.

ENERGIE - GETRAENK
(Energy Drink)

Ingredients:

1		egg yolk
2	tablespoons	sugar
		beer

Directions:

Using a tall glass, stir egg yolk and sugar together, and mix well. Slowly stir in cold beer to fill glass.

Serves 1.

* This is a good beverage to gain strength. My mother would often come down with phlebitis right after giving childbirth. I guess it was mainly because during those days women would have about 10-12 days of strict bed rest after giving childbirth, which is not too good for someone who has varicose veins. I remember one time Mother was confined to bed for four weeks due to childbirth and phlebitis. When she finally was well again, she could not stand up due to weakness. The doctor prescribed the above energy drink to take for three days, three times a day. Needless to say, it worked. Years later my mother would prepare the same energy drink whenever someone in the family needed an energy booster.

FICHTENNADELSAFT
(Spruce Needle Juice)

Ingredients:

new Spring shoots from the spruce
sugar
water

Directions:

Wash spruce Spring shoots, and place in large pot.
Add just enough water to cover spruce Spring shoots.
Bring to a boil, then simmer for 20-30 minutes.
Set aside to cool.
Strain juice through triple cheese cloth and squeeze remaining juice out of Spring shoots before discarding.
Sweeten juice to your taste and bring to boil.
Simmer for 10 minutes, and remove foam with skimming ladle.
Pour into clean and hot canning jars, and process in water bath.

* Growing up during World War II and right after in Germany, there was no such luxury as soft drinks. So our main beverage besides water were the juices my mother made every year. Looking back now, it was a lot better and healthier than what we have now.

I am sure, no one ever heard of my mother's spruce needle juice, but it is a very healthy beverage. I have made it in the United States. It has a citrus flavor. However, there is a mentioning in Webster's Dictionary of "Spruce Beer", a fermented liquor made with an extract of spruce needles and twigs. I guess my mother was not that far off after all.

HOLUNDERBEERENSAFT
(Elderberry Juice)

Ingredients:

> ripe black elderberries
> water
> sugar or honey

Directions:

Rake elderberries with a fork or fingers from clusters.
Rinse and place in large pot.
Cover elderberries with water about 1-2 inches above berries.
Bring to boil, then simmer for 15 minutes.
Set aside to cool completely.
Strain juice through triple cheese cloth overnight.
Squeeze out remaining juice from elderberries the next day.
Sweeten juice only slightly with sugar or honey.
Pour into clean and hot canning jars and process in water bath.
When ready to use, sweeten juice with more sugar or honey.

Note: Holunderbeerensaft is also known as "Hollersaft". Leave at least 1 inch headspace in canning jars in case of expansion. Juice can be used hot or cold. Good for colds or for making elderberry jelly. We used it as a juice and it was great to serve with Mother's dampfnudeln as a dip.

*   This reminds me of another true story. My mother would make three kinds of juice every year; spruce-needle, rhubarb and elderberry juice.

My family was not rich and during World War II, one could not find canning jars very easily. So Mother canned all the juice in old fashioned beer bottles, the kind with a flip-top. All her canning was stored in the cool cellar. It was not uncommon to hear a bottle of elderberry juice burst every once in awhile. Well, every year the painter came to paint the kitchen and the hallway. Mother would clean all day, and by the evening, we would have a freshly painted and very clean kitchen.

So one time while the painter did his annual job, Mother prepared dampfnudeln for dinner and wanted to serve it with elderberry juice. The painter had just left, the kitchen was nice and clean and dinner was ready. Quickly, Mother went to the cellar for elderberry juice. She stood in the middle of the kitchen when she opened the bottle. To her surprise, there was a champagne like gush, and half of the kitchen ceiling was covered with purple juice. From then on, no matter how bad the weather was, Mother would go outside to open a bottle of elderberry juice.

ICE CREAM SODA

Ingredients:

12	scoops	vanilla ice cream
3	cans	Pepsi Cola or Ginger Ale, 12 oz.
		Cool Whip

Directions:

Place in each tall glass 3 scoops of ice cream.
Fill with Pepsi Cola or Ginger Ale.
Top with Cool Whip.
Serve with straw and small spoon.

Serves 4.

PEACH SHAKE

Ingredients:

8	scoops	peach, or vanilla ice cream
1		banana
1-2	cups	peaches, fresh or frozen
2	cups	milk
		Cool Whip

Directions:

Place first 4 ingredients into blender or food processor, and blend until smooth.
Pour into tall glasses, and top with Cool Whip.

Serves 2 - 4.

Note: Other fruit combinations can be used as well.

RHABARBERSAFT
(Rhubarb Juice)

Ingredients:

rhubarb, cleaned and cut about 1 inch thick
water
sugar or honey

Directions:

Place rhubarb in large pot and cover with water, about 1 - 2 inches above rhubarb.
Bring to a boil, then simmer for about 20 minutes.
Set aside to cool.
Strain juice through triple cheese cloth and squeeze remaining juice out of rhubarb.
Sweeten juice with sugar or honey to taste and heat to boiling point.
Pour into clean and hot jars, adjust hot lids and process in water bath.

*   This juice is high in minerals. It reminds me of when I was very sick during my childhood. I could not hold anything down, including the medicine. The doctor didn't know was wrong with me and after a few weeks he simply gave up. I had a very high fever. Every night I was delirious, and every night my parents thought this would be the night I would die. Then, my mother tried rhubarb juice and to her surprise, it worked. Within days the fever was gone and the doctor, puzzled, had no answer.

Maria Swaringen

Baking with Yeast, Baking Powder and Some - Deep Fried

HEFETEIG # 1
(Yeast Dough # 1)

Ingredients:

1	package	dry yeast
1⅔	cups	warm milk
3	tablespoons	butter, melted
¼	cup	sugar
4¼	cups	flour
1	teaspoon	salt
1		egg
⅓	cup	raisins

Directions:

Soften dry yeast in ¾ cup of warm milk and 1 tablespoon of sugar.
Stir softened yeast into 1 cup of flour and mix well.
Cover and set aside in warm place for 20-30 minutes.
Add egg, remaining sugar, melted butter and mix well.
Add remaining flour, salt, milk and raisins, and mix well.
Beat dough 6-8 minutes or until dough "blows" bubbles.
Cover dough and let rise in warm place until double in size.
Punch down risen dough and use according to recipe.

Note: Dough rises well in pre-heated light warm oven. This yeast dough is used for steamnoodles and/or panrolls.

HEFETEIG # 2
(Yeast Dough # 2)

Ingredients:

1	package	dry yeast
⅔	cup	warm milk
⅓	cup	sugar
½	cup	butter, melted
4	cups	flour
3		eggs
1	teaspoon	salt
1	teaspoon	vanilla extract
1	teaspoon	grated orange peel
½	cup	golden raisins

Directions:

Soften dry yeast in warm milk and 1 tablespoon of sugar.
Stir softened yeast into ¾ cup of flour.
Cover and set aside in warm place for 20-30 minutes.
In separate bowl beat together butter, eggs, orange peel, vanilla extract and remaining sugar.
Add to yeast dough and mix well.
Add remaining flour, salt and raisins.
Beat dough 6-8 minutes or until dough "blows" bubbles.
Cover and let rise until double in size.
Punch down risen dough and use according to recipe.

Note: To be used for sweet pastry breads, braids, etc.

HEFETEIG # 3
(Yeast Dough # 3)

Ingredients:

1	package	dry yeast
1⅛	cups	milk
⅓	cup	sugar
4¼	cups	flour
⅔	cup	butter, melted
1		egg
1	teaspoon	vanilla extract
1	teaspoon	dry orange or lemon peel
1	teaspoon	salt

Directions:

Soften dry yeast in ¾ cup of warm milk and 1 tablespoon of sugar.
Stir softened yeast into 1 cup of flour.
Cover and set aside in warm place for 20-30 minutes.
Add egg, remaining sugar, vanilla extract, dry orange or lemon peel and mix well.
Stir in melted butter.
Add remaining flour, salt and milk, and mix well.
Knead dough for 6-8 minutes.
Cover dough and let rise in warm place until double in size.
Punch down risen dough and use according to recipe.

Note: Yeast dough to be used for apple and plum cake, plus for bee sting cake and butter cake.

APFELDATSCHI # 1
(Apple Cake # 1)

Ingredients:

		Yeast Dough # 3, pg. 190
2	pounds	apples
2	teaspoons	Vanilla Sugar, pg. 262
½	teaspoon	cinnamon
½	cup	sugar
⅓	cup	raisins

Directions:

Preheat oven to 350 degrees.
Prepare yeast dough # 3 as directed.
Wash, peel, core and slice apples; set aside.
Spread yeast dough onto very large cookie sheet.
Place apple slices (standing up) close together on top of yeast dough.
Combine vanilla sugar, cinnamon, sugar, and raisins and spread over sliced apples.
Bake at 350 degrees for 30-40 minutes.
Cool, cut into squares and serve.

Serves 8.

Note: Vanilla sugar is a German product. One may find vanilla sugar in major grocery stores in their foreign food section. See pg. 262 for vanilla sugar recipe and note.

BIENENSTICH
(Bee Sting Cake)

Ingredients:

		Yeast Dough # 3, pg. 190
7½	ounces	slivered almonds
½	cup	butter
1	cup	sugar
1	teaspoon	vanilla extract
1	teaspoon	rum extract
3	tablespoons	milk
1	box	vanilla pudding, 3 oz. (cook & serve)
2	cups	milk

Directions:

Preheat oven to 325 degrees.
Prepare yeast dough # 3 as directed.
Divide dough in half and spread into 2 greased 10 inch round spring-form pans.
Let rise once for about 20 minutes.
Meanwhile, heat butter, sugar and almonds in saucepan.
Mix well, then remove from stove.
Stir in 3 tablespoons of milk, vanilla and rum extract, then set aside to cool.
Spread mixture over both tops of yeast dough.
Bake at 325 degrees for 30-35 minutes.
Meanwhile, cook vanilla pudding as directed and cool.
Cut through thickness of both cool cakes, and fill with vanilla pudding.
Cut into slices and serve.

Serves 8 - 10.

Note: This cake is well known in southern Germany and sold in almost every bakery. When baking, place a cookie sheet under spring-form pans to catch sugar and butter drippings, if any. Cake may also be baked on a large, deep cookie sheet.

BUTTERKUCHEN
(Butter Cake)

Ingredients:

		Yeast Dough # 3, pg. 190
½	cup	butter, softened
1		egg yolk
½	cup	sugar
2	teaspoons	Vanilla Sugar, pg. 262
½	teaspoon	cinnamon
1	dash	nutmeg
¼	cup	slivered almonds, chopped or ground
⅓	cup	sour cream

Directions:

Preheat oven to 350 degrees.
Prepare yeast dough # 3 as directed.
Spread yeast dough into greased 10 inch round spring-form pan.
Let rise again in warm place for about 30 minutes.
Cream together butter and egg yolk.
Prick dough with fork several times, then spread with butter egg mixture.
Combine sugar, cinnamon, nutmeg and almonds, and sprinkle on top of butter egg mixture.
Mix vanilla sugar with sour cream, than spread over top of cake.
Bake at 350 degrees for 40-50 minutes.

Serves 6 - 8.

Note: This is a nice cake to have with coffee. If 10 inch spring-form pan is not available, use two smaller cake pans. A deep cookie sheet can also be used. Remember this is a yeast dough and will rise when baking. Therefore, sides should be at least 2 inches high depending on how much dough is used per pan. Place a regular cookie sheet under spring-form pan, or two smaller cake pans, in case any drippings should occur.

HEFEZOPF
(Braided Sweet Bread)

Ingredients:

Yeast Dough # 2, pg. 189
Sugar Glaze, pgs. 256 and 257
or confectioners sugar

Directions:

Preheat oven to 350 degrees.
Prepare yeast # 2 dough as directed in recipe.
To make the braid, use a floured board and divide yeast dough into three equal parts.
Roll each part out to about 15 inch-long strips.
Press 3 strips together on one end, and then proceed making the braid.
Seal ends of braid by pinching firmly together, and tuck under.
Place braid onto greased cookie sheet.
Bake at 350 degrees for 35-45 minutes, or until done.
Brush with sugar glaze or dust with confectioners sugar while still hot.

Serves 8.

Note: One may want to bake the sweet bread in a Bundt cake form, or any other form for that matter, but the time for baking may change somewhat.

HEFESTOLLEN
(Yeast Stollen or Yuletide Bread)

Ingredients:

1	package	dry yeast
½	cup	warm milk
½	cup	butter, melted
¾	cup	milk, scalded
⅓	cup	sugar
1	teaspoon	salt
¼	teaspoon	cardamom
1	dash	nutmeg
4½	cups	flour
1		egg
1½	tablespoons	grated orange peel
1	tablespoon	grated lemon peel
½	teaspoon	vanilla extract
½	teaspoon	rum extract
1½	cups	seedless raisins
¾	cup	dried apricots and candied cherries, chopped
¼	cup	blanched almonds, chopped
		Sugar Glaze, pgs. 256 and 257 or confectioners sugar

Directions:

Preheat oven to 350 degrees.
Soften dry yeast in ½ cup of warm milk and 1 teaspoon of sugar.
Stir together scalded milk, butter, remaining sugar, salt and spices.
Cool to lukewarm.
Add 2½ cups of flour, softened yeast, egg, vanilla and rum extract, and mix well.
Set aside for 15 minutes.
Add raisins, apricots, cherries, peels and nuts.
Mix well.
Add remaining flour to make soft dough.

Knead dough for about 6 minutes or until very smooth.

Place in lightly floured bowl.

Cover and let allow to rise in warm place until double in size, about 75 minutes.

Punch down risen dough, turn out on lightly floured surface, and divide into 3 equal parts.

To make the stollen shape, roll each part to a rounded rectangle, about 12 x 7 inch in size.

Fold long side over within 1 inch of opposite side.

Seal edges by dampening with water.

Place on greased baking sheets.

Cover and allow to rise until double in size, about 30-45 minutes.

Bake at 350 degrees for 20-25 minutes, or until golden brown.

Cover with sugar glaze or confectioners sugar while still hot.

Makes 3 yeast stollen.

Note: Can be made in advance and frozen for later use.

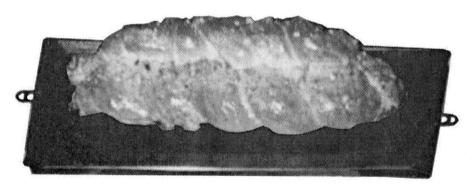

Braided Sweet Bread, pg. 194

ROHRNUDELN
(Pan Rolls)

Ingredients:

> Yeast Dough # 1, pg. 188
> butter
> sugar

Directions:

Preheat oven to 350 degrees.
Prepare yeast dough # 1 as directed.
Form little balls, about 2½ inches in diameter.
Place onto floured board, cover and let rise for 20-30 minutes.
Place yeast dough balls into generously buttered casserole dish, small roasting pan or deep cake pan.
Bake at 350 degrees for 25-35 minutes or until done.
Turn rolls upside-down onto large plate while still hot and sprinkle generously with sugar.

Serves 6 - 8.

Note: Use a generous amount of butter so rolls will be crusty on the bottom. One may want to use half of the dough for steamnoodles, and half for pan rolls. This is a Sunday breakfast in Germany.

ZWETSCHGENDATSCHI
(Plum Cake)

Ingredients:

		Yeast Dough # 3, pg. 190
2½	pounds	ripe damson plums
2	teaspoons	Vanilla Sugar, pg. 262
½	teaspoon	cinnamon
⅓	cup	sugar

Directions:

Wash damson plums, remove stones and cut into quarters.
Spread yeast dough onto large greased cookie sheet.
Place plum quarters close together (standing up) on top of yeast dough.
Combine sugar, vanilla sugar and cinnamon, then divide in half.
Sprinkle one half of sugar mixture on top of damson plums.
Bake at 350 degrees for 20 minutes.
Sprinkle remaining sugar mixture on top of cake, then continue baking for another 10-15 minutes or until done.
Cool, cut in squares and serve with whipping cream.

Serves 8 - 10.

Note: Use only fresh and well ripened damson plums. Plums are very juicy when baking with sugar. Therefore, it is advisable not to use all of the sugar in the beginning of baking. This plum cake, somewhat tart in taste in the beginning, is not only delicious, but found in every bakery throughout southern Germany during plum season.

APFELKUECHL
(Fried Apple Rings)

Ingredients:

2¼	cups	flour
3		eggs
2	tablespoons	sugar
1	dash	salt
1	cup	milk, or half & half
1	teaspoon	rum extract
2	tablespoons	sour cream
2	tablespoons	warm butter or margarine
6		apples
		shortening or oil for frying
1	tablespoon	Vanilla Sugar, pg. 262
		sugar to sprinkle fried apple rings

Directions:

Combine sugar flour and salt.
Add eggs, milk, rum extract and sour cream.
Stir until batter is smooth and free of lumps.
Stir in warm butter or margarine, then set aside.
Peel apples, remove core, and slice into apple rings, about ¼ inch thick.
Dip apple rings into batter, and fry in hot shortening or oil on both sides until golden color.
Mix sugar with vanilla sugar and sprinkle over hot fried apple rings.
Serve hot with apple sauce, your favorite compote, Cool Whip, ice cream or vanilla sauce.

Serves 4.

Note: Apple rings should float in hot shortening or oil when frying. Another way to make fried apple rings is by using German pancake dough.

* This dessert reminds me of a joke, my mother played on my dad. My father loved fried apple rings. So one day, Mother substituted a piece of cloth, the size and form of an apple ring, for an apple ring. She dipped the cloth into the batter, fried it, and made sure this apple ring was within my fathers reach.

All of us children knew what Mother had done and were waiting to see what was going to happen. The suspense was almost more than we could bear. Finally Dad reached for the cloth apple ring and took a bite, but since it was so tough, and without thinking, he stuffed the whole apple ring into his mouth. Dad chewed and chewed until finally he came to the conclusion that there was something wrong. He took a good look at his favorite dessert, which by then was nothing but a chewed up and worn-out piece of cloth. At that point we were all in stitches. Mother was in tears from laughing so hard.

My father was a very stern person, and there was not much, one could put over him. But this one finally made up for all those tries in the past.

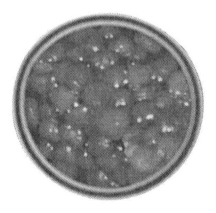

Strawberry Compote, pg. 268

HASENOHREN
(Rabbit Ears)

Ingredients:

1	cup	flour
dash		salt
dash		nutmeg
¼	cup	butter, melted
1		egg
1	tablespoon	sour cream
		shortening or oil for deep frying
		cinnamon and sugar

Directions:

Combine dry ingredients and place onto pastry board.
Add butter, egg, and sour cream, and work together well.
Set aside for about 10 minutes.
Using floured pastry board, roll out dough ⅛ inch thick, and cut out narrow shapes (like rabbit ears).
Deep fry until golden color on both sides.
Sprinkle with cinnamon and sugar.
Serve hot with coffee or compote.

Serves 2.

Note: Rabbit ears can be served without cinnamon and sugar, as a side dish with a meat entrée.

Maria Swaringen

MITTELBERG - NUDELN
(Mittelberg - Noodles)

Ingredients:

4	cups	flour
1	package	dry yeast
1	tablespoon	sugar
1½	cups	milk
1	tablespoon	butter or margarine, softened
2		eggs
½	teaspoon	vanilla extract
½	cup	raisins
1	teaspoon	salt
		shortening or oil for deep frying

Directions:

Soften dry yeast in ¾ cup of warm milk and sugar.
Stir softened yeast into 1 cup of flour, mix well and set aside for 20-30 minutes.
Add eggs and vanilla extract and mix well.
Stir in remaining flour, milk, salt, butter or margarine and raisins.
Beat dough 6-8 minutes or until dough "blows" bubbles.
Cover and allow dough to rise until double in size.
Divide into 14 to 16 parts.
Form balls and place on floured surface.
Cover and let rise for about 30 minutes.
Meanwhile, in large pot or Dutch oven, heat enough shortening or oil for deep frying (mittelberg noodles need to float in shortening or oil).
With your fingers, stretch each dough ball as you keep turning dough until the outer ring is no more then about ½ - ¾ inch thick, and the inner part of the dough is paper thin.
Place in hot shortening or oil.
Use a large spoon to ladle hot grease over dough so mittelberg noodle will rise while bottom side deep-fries until golden color.
Turn over carefully and finish deep frying.

202

Sprinkle with confectioners sugar and serve while still warm with coffee, applesauce, or plum compote.

Serves 6 - 8.

Note: When finished, it will look like a giant doughnut with a thin dome in the middle or you might call it a flying saucer. Therefore, it is important not to break the thin dough in the center before frying.

* In Germany, this is a meatless main meal, but one may use it also as a dessert. This recipe is known throughout southern Germany under several recipe names, such as "Bayerische Kuechel" (Bavarian deep fried Pastry), "Auszog'ne" (Stretch Noodles), "Kirtanudeln" or Kirchweihnudeln" (Church Festival Noodles), also "Kniekuechel" (Knee Noodles), because some ladies at times actually wrapped the dough around the knee to achieve the thin middle part of the dough, and a nice round doughnut shape on the outer ring (so I was told). It would have been easier to use a small glass and push down in the center of each dough ball as a good start for forming the mittelberg noodle.

My family back in Germany calls them "Mittelberg-Nudeln". If I remember correctly, my oldest brother, while still a young boy, was very sick once, and hospitalized in the Alps at a place called "Mittelberg". My mother used to make these noodles and she would mail them to my brother faithfully during his stay at the hospital. So the rest of us children gave the noodles the name "Mittelberg-Nudeln", and to this day we still use that name.

SCHMALZNUDELN
(Deep Fried Noodles)

Ingredients:

1	package	dry yeast
½	cup	warm milk
1	teaspoon	sugar
2¼	cups	white flour
2	cups	rye flour
1½	cups	buttermilk
1		egg
1½	teaspoons	salt
		butter shortening or canola oil for deep frying

Directions:

Soften dry yeast in warm milk and sugar.
Stir softened yeast into 1 cup of white flour, and set aside for 20-30 minutes.
Meanwhile, combine remaining white flour, rye flour and salt.
Add egg and dry ingredients, alternating with buttermilk, to soft dough and mix well.
Knead dough 8-10 minutes.
Cover and let rise in warm place for about 30 minutes.
Form little balls, about 2½ inches in diameter and place on floured pastry board.
Cover and allow to rise once more for 30 minutes.
Heat butter shortening or canola oil in large pot or Dutch oven, (enough so noodles will float).
Place a few balls upside-down into hot fat.
Use a large spoon to ladle hot fat over balls so dough will rise.
Deep fry on both sides until golden color.

Serves 6.

Note: In Bavaria the schmalznudel is very well known and available throughout the year in bakeries. Farmers always prepare the schmalznudel among other baked goods during holidays and other big festivals. Butter shortening offers a much better flavor when deep frying. However, one cannot get it in the United States. To make this pure butter shortening, simply heat the butter and skim off the foam from the hot butter. Save the foam or so-called sour butter, and use for other dishes such as for frying potato patties made from cooked potatoes.

Mittelberg Noodles, pg. 202

SCHUCHSEN
(Cottage Cheese Noodles)

Ingredients:

1	package	dry yeast
½	cup	warm milk
1	teaspoon	sugar
1		egg
¼	cup	soft butter
2	tablespoons	evaporated milk
1¾	cups	buttermilk
8	ounces	cottage cheese, small curd
3	cups	white flour
3	cups	rye flour
1	tablespoon	salt
		shortening or oil for deep frying

Directions:

Soften dry yeast in warm milk and sugar.
Using a large bowl, stir 1 cup of buttermilk into 2 cups of white flour.
Add softened yeast, egg, evaporated milk, butter and cottage cheese, and mix well.
Add remaining ingredients and knead together (do not stir).
Cover and allow to rise in warm place for about 1 hour.
Spoon out small portions of dough onto floured pastry board, and roll out rectangular to about ⅓ inch thick.
Heat 2-3 cups of shortening or oil in large pot or Dutch oven.
Deep fry schuchsen, basting top of schuchsen with hot fat until bottom is golden brown.
Turn over schuchsen and finish deep frying.

Serves 8.

*   This is a very old recipe dating back to the year 1500 AD. It had something to do with Mardi Gras. In those days, the Saturday before

Shrove Tuesday was the so-called "Greasy Saturday". That was the day when the old "Schuchsen" was prepared, deep fried in lard, then passed out to the people and eaten Sunday through Shrove Tuesday. All this was done in preparation of Lent. People would use up their eggs and fat, which were prohibited foods during Lent.

It took me at least 20 years to find this recipe, as very few bakeries in Germany still make the schuchsen. I love to dunk the schuchsen into coffee. It is a perfect breakfast for me while vacationing in Germany. The schuchsen can be frozen, and reheated in the oven.

APFELDATSCHI # 2
(Apple Cake # 2)

Ingredients:

½	cup	butter or margarine
2		eggs
¾	cup	sugar
1	teaspoon	vanilla extract
3¼	cups	flour
2	teaspoons	baking powder
½	cup	milk
2½	pounds	apples, peeled, cored & sliced
⅓	cup	raisins
½	cup	sugar to sprinkle on cake
1	teaspoon	cinnamon

Directions:

Preheat oven to 350 degrees.
Cream butter or margarine.
Add sugar, eggs and vanilla extract, and beat well.
Sift together flour and baking powder and stir into batter, alternating with milk.
Spread cake batter evenly onto large greased and floured cookie sheet.
Place apple slices (standing up) close together on top of cake batter.
Sprinkle raisins on top of apples.
Blend cinnamon with ½ cup of sugar, and sprinkle apples sparingly before baking.
Bake at 350 degrees for 30-40 minutes or until done.
Sprinkle with remaining cinnamon sugar after baking.

Serves 10.

Note: Other fruits may be used instead of apples.

APFELKUCHEN
(Apple Cake)

Ingredients:

1¾	cups	flour
½	teaspoon	baking powder
½	cup	butter or margarine
¾	cup	sugar
1	teaspoon	vanilla extract
1	teaspoon	grated lemon rind
1		egg

Filling:

⅓	cup	bread crumbs
5	medium	apples, peeled, cored & sliced thin
¼	cup	sugar

Topping:

3		egg yolks
3	tablespoons	sugar
½	teaspoon	vanilla extract
8	ounces	sour cream
¼	cup	ground almonds, optional
3		egg whites

Directions:

Preheat oven to 350 degrees.
Sift together flour and baking powder.
Cut butter or margarine into flour mixture.
Add sugar, vanilla extract and grated lemon rind.
Mix ingredients until crumbly.
Mix in egg, then knead until dough is smooth.
Set dough aside for 15 minutes.
Roll out dough on floured surface.

Press onto greased and floured bottom and side of 10 inch round spring-form pan.

Prick bottom of dough a few times and sprinkle with bread crumbs.

Add sliced apples and sprinkle with ¼ cup of sugar.

Beat egg whites until very stiff and set aside.

In separate bowl beat egg yolks and sugar together.

Stir in vanilla extract, sour cream, and ground almonds, optional.

Blend in stiff egg whites, then spread topping over apples.

Bake at 350 degrees for 40-45 minutes.

Remove ring from spring-form pan and cool completely.

Refrigerate cake for a few hours, or better yet, overnight before cutting.

Serves 8 - 10.

Note: If apples are very hard, steam slices for a few minutes before using for cake. One may want to use other fruit than apples. When using rhubarb, more sugar is needed.

APFEL STREUSELKUCHEN
(Apple Crumb Cake)

Ingredients:

½	cup	butter
⅔	cup	sugar
2		eggs
½	teaspoon	vanilla extract
1	cup	flour
½	teaspoon	baking powder
3-4		apples, peeled, cored, and sliced thin
3	tablespoons	sugar
1	recipe	for Sugar Crumbs, pg. 261

Directions:

Preheat oven to 350 degrees.
Cream together butter, sugar, eggs and vanilla extract.
Beat until batter is light and fluffy.
Sift together flour and baking powder and stir into batter.
Spread batter into greased and floured 10 inch round spring-form pan.
Place apple slices (standing up) on top of batter.
Sprinkle with 3 tablespoons of sugar.
Sprinkle sugar crumbs over sugared apples.
Bake at 350 degrees for 35-40 minutes.

Serves 6 - 8.

Note: One may substitute apples with cherries, peaches, blueberries, etc., but sprinkle with less sugar. A cookie sheet can be used instead of a spring-form pan.

GLASIERTER APFELKUCHEN
(Glazed Apple Cake)

Ingredients:

1	cup	butter
¾	cup	sugar
½	teaspoon	vanilla extract
5		eggs
2	cups	flour
2	teaspoons	baking powder
2	pounds	apples, peeled, cored and sliced
1½	teaspoons	apricot marmalade
1	tablespoon	water

Sugar Glaze:

1	cup	confectioners sugar
2	tablespoons	rum, or lemon juice
1½	teaspoons	hot water (give or take)

Directions:

Preheat oven to 350 degrees.

Cream butter.

Add sugar, alternating with eggs one at a time, vanilla extract, and beat until creamy.

Combine flour and baking powder.

Stir into batter in small portions.

Spread half of the batter evenly into greased 10 inch round spring-form pan.

Arrange a double layer of apple slices on top of batter.

Spread remaining batter evenly over apple slices.

Bake at 350 degrees for 75 minutes or until done (second oven shelf).

After cake is done, stir together apricot marmalade and water and bring to a quick boil.

Remove from stove and immediately brush on hot baked cake.

When cake is cool stir together confectioners sugar with rum, or lemon juice, and enough hot water to make a thin sugar glaze.
Cover cake with sugar glaze.

Serves 8 - 10.

RUSSISCHER APFELKUCHEN
(Russian Apple Cake)

Ingredients:

1	cup	butter or margarine
1¼	cups	sugar
3		eggs
1	teaspoon	vanilla extract
1½	teaspoons	cinnamon
	dash	salt
2½	cups	flour
2½	teaspoons	baking powder
4	ounces	chopped nuts
3	medium	apples, peeled, cored and grated
4	tablespoons	rum

Glaze:

2	cups	confectioners sugar
2	tablespoons	rum
2	tablespoons	hot water

Directions:

Preheat oven to 350 degrees.
Cream butter or margarine.
Add sugar, eggs and vanilla extract, and beat well.
Combine flour, salt, cinnamon and baking powder, and stir into batter.
Combine rum with grated apples.
Stir in grated apples and chopped nuts.
Spoon batter into greased and floured 9 or 10 inch spring-form pan.
Bake at 350 degrees for 60-70 minutes, or until done.
When cake has cooled off somewhat, remove outer ring, turn up side down onto plate, and remove bottom part of spring-form pan.
Combine ingredients for glaze and proceed glazing cool apple cake.

Serves 8 - 10.

ERDBEERKUCHEN
(Strawberry Shortcake)

Ingredients:

Topping:

3	pints	fresh, clean strawberries
6	tablespoons	sugar
1	package	of Tortenguss, or Fruit Glaze whipping cream

Shortcake:

1	cup	butter or margarine
1¼	cups	sugar
4		eggs
1	teaspoon	vanilla extract
2	cups	flour
1	teaspoon	baking powder
1	dash	salt

Directions:

Preheat oven to 350 degrees.
Blend clean strawberries with 6 tbsp. of sugar (cutting large strawberries in half) and set aside.
Cream butter or margarine.
Add sugar, eggs (one at a time) and vanilla extract, and beat until batter is nice and creamy.
Sift dry ingredients together and stir into batter.
Spread batter onto greased and floured cookie sheet.
Bake at 350 degrees for 15-20 minutes.
Cool cake on cookie sheet.
Meanwhile, drain sugared strawberries (setting aside liquid).
Place sugared strawberries nicely on top of cool cake.
Prepare Tortenguss, or Fruit Glaze according to directions, using up strawberry liquid that was set aside.

Spoon hot Tortenguss, or Fruit Glaze over sugared strawberries.
Refrigerate strawberry shortcake until ready to use.
Top with whipping cream just before serving.

Serves 8 - 10.

Note: This cake is ideal for a large get-together during strawberry season. Only fresh strawberries are recommended. One may find the German Fruit Glaze, or Tortenguss in major grocery stores in the foreign food section. Other fresh fruits may be used, such as bananas, grapes, raspberries, blueberries, or peaches. Canned peaches work well too, but need to be drained very well. One may also arrange several fruits on the cake. If less cake is needed at a time, one may bake two 9 inch round cake layers from above recipe, and freeze one layer for later use.

Strawberry Shortcake, pg. 215

ZWETSCHGENKUCHEN
(Plum Cake)

Ingredients:

2⅓	cups	flour
1	teaspoon	baking powder
1	cup	cottage cheese, small curd, or sour cream
1		egg
¾	cup	sugar
6	tablespoons	oil
1	teaspoon	vanilla extract
7	tablespoons	milk
3	tablespoons	bread crumbs
2	pounds	damson plums, pitted and quartered
3	tablespoons	sugar
1	recipe	of Sugar Crumbs, pg. 261
		Cool Whip or whipping cream

Directions:

Preheat oven to 375 degrees.

Sift together flour and baking powder, and set aside.

Stir together cottage cheese or sour cream, sugar, egg, oil and vanilla extract, and beat until creamy.

Add flour mixture and milk, and mix well.

Spread batter evenly onto large greased and floured cookie sheet.

Sprinkle with bread crumbs.

Arrange pitted and quartered damson plums nicely on top of bread crumbs.

Sprinkle 3 tablespoons of sugar over damson plums and top with sugar crumbs.

Bake at 375 degrees for 45-60 minutes, or until done.

Slice cake when cool and serve with Cool Whip or whipping cream.

Serves 8 - 10.

Note: In the United States the small curd cottage cheese is still not fine enough to use for baking; therefore, use an electric food chopper to achieve a finer texture of cottage cheese. One may use 2 round cake pans instead of a large cookie sheet or cut the recipe in half to use only one round cake pan. If plums are very juicy, sprinkle with a little less sugar.

* Wasps and yellow jackets love juicy sweet plums. They are a nuisance at the bakeries during the summer months when plum cakes are displayed in the bakery windows.

It also reminds me of a story that may be very beneficial one day to some of my readers. Years ago, we had a tall oak tree in our front yard. The tree was somewhat hollow inside, and to our surprise, large yellow hornets decided to move in. It would have been fine with us, if only those hornets would not have been so attracted to lights; it got so bad we could not leave an outside light on in the evening. When we did, upon our arrival at home we could not open the garage door due to the swarm of hornets.

So how does one get rid of these pesky insects? We hung our "blue light bug and insect zapper" underneath the light at the front door. In one week we rid ourselves of the entire hornets' nest in the tree. My husband cleaned up the blue light zapper every morning, and counted a total of 700 hornets.

A few years later, a swarm of wasps or yellow jackets moved into the back of our house, underneath the siding. They were really busy coming and going, and it was difficult for us to use the patio steps. We had no outside light in that area, so we had to trap them during the day. Again we used the same blue light bug and insect zapper. But this time we turned the zapper upside-down, fasten a hook or ring to the top of it, slid an old short broom handle through the opening and placed it between the house and the steps, so the blue light zapper would hang near the low area where the wasps or yellow jackets were coming and going. Since we didn't have a night-light, we used honey on the upside-down bottom of the blue light zapper. It worked like a

2 for Recipe. Visit the Meal Station in our
epartment for ingredients and cooking tips.

SWORDFISH NICOISE SALAD
PAGE 3

BAVARIAN HAM ON WHOLE
WHEAT WITH EGGS & GRUYÈRE
PAGE 5

BELLELAY

BERN

EMMENTAL

INCREDIBLE CHEESES
OF SWITZERLAND
PAGE 6

Wegmans

helping you make great meals easy

45131 Columbia Place
Sterling, VA 20166
(703) 421-2400

SAUERBRATEN
CAULIFLOWER & SPINACH GRATIN

Sauerbraten

SERVES 6   ACTIVE TIME: 15 MIN
TOTAL TIME: 26 HOURS 45 MIN

3   lbs beef short ribs
1   Tbsp Wegmans Cracked Pepper Blend
¾   cup red wine
¾   cup red wine vinegar
¾   cup water
1   medium (about ½ lb) onion, peeled, sliced
5   Tbsp Wegmans Pan Searing Flour, divided
2   Tbsp olive oil
1   can (14 oz) reduced-sodium beef broth
10   gingersnaps, crushed (about ½ cup crumbs)
1   pkg (12 oz) wide egg noodles, cooked

1. **Cut** each rib in half (if full rib); season ribs with cracked pepper blend. Combine wine, wine vinegar, water, and onion in medium bowl. Pour over ribs in large plastic bag or large bowl. Close bag or cover bowl; refrigerate 24 hours.

2. **Preheat** oven to 350 degrees. Remove meat from marinade, saving marinade. Dry meat with paper towels; dust with about 4 Tbsp pan searing flour; pat off excess.

3. **Heat** oil on MEDIUM in large braising pan, until oil faintly smokes. Add ribs and sear, turning to sear all sides, until lightly browned, 2-3 min on each side. Remove from pan.

4. **Add** onions from marinade to pan and cook, stirring frequently, until lightly browned, 2-3 min. Add reserved marinade and beef broth; heat to simmering. Return meat to pan; cover. Place on center rack of oven and braise 2 hours, until tender; remove from oven.

5. **Skim** fat from surface and discard. Remove meat from pan; add crushed gingersnaps and remaining 1 Tbsp pan searing flour to sauce. Heat to simmering on MEDIUM-HIGH, stirring continuously. Puree 1-2 min with hand or regular blender until gingersnaps are smooth.

6. **Spoon** noodles onto deep platter. Slice sauerbraten; serve with sauce over cooked noodles.

Nutrition Info: Each Serving (4 oz meat, 1 cup vegetables w/sauce, 1 cup noodles) contains 650 calories, 59g carbohydrate (2g fiber), 37g protein, 41g fat (15g saturated fat), 155mg cholesterol and 670mg sodium.

Wine Selection:
BONNY DOON SYRAH 2001

When you think Syrah you think Southern France - well think again! The fun and not-so-traditional wine makers at Bonny Doon (in California) have captured the Old World style that matches perfectly with this meal.

Cauliflower & Spinach Gratin

SERVES 6   ACTIVE TIME: 25 MIN
TOTAL TIME: 1 HOUR, 20 MIN

Juice of ½ lemon (about 1 Tbsp)
1   medium head cauliflower (about 1½ lbs), separated into florets
1   tsp plus 1 Tbsp butter
1   small fennel bulb (about ½ lb), trimmed, cored, cut in ¼-inch strips (about 2½ cups)
2   cloves garlic, peeled, chopped
1   pkg (10 oz) *Food You Feel Good About* Spinach
¼   cup water
2   Tbsp cornstarch
2   cups half-and-half
3   Tbsp seasoned bread crumbs
⅓   cup shredded Gruyère cheese (about 1.5 oz)

Preheat oven to 350 degrees.

1. **Bring** large pot of salted water to a boiling high. Add lemon juice and cauliflower; blanch, covered, 3-4 min. Drain. Shock (to stop cooking process) by transferring to bowl of ice water; drain. (This step can be done ahead of time.)

2. **Butter** 11 x 7-inch baking dish with 1 tsp butter; add drained cauliflower.

3. **Melt** remaining 1 Tbsp butter in skillet on MEDIUM. Add fennel; cook 3-4 min, stirring occasionally. Add garlic; cook 2 min, stirring frequently, until softened. Add spinach; cook 1-1½ min, until wilted. Season to taste with salt and pepper.

4. **Combine** water and cornstarch in small bowl; set aside.

5. **Add** half-and-half to skillet. Increase heat to MEDIUM-HIGH and cook, stirring occasionally, 3-5 min. Stir in cornstarch-water mixture. Spoon over cauliflower. Sprinkle with half the bread crumbs, cheese, then remaining bread crumbs.

6. **Bake** on center rack of oven 35-45 min, until lightly browned and bubbling.

Chef tip: Blanching cauliflower covered helps keep it white.

Nutrition Info: Each Serving (about 1 cup) contains 230 calories, 20g carbohydrate (6g fiber), 9g protein, 15g fat (9g saturated fat), 45mg cholesterol and 420mg sodium.
🔵 **High Fiber** 🔵 **High Calcium**

charm; in one week we were rid of all the wasps or yellow jackets, about a 1000 of them. The blue light zapper had to be cleaned up every day, and new honey had to be applied.

Needless to say, this method is the easiest way to get rid of the problem.

BANANEN - NUSSKUCHEN
(Banana Nut Cake)

Ingredients:

1	cup	butter or margarine
1¾	cups	sugar
6		eggs
1	teaspoon	vanilla extract
1	teaspoon	rum extract
3¼	cups	flour
⅛	teaspoon	salt
1½	teaspoons	baking powder
1½		bananas, mashed
2	tablespoons	milk
1	cup	ground nuts; almonds, hazelnuts or mixed
⅓	cup	raisins

Directions:

Preheat oven to 350 degrees.
Cream butter or margarine.
Add sugar, eggs (one at a time) and beat until batter is light and fluffy.
Add vanilla and rum extract.
Combine flour, salt and baking powder, and stir into batter.
Add mashed banana and milk.
Blend in ground nuts and raisins.
Spoon batter into greased and floured Bundt cake pan.
Bake at 350 degrees for 65-70 minutes or until done.
Cool cake for 10 minutes.
Turn upside-down onto cake rack, cool completely and dust with confectioners sugar.

Serves 8.

Note: This cake can be frozen for later use.

BUTTERCREME ROLLE
(Butter Cream Roll)

Ingredients:

4		eggs
1	cup	sugar
¼	cup	water
1	teaspoon	vanilla extract
½	teaspoon	rum extract
1¼	cups	flour
1	teaspoon	baking powder
1	dash	salt
1	recipe	for Butter Cream, pgs. 250 to 255

Directions:

Preheat oven to 375 degrees.
Beat eggs until lemon colored.
Add sugar gradually, continuing to beat until mixture is light and fluffy.
Add water, vanilla and rum extract.
Sift together flour, baking powder and salt.
Slowly add to batter and blend until smooth.
Pour batter onto large greased cookie sheet lined with greased wax paper.
Bake at 375 degrees for 12-15 minutes.
Turn hot cake onto clean dishtowel sprinkled generously with confectioners sugar.
Carefully peel off wax paper.
Roll up cake together with dishtowel.
When cake is completely cool, unroll and spread with butter cream.
Roll up cake again without dishtowel, and decorate with remaining butter cream.

Serves 6 - 8.

Note: This recipe is ideal for creating a decorative and delicious Yule-log cake during the Christmas holidays. During the summer months, use fresh strawberries or peaches and whipping cream instead of butter cream, and dust with confectioners sugar.

Butter Cream Torte, pg. 223

BUTTERCREMETORTE
(Butter Cream Torte)

Ingredients:

2	boxes	of cake mix, (yellow, chocolate or one of each)
2	recipes	for Butter Cream, pg. 253 or 254 (rum or chocolate flavor)
½	cup	marmalade, optional

Directions:

Preheat oven to 350 degrees.
Prepare cake batter (one at a time) as directed on box.
Use a greased and floured 10 inch spring-form pan, and bake two cake layers at 350 degrees for 20-25 minutes.
Repeat with second cake mix.
Let cakes cool for several hours or overnight before spreading with butter cream.
Spread first layer with butter cream.
Place second layer on top of first layer, then spread with butter cream.
Place third layer on top of second layer, then spread with butter cream.
Place fourth layer on top of third layer.
Decorate cake on top and sides with butter cream to your desire.
One may want to use marmalade, optional on one cake layer instead of butter cream.

Serves 16.

Note: One may want to decorate top of cake with chocolate shavings or nuts on top of butter cream. Or one may want to use less butter cream on sides of cake, and cover with roasted almonds or oatmeal.

*   Butter Cream Torte brings back a wonderful memory. It reminds me of my mother's birthday and Mother's Day. Long before these special days came around every year, all of us children would be busy getting all the ingredients together for two butter cream cakes. The bakery would give us a list of ingredients needed for these cakes. Then we would go to our neighboring farmers and literally beg for flour, butter sugar, etc.

We had no money for none of us six children (ages 5 through 12) ever received an allowance for doing chores around the house. So upon asking Mother, she always would give us enough money to cover the cost that the bakery charged for baking the cakes.

Then we had to gather all of the flowers. Besides one or two potted flowers, we again went to all of our neighbors for fresh cut flowers for our Mother. None of the neighbors ever said "No" to us, and all of us greatly enjoyed the secret of planning and gathering for these special days.

Finally the occasion had arrived. Mother would wake us up in the morning just before she left for early Mass for she knew what we were up to, but wasn't aware of all of the details.

While Mother was in Church, we would all hurry as fast as we could to set the table, place the two butter cream cakes in the center, and put flowers everywhere in our large eat-in kitchen. As the coffee was just about ready, Mother would come home from Church. There she was, standing in the kitchen door with tears running down her cheeks and full of joy.

After all the congratulations, the reading of the homemade cards and the wonders of the beautiful fresh cut spring flowers, we soon would sit around the table enjoying mother's delicious butter cream torte.

EIERLIKOERKUCHEN
(Eggnog Cake)

Ingredients:

5		eggs
1⅞	cups	confectioners sugar
1	cup	eggnog mixed with rum (see note)
1	cup	canola oil
2	cups	flour
1½	teaspoons	baking powder
		Chocolate Glaze # 2, pg. 257

Directions:

Preheat oven to 350 degrees.
Beat eggs until lemon colored.
Add confectioners sugar and beat until light and fluffy.
Stir in eggnog.
Sift together flour and baking powder.
Add flour and canola oil alternately in small amounts, and blend well.
Pour batter into greased and floured ring cake form.
Bake at 350 degrees, (bottom shelf) for 50-60 minutes or until done.
Cover cool cake with chocolate glaze.

Serves 8.

Note: German eggnog always contains liqueur. It is served in a shot glass instead of a cup and not recommended for children. It is more like a brandy. So for above recipe, use ¾ cup of American eggnog, and mix with ¼ cup of rum.

Maria Swaringen

EINFACHE PUNSCHTORTE
(Simple Punch Torte)

Ingredients:

1	box	lemon cake mix

To sprinkle cake layers:

3	tablespoons	black tea (beverage)
4	tablespoons	rum
1	teaspoon	sugar

Filling:

1	cup	peach, apricot or strawberry marmalade
3	tablespoons	pear or peach schnapps
¾	cup	drained canned fruit, chopped (fruit cocktail, peaches, etc.)
1	cup	Cool Whip, or whipping cream
		Sugar Icing, pg. 263 to cover cake

Directions:

Preheat oven to 350 degrees.
Prepare cake batter, adding ingredients as directed on box.
Pour batter into four 9 inch greased and floured cake pans.
Bake at 350 degrees for 15-20 minutes.
Turn onto cake rack and let cool completely.
Blend marmalade with pear or peach schnapps and set aside.
Blend fruit with Cool Whip or whipping cream, and set aside.
Stir together tea, rum and sugar.
Sprinkle 2 tablespoons of liquid on top of first cake layer.
Spread with marmalade mixture.
Place second cake layer on top of first cake layer.
Sprinkle with 1½ tablespoons of liquid.
Top with fruit and Cool Whip, or whipping cream mixture.
Place third cake layer on top of second cake layer.

Sprinkle with 1 ½ tablespoons of liquid.

Spread with marmalade mixture.

Place fourth cake layer on top of third cake layer.

Sprinkle with 2 tablespoons of liquid.

Place large plate on top of cake, and set aside for a few hours or overnight in refrigerator.

Remove large plate and cover cake with sugar icing, using rum extract instead of vanilla extract.

Serves 8.

EINFACHE SCHOKOLADENTORTE
(Simple Chocolate Torte)

Ingredients:

1	box	German chocolate cake mix
1	recipe	for Butter Cream, pgs. 250 to 255 any flavor
1	recipe	for Chocolate Glaze # 2, pg. 257

Directions:

Preheat oven to 350 degrees.
Prepare batter for German chocolate cake, adding ingredients as directed on box.
Pour batter into three 9 inch greased and floured cake pans.
Bake at 350 degrees for 15-20 minutes.
Turn out onto cake rack and cool completely before filling with prepared butter cream.
Cover cake with chocolate glaze # 2.

Serves 8.

Note: This cake is very easy to make. One may bake the cake earlier and freeze for later use. When using the butter cream, make sure cake is defrosted and at room temperature.

EINFACHER GESUNDHEITSKUCHEN
(Simple Pound Cake)

Ingredients:

1	cup	butter
1¼	cups	sugar
4		eggs
1	teaspoon	vanilla extract
2	cups	flour
1	teaspoon	baking powder
1	dash	salt

Directions:

Preheat oven to 350 degrees.
Cream butter.
Slowly add sugar, eggs (one at a time) and vanilla extract.
Beat until batter is nice and creamy.
Combine flour, salt and baking powder, and stir into batter.
Spoon batter into greased and floured 4 x 10 inch loaf pan.
Bake at 350 degrees for 60-70 minutes or until done.

Serves 6 - 8.

Note: For quick strawberry shortcakes, slice cake 1 inch thick, top with fresh strawberries and whipping cream. Cake can be frozen for later use.

Maria Swaringen

FEINER GESUNDHEITSKUCHEN
(Chocolate Chip Pound Cake)

Ingredients:

1	cup	butter
4		eggs
1¼	cups	sugar
1	teaspoon	vanilla extract
1	teaspoon	rum extract
2	cups	flour
1	teaspoon	baking powder
1	dash	salt
⅓	cup	raisins
⅓	cup	chocolate chips

Directions:

Preheat oven to 350 degrees.
Cream butter.
Slowly add sugar and eggs (one at a time) and beat until very creamy.
Add vanilla and rum extract.
Sift together flour, salt and baking powder, and stir into batter.
Blend raisins and chocolate chips into batter.
Spoon batter into greased and floured 4 x 10 inch loaf pan.
Bake at 350 degrees for 60-70 minutes, or until done.

Serves 6 - 8.

HASELNUSSKUCHEN
(Hazelnut Cake)

Ingredients:

1	cup	butter or margarine
1½	cups	sugar
6		eggs
1	teaspoon	vanilla extract
3¼	cups	flour
1	cup	ground hazelnuts
1½	teaspoons	cinnamon
1	teaspoon	baking powder
¼	cup	milk

Directions:

Preheat oven to 350 degrees.
Cream butter.
Add sugar, eggs (one at a time) and vanilla extract, and beat well until batter is creamy.
Combine flour, cinnamon and baking powder.
Stir into batter with milk.
Blend in ground hazelnuts.
Spoon batter into greased and floured Bundt cake pan.
Bake at 350 degrees for 65-70 minutes or until done.
Cool cake for 10 minutes, then turn upside-down onto cake rack.
Dust with confectioners sugar.

Serves 8 - 10.

HASELNUSSTORTE
(Hazelnut Torte)

Ingredients:

1	cup	butter
1	cup	sugar
4		eggs
1	teaspoon	almond extract
¼	cup	sour cream
2	cups	flour
1	cup	ground hazelnuts
1	teaspoon	baking powder
1	dash	salt
1	recipe	for Nut Butter Cream, pg. 252

Directions:

Preheat oven to 350 degrees.
Cream butter.
Add eggs (one at a time) and sugar, and beat until very creamy.
Add almond extract and sour cream, and mix well.
Sift together flour, salt and baking powder and stir into batter.
Stir in ground hazelnuts.
Spoon batter into three 8 inch round greased and floured cake pans.
Bake at 350 degrees for 18-20 minutes.
Cool cake completely before filling, and/or decorating with nut butter cream.

Serves 8.

Note: One may use only a thin coat of nut butter cream on sides of torte, then cover with ground hazelnuts mixed with sugar (2 tablespoons of sugar to ½ cup of ground hazelnuts).

HAUSMACHERTORTE
(Hausmacher Torte)

Ingredients:

13	tablespoons	butter or margarine
1⅝	cups	sugar
4	ounces	Baker's or Nestlé's semi sweet chocolate, grated coarse
4		eggs
7	ounces	ground hazelnuts
1⅔	cups	flour
	dash	salt
1	teaspoon	baking powder
2	tablespoons	milk
1	tablespoon	cocoa
¼	teaspoon	cinnamon
1	teaspoon	coffee, ground very fine
		confectioners sugar

Directions:

Preheat oven to 350 degrees.
Cream butter.
Add sugar and eggs (one at a time), and beat until very creamy.
Add coarsely grated chocolate, milk, cocoa, cinnamon and ground coffee.
Sift together flour, salt and baking powder, and stir into batter.
Blend in ground hazelnuts.
Spoon batter into greased and floured 9 inch spring-form pan.
Bake at 350 degrees for 60 minutes or until done.
Turn upside-down onto cake rack to cool.
Dust with confectioners sugar.

Serves 8 to 10.

NUSS-SCHOKOLADEKUCHEN
(Nut-Chocolate Cake)

Ingredients:

1	cup	butter or margarine
1	cup	sugar
6		eggs, separated
7	ounces	Baker's or Nestlé's semi sweet chocolate, melted
5	tablespoons	hot water
5	tablespoons	rum
1½	cups	flour
2	teaspoons	baking powder
6	ounces	ground almonds or hazelnuts
		Chocolate Glaze # 1, pg. 256 or confectioners sugar

Directions:

Preheat oven to 350 degrees:
Cream butter.
Add sugar and egg yolks (one at a time), and beat until very creamy.
Add melted semi sweet chocolate.
Sift together flour and baking powder.
Add flour, water and rum to batter, and mix well.
Stir in ground almonds or hazelnuts.
Beat egg whites very stiff and fold into cake batter.
Spoon batter into greased and floured Bundt cake pan.
Bake at 350 degrees for 60-70 minutes or until done.
Turn cake upside-down and cool.
Use chocolate glaze # 1 or dust with confectioners sugar.

Serves 8 - 10.

Note: Use an electric coffee grinder to pulverize nuts.

PRINZREGENTENTORTE
(Prinzregenten Torte)

Ingredients:

1	cup	butter
1	cup	sugar
4		eggs
1	teaspoon	vanilla extract
1	teaspoon	baking powder
2	cups	flour
2	tablespoons	milk
1	recipe	Chocolate Butter Cream, pg. 254
1	recipe	Chocolate Glaze # 1, pg. 256

Directions:

Preheat oven to 375 degrees.
Cream butter.
Add sugar, eggs (one at a time) and vanilla extract, and beat until creamy.
Sift together flour and baking powder.
Add flour and milk to batter and stir well.
Spread ⅓ cup of cake batter onto greased 9 inch bottom of spring-form pan (without sides).
Bake at 375 degrees for 6 minutes.
Transfer cake layer onto large plate to cool off, then transfer to another cake plate and spread with a thin layer of chocolate butter cream.
Bake second layer, transfer to large plate to cool off, then transfer onto top of first layer and spread with a thin layer of chocolate butter cream.
Repeat until all cake batter and chocolate butter cream is used up. (Do not spread chocolate butter cream on top of last layer).
Should make 10 cake layers.
Prepare chocolate glaze # 1 and glaze entire cake.
Refrigerate.

Serves 8 - 10.

Note: Have butter cream ready before baking cake. This cake takes a long time to make, but it is very good. One may use ½ cup of batter for each layer to achieve 6-7 layers. Bake each layer for about 8 minutes, and frost cake with leftover butter cream, instead of using chocolate glaze.

Prinzregenten Torte, pg. 235

SCHOKOLADE - HASELNUSSKUCHEN
(Chocolate Hazelnut Cake)

Ingredients:

1½	cups	butter
1¾	cups	sugar
6		eggs
3	cups	flour
1	cup	ground hazelnuts
1	teaspoon	baking powder
¼	teaspoon	salt
2	teaspoons	rum extract
2	teaspoons	chocolate extract
¼	cup	raisins
¼	cup	chocolate chips
		Chocolate Glaze # 1, pg. 256

Directions:

Preheat oven to 350 degrees.
Cream butter.
Add sugar, eggs, (one at a time) rum and chocolate extract, and beat well.
Combine flour, salt and baking powder, and stir into batter.
Add ground hazelnuts.
Dust raisins with flour and add with chocolate chips to batter.
Spoon batter into greased and floured Bundt cake pan.
Bake at 350 degrees for 70-75 minutes or until done.
Cool cake for 10 minutes.
Turn upside-down onto cake rack.
Cover cool cake with chocolate glaze # 1.

Serves 8 - 10.

Note: If ground hazelnuts are not available, use an electric coffee grinder to pulverize the nuts.

SCHWARZWAELDER KIRSCHTORTE
(Black Forest Cherry Torte)

Ingredients:

1		German chocolate cake mix
1	can	cherry pie filling, 21 oz.
4	tablespoons	cherry brandy
4	tablespoons	water
1	envelope	Knox Unflavored Gelatine
1½	pints	whipping cream
⅓	cup	sugar
1	teaspoon	vanilla extract
		small amount of cherry brandy to spray on cake layers
		chocolate shavings

Directions:

Preheat oven to 350 degrees.

Prepare German chocolate cake batter as directed on box.

Divide batter into three 9 inch round cake pans.

Bake at 350 degrees for 15-20 minutes.

Rinse 8-12 cherries and mix with 1 tablespoon of cherry brandy and set aside.

Mix remaining cherry pie filling with 3 tablespoons of cherry brandy and set aside.

Sprinkle Knox Unflavored Gelatine over 4 tablespoons of water and set aside.

Beat whipping cream to halfway point.

Heat Knox Unflavored Gelatine until dissolved, stirring constantly (do not boil).

Cool off Knox Unflavored Gelatine, stirring constantly.

Add Knox Unflavored Gelatine to whipping cream along with sugar and vanilla extract, and finish beating whipping cream until stiff.

Spray first cake layer sparingly with cherry brandy.

Spread small amount of whipping cream on first cake layer.

Top with half of cherry pie filling.

Spread whipping cream on top of cherry pie filling.
Place second cake layer on top.
Spray with cherry brandy, and repeat as with first cake layer.
Top with third cake layer.
Spread whipping cream around side of torte.
Decorate top of torte with remaining whipping cream, cherries set aside and chocolate shavings.

Serves 8-10.

Note: Omit water and unflavored Knox Unflavored Gelatine if torte is used the same day. Most remaining whipping cream should be used to crown torte. In Germany one can use "Sahne Steif" instead of Knox Unflavored Gelatine. It keeps the whipping cream stiff. It may be found in grocery stores carrying foreign foods. Also "Kirschwasser" is used instead of cherry brandy. It is a somewhat stronger cherry liqueur, which is hard to find in the United States.

Black Forest Cherry Torte, pg. 238

ZUCCHINIKUCHEN
(Zucchini Bread)

Ingredients:

4		eggs
1	cup	oil
1	cup	brown sugar
1	cup	white sugar
½	teaspoon	baking powder
2	teaspoons	baking soda
1	teaspoon	salt
1	tablespoon	cinnamon
1	dash	nutmeg
¼	teaspoon	allspice
2¾	cups	flour
2	cups	grated zucchini
1	tablespoon	vanilla extract
1	cup	chopped walnuts or pecans
½	cup	raisins

Directions:

Preheat oven to 350 degrees.
Combine and beat first 4 ingredients until creamy.
Sift together next 7 ingredients and gradually add to batter.
Stir in remaining 4 ingredients.
Pour batter into 3 greased 8 x 4 inch or 2 greased 9 x 5 inch loaf pans.
Bake at 350 degrees for 45-60 minutes, depending on size of loaf pan.

Serves 12.

Note: Zucchini bread can be baked long before the holidays and frozen. One may grate the zucchini in the summer when there is plenty, then measure 2 cups per container to freeze for later use. When defrosting, use all the water with the grated zucchini in the container.

KAESEKUCHEN MIT BUTTERMILCH
(Cheese Cake with Buttermilk)

Ingredients:

7	tablespoons	butter
3	tablespoons	sugar
1		egg
1½	cups	flour
1	teaspoon	baking powder

For cheese filling:

11	tablespoons	margarine
2		eggs
¾	cup	sugar
16	ounces	cottage cheese, small curd
1	box	vanilla pudding, 3 oz.(cook & serve)
2	cups	buttermilk
1	teaspoon	vanilla extract
		grated lemon peel of a ½ lemon

Directions:

Preheat oven to 350 degrees.
Combine flour, sugar and baking powder.
Cut in butter with 2 knives or pastry blender.
Add egg and knead dough well.
Use ⅔ of dough to roll out and place on bottom of 9 inch spring-form pan.
Use remaining dough to place on sides of spring-form pan, about 2½ to 3 inches high.
To make cheese filling.
Use a food processor to cream cottage cheese, and set aside.
Cream margarine and sugar together.
Add vanilla extract, eggs and cottage cheese, and beat well.
Add grated lemon peel, vanilla pudding and buttermilk, and beat until very creamy.

Spread cheese filling into prepared spring-form pan.
Bake at 350 degrees for 70-90 minutes.
Cool cheese cake, remove outer ring, then turn upside-down onto plate and remove bottom part of pan.
Turn again right side up and dust with confectioners sugar and serve.

Serves 8 - 10.

Cheese Torte, pg. 243

KAESETORTE
(Cheese Torte)

Ingredients:

For cake batter:

¼	cup	soft butter
⅓	cup	sugar
1		egg
1	teaspoon	water
½	cup	flour
½	teaspoon	baking powder
⅛	teaspoon	lemon extract

For cheese filling:

2	cups	whipping cream
2	envelopes	Knox Unflavored Gelatine
⅓	cup	water
16	ounces	soft cream cheese
1	teaspoon	vanilla extract
3		egg yolks
¾	cup	sugar
3	tablespoons	lemon juice
1	dash	salt

For topping:

2	tablespoons	orange or peach marmalade
½	tablespoon	water
		orange or peach slices

Directions:

Preheat oven to 350 degrees.
Beat butter, sugar and egg together until creamy.
Add water and lemon extract.

Sift together flour and baking powder and stir into batter.

Spread batter into greased and floured 9 inch spring-form pan.

Bake at 350 degrees for 10-12 minutes or until done.

Cool cake completely in spring-form pan before preparing cheese filling.

Using cool beaters, whip 2 cups of whipping cream until stiff.

Refrigerate whipping cream until ready to use.

Sprinkle Knox Unflavored Gelatine over ⅓ cup of water and set aside.

Cream together cream cheese, vanilla extract, egg yolks, sugar, lemon juice and salt.

Heat Knox Unflavored Gelatine to boiling point, stirring constantly.

Quickly stir Knox Unflavored Gelatine into cream cheese filling and mix well.

Fold in whipping cream.

Remove cool cake from spring-form pan.

Place cake on flat plate.

Place greased ring of spring-form pan around cake.

Spread cream cheese filling evenly on top of cake layer.

Refrigerate for 4 hours or overnight.

Remove ring from spring-form pan.

Mix orange or peach marmalade with water.

Spread marmalade on top of cheese torte and decorate with orange or peach slices.

Serves 12 - 14.

Note: If preferred, one may leave cake in spring-form pan, grease ring slightly, proceed with cheese filling and refrigerate. This is also an easier way to transport cheese torte. Canned sliced peaches work very well. One may also use other fruit, such as fresh strawberries, blueberries or raspberries with marmalade of same flavor. One my also use sugar crumbs (streusel) instead of the cake batter and bake as a layer for the cheese torte.

MARMOR KAESETORTE
(Marble Cheese Torte)

Ingredients:

For cake batter:

¼	cup	butter
⅓	cup	sugar
1		egg
1	teaspoon	water
½	cup	flour
½	teaspoon	baking powder
⅛	teaspoon	rum extract

For cheese filling:

2	cups	whipping cream
2	envelopes	Knox Unflavored Gelatine
⅓	cup	water
16	ounces	soft cream cheese
1	teaspoon	vanilla extract
3		egg yolks
¾	cup	sugar
2	tablespoons	lemon juice
2	teaspoons	rum extract
1	dash	salt
2	tablespoons	cocoa
1	tablespoon	sugar
1	teaspoon	rum extract
1½	tablespoons	milk

Chocolate Glaze:

¾	cup	confectioners sugar
2½	tablespoons	cocoa
¼	teaspoon	rum extract
1½-2	tablespoons	hot water

245

Directions:

Preheat oven to 350 degrees.
Beat butter, sugar and egg together until creamy.
Add water and rum extract.
Sift together flour and baking powder and stir into batter.
Spread batter into greased and floured 9 inch spring-form pan.
Bake at 350 degrees for 10-12 minutes, or until done.
Cool cake completely in spring-form pan before preparing cheese filling.
Using cool beaters, whip 2 cups of whipping cream until stiff.
Refrigerate whipping cream until ready to use.
Sprinkle Knox Unflavored Gelatine over ⅓ cup of water and set aside.
Cream together cream cheese, vanilla extract, egg yolks, sugar, lemon juice, 2 teaspoons of rum extract and salt.
Heat Knox Unflavored Gelatine to boiling point, stirring constantly.
Quickly stir Knox Unflavored Gelatine into cream cheese filling and mix well.
Fold in whipping cream.
In separate bowl, stir together cocoa with 1 tablespoon of sugar, 1 teaspoon of rum extract and milk.
Stir chocolate mixture into 2 cups of cheese filling and set aside.
Remove cool cake from spring-form pan.
Place cake layer on flat plate.
Place greased ring of spring-form pan around cake.
Spread white cream cheese filling on top of cake layer.
Spoon chocolate cheese filling on top of white cream cheese filling, then lightly fold under with a fork or spoon, and spread filling on top evenly.
Refrigerate for 4 hours or overnight.
Remove ring from spring-form pan.
Prepare chocolate glaze and dribble over top of cheese torte just before serving.

Serves 12 - 14.

QUARK - STREUSELKUCHEN
(Cheese Crumb Cake)

Ingredients:

For Crumbs:

¾	cup	butter
2⅓	cups	flour
⅔	cup	sugar
2	teaspoons	Vanilla Sugar, pg. 262

For Cheese Filling:

⅔	cup	butter
¾	cup	sugar
2	teaspoons	vanilla extract
4		eggs, separated
	dash	salt
		grated lemon peel of 1 large lemon
3	tablespoons	fresh lemon juice
1½	pounds	fat free cottage cheese, small curd
2	tablespoons	sour cream
⅓	cup	golden raisins
¼	cup	semolina
		confectioners sugar

Directions:

Preheat oven to 350 degrees.
To prepare crumbs:
Melt butter.
Combine flour, sugar and vanilla sugar.
Add melted butter and mix until dough turns into crumbs.
Press half of crumbs onto greased bottom and side of spring-form pan
and set aside.

To prepare cheese filling:

Cream butter, sugar, egg yolks, vanilla extract and salt.
Add grated lemon peel and juice, cottage cheese, (see Note) sour cream, raisins and semolina, and mix well.
Beat egg whites and carefully blend into cheese filling.
Spread cheese filling evenly on top of crumbs in spring-form pan.
Top cheese filling with remaining crumbs.
Bake on second shelf at 350 degrees for 70-75 minutes.
Turn off oven and allow cake to cool with oven door ajar.
Use knife to loosen cake on top edge of spring-form pan after cake has cooled off.
Remove side (ring) from spring-form pan and cool cake completely.
Dust with confectioners sugar just before serving.

Serves 8 - 10.

Note: In the United States small curd cottage cheese does not have a fine texture. Therefore, use a food processor to achieve a better texture before mixing cottage cheese with other ingredients. You may want to cover cake during last 15 minutes of baking.

Cheese Crumb Cake, pg. 247

Creams, Garnish, Glazes And Icing

Plus

Marzipan, Spices And Streusel

Please note: When making "Butter Cream", it is very important for butter and pudding to be at the same room temperature. Therefore, it is advisable to take the butter out of the refrigerator in the morning and prepare the pudding about the same time. Stir the pudding occasionally during the day to prevent skin from forming. By afternoon, butter and pudding will be at the same room temperature.

MOKKABUTTERCREME
(Mocha Butter Cream)

Ingredients:

1	box	vanilla pudding 3 oz., (cook & serve)
1⅔	cups	milk
3	tablespoons	sugar
2	teaspoons	instant coffee
1	cup	sweet butter, at room temperature

Directions:

Cook vanilla pudding, using only 1⅔ cups of milk.
While still hot, stir in sugar and instant coffee and set aside.
Cool pudding to room temperature, stirring often to prevent skin from forming.
Cream butter.
Stir 1-2 tablespoons of pudding at a time into butter, and mix well each time.
Continue until all pudding has been thoroughly mixed with butter.
Decorate cool cake.

Note: Leftover butter cream may be used to spread between graham crackers. Cover and refrigerate for dessert later.

MOKKA - SCHOKOLADENBUTTERCREME
(Mocha - Chocolate Butter Cream)

Ingredients:

1	box	chocolate pudding 3 oz. (cook & serve)
1⅔	cups	milk
2	ounces	Baker's semi sweet chocolate squares
1½	teaspoons	instant coffee
3	tablespoons	sugar
1	cup	sweet butter, at room temperature

Directions:

Cook chocolate pudding, using only 1⅔ cups of milk.
While still hot, stir in Baker's semi sweet chocolate squares, instant coffee and sugar, and set aside.
Cool pudding to room temperature, stirring often, to prevent skin from forming.
Cream butter.
Stir 1-2 tablespoons of pudding at a time into butter, and mix well each time.
Continue until all pudding has been thoroughly mixed with butter.
Decorate cool cake.

Note: Warm hands holding decorating material will soften butter cream. All butter cream cakes and/or torte need to be refrigerated. Once you have tested butter cream you will want to use it often, to say the least.

NUSSBUTTERCREME
(Nut Butter Cream)

Ingredients:

1	box	vanilla pudding 3 oz. (cook & serve)
1⅔	cups	milk
2	tablespoons	sugar
3	teaspoons	almond extract
1	cup	sweet butter, at room temperature

Directions:

Cook vanilla pudding, using only 1⅔ cups of milk.
While still hot, stir in sugar, and almond extract.
Cool pudding to room temperature, stirring often so no skin will form.
Cream butter.
Stir 1-2 tablespoons of pudding at a time into butter, and mixing well each time.
Continue until all pudding has been thoroughly mixed with butter.
Decorate cool cake.

RUMBUTTERCREME
(Rum Butter Cream)

Ingredients:

1	box	vanilla pudding 3 oz. (cook & serve)
1⅔	cups	milk
2	tablespoons	sugar
3	teaspoons	rum extract
1	cup	sweet butter, at room temperature

Directions:

Cook vanilla pudding, using only 1⅔ cups of milk.
While still hot, stir in sugar and rum extract, and set aside.
Cool pudding to room temperature, stirring often so no skin will form.
Cream butter.
Stir 1-2 tablespoons of pudding at a time into butter, mixing well each time.
Continue until all pudding has been thoroughly mixed with butter.
Decorate cool cake.

Note: It is important for butter and pudding to be at room temperature. If it varies, the butter will run, and separate from the pudding. It will look like little beads of butter on the cake. If it should happen, slightly warm butter cream, by sitting bowl on top of double boiler containing ONLY warm water, and stirring constantly. DO NOT LET BOWL GET HOT. Remove when butter cream is back to creamy again.

SCHOKOLADENBUTTERCREME
(Chocolate Butter Cream)

Ingredients:

1	box	chocolate pudding 3 oz. (cook & serve)
1⅔	cups	milk
2	tablespoons	sugar
2	ounces	Baker's semi sweet chocolate squares
1	cup	sweet butter, at room temperature

Directions:

Cook chocolate pudding, using only 1⅔ cups of milk.
While still hot, stir in sugar and Baker's semi sweet chocolate squares, and set aside.
Cool pudding to room temperature, stirring often to prevent skin from forming.
Cream butter.
Stir 1-2 tablespoons of pudding at a time into butter, and mix well each time.
Continue until all pudding has been thoroughly mixed with butter.
Decorate cool cake.

VANILLEBUTTERCREME
(Vanilla Butter Cream)

Ingredients:

1	box	vanilla pudding 3 oz. (cook & serve)
1⅔	cups	milk
2	tablespoons	sugar
1	teaspoon	vanilla extract
1	cup	sweet butter, at room temperature

Directions:

Cook vanilla pudding, using only 1⅔ cups of milk.
While still hot, stir in sugar and vanilla extract, and set aside.
Cool pudding to room temperature, stirring often to prevent skin from forming.
Cream butter.
Stir 1-2 tablespoons of pudding at a time into butter, and mix well each time.
Continue until all pudding has been thoroughly mixed with butter.
Decorate cool cake.

EINFACHE ZUCKERGLASUR
(Simple Sugar Glaze)

Ingredients:

1	cup	confectioners sugar
2	tablespoons	milk
1	teaspoon	vanilla or rum extract

Directions:

In small bowl stir together all ingredients.
If glaze is too thin, add a little more sugar.
If glaze is too thick, add a few more drops of milk.
Brush on cookies or pastries.

SCHOKOLADENGLASUR # 1
(Chocolate Glaze # 1)

Ingredients:

1¼	cups	confectioners sugar
3½	ounces	semi sweet chocolate squares
4½	tablespoons	hot water
1	tablespoons	butter

Directions:

Melt semi sweet chocolate squares and butter together in microwave oven.
Add to confectioners sugar.
Stir in enough hot water to make a thick creamy glaze.
If glaze is too thick, add 1-2 drops of hot water at a time to reach the desired consistency.
Use immediately.

SCHOKOLADENGLASUR # 2
(Chocolate Glaze # 2)

Ingredients:

1½	cups	confectioners sugar
⅓	cup	cocoa
2½-3	tablespoons	hot water or milk

Directions:

Sift together confectioners sugar and cocoa.
Stir in 2½ tablespoons of hot water or milk, adding a little more if needed, to reach the desired consistency.

Note: For rum flavoring, omit ¼ to ½ teaspoon of hot liquid and add rum extract instead.

ZUCKERGLASUR FUER KLEINGEBAECK
(Sugar Glaze for Cookies or Sweet Breads)

Ingredients:

2	cups	confectioners sugar
3	tablespoons	hot water
1	teaspoon	butter, melted
¾	teaspoon	vanilla, rum, or lemon extract, optional

Directions:

Stir together all ingredients until smooth.
Brush on cookies or sweet breads.

GEROESTETE HAFERFLOCKEN
(Roasted Oatmeal)

Ingredients:

2	tablespoons	butter or margarine
1	cup	oatmeal, old fashioned
¼	cup	sugar

Directions:

Melt butter or margarine in frying pan.
Add oatmeal, stirring constantly until oatmeal turns light brown.
Add sugar and stir for about 1 minute.
Let cool completely before decorating cake.
Apply roasted oatmeal on top of frosted sides of cake.

Note: If oatmeal sticks together, crumble before decorating cake.

GEROESTETE MANDELN
(Roasted Almonds)

Ingredients:

1	tablespoon	butter or margarine
1	cup	almonds, chopped or slivered
¼	cup	sugar

Directions:

Melt butter or margarine.
Add almonds, stirring constantly until pale brown.
Add sugar and stir for about 1 minute or until sugar is melted.
Let cool completely, then crumble roasted almonds.
Apply roasted almonds on top of frosted sides of cake and/or decorate
to your desire.

LEBKUCHENGEWUERZ
(Gingerbread Spice)

Ingredients:

1½	tablespoons	cinnamon
¼	teaspoon	nutmeg
¼	teaspoon	cardamom
¾	teaspoon	ground anise
¼	teaspoon	ginger
¼	teaspoon	allspice
¼	teaspoon	ground cloves

Directions:

Combine all ingredients and place in air tight container until ready to use for lebkuchen cookies.

ROHMARZIPAN
(Raw Marzipan)

Ingredients:

2	cups	confectioners sugar
1¾	cups	ground blanched almonds
½	teaspoon	vanilla extract, optional
2⅓	tablespoons	water
½	teaspoon	oil

Directions:

Use an electric coffee grinder to pulverize blanched almonds.
Blend together confectioners sugar and ground almonds.
Add vanilla extract optional and water mixed with oil.
Mix and knead until dough-like mixture forms.
Use in cookie recipes or roll out marzipan very thin to cover cakes or pastries.
One may want to form different kinds of fruit, small wreath, etc. with raw marzipan.
Place fruit or other designs on cookie sheet covered with wax paper.
Dry in oven with low heat and door ajar for 15 minutes.

Note: Raw marzipan is actually made with "Rosewater" instead of water and oil as written above. However, "Rosewater" is not as easily available in the United States as it is in Germany in the drug stores and/or pharmacies. For small fruits or other designs one may use a little flavoring such as rum or vanilla extract. In Germany one can find raw marzipan in stores much easier then in the United States.

STREUSEL
(Sugar Crumbs)

Ingredients:

1½	cups	flour
¾	cup	butter
¾	cup	sugar
4	teaspoons	Vanilla Sugar, pg. 262

Directions:

Combine flour, sugar and vanilla sugar.
Add cold butter (cut into small pieces) and mix well.
Work dough with fingers to achieve crumbs.
Sprinkle on top of cake and/or fruit before baking.

Note: One may want to use cinnamon and a dash of nutmeg instead of vanilla sugar.

VANILLE ZUCKER
(Vanilla Sugar)

Ingredients:

2	cups	sugar
4		vanilla beans

Directions:

Cut vanilla beans in half and cut open lengthwise.
Place all 8 pieces in pint jar.
Pour sugar over vanilla beans.
Close pint jar tight for about 8 weeks.
Vanilla sugar will be ready to use after 8 weeks; (use in place of vanilla extract).
Use 4 teaspoons per cake recipe, or use with sugar crumbs and other dry sprinklings on bake goods.

Note: In Germany vanilla sugar is used for all kinds of baking and is available in grocery stores. One small paper pouch contains 2 teaspoons of vanilla sugar, enough for one pound of flour. However, homemade vanilla sugar is somewhat weaker. Therefore, use 4 teaspoons per recipe. One may find vanilla sugar in major grocery stores in the foreign food section.

ZUCKERGUSS
(Sugar Icing)

Ingredients:

1½	cups	confectioners sugar
2½-3	tablespoons	hot water
1	teaspoon	vanilla extract

Directions:

Sift confectioners sugar.
Stir in vanilla extract and 2½ tablespoons of hot water, adding a little more if needed, to reach the desired consistency.
Use immediately.

Note: It is important to add only small amounts of liquid at a time to achieve the desired thickness of icing. Too much liquid, perhaps only a few drops, will make the icing too thin and runny. If icing is too thick, add only a few drops of liquid at a time. To use rum or lemon flavor, omit vanilla extract for desired flavor extract. For coffee flavor, use instant hot coffee instead of water. Even though sugar icing is a little thicker then sugar glaze, one might want to spread a very thin layer of marmalade or jelly on cake before spreading icing to prevent sugar icing from soaking into cake.

Maria Swaringen

Fruit

Desserts

Maria Swaringen

GROSSMUTTERS RUMTOPF
(Grandmas Rum Pot)

Ingredients:

2	cups	strawberries
1	cup	cherries
2	cups	raspberries
1	cup	apricots, pitted and sliced
1	cup	peaches, peeled, pitted and sliced
1	cup	pears, peeled, cored and sliced
1	cup	plums, any kind, pitted and quartered
½	cup	walnuts, chopped, optional
9	cups	sugar
		rum

Directions:

Use a porcelain or an old fashioned crock pot with a tight lid.
Use only fruit without blemishes and fully ripe.
Clean fruit thoroughly.
Start with fresh strawberries and add the same amount of sugar.
Meaning, 2 cups of strawberries with 2 cups of sugar.
Add enough rum to cover fruit and sugar.
Stir fruit mixture before adding next fruit to pot.
Continue adding fruit and sugar.
Add rum if more liquid is needed to cover fruit.
Fruits not suitable for the rum pot are apples, currants, blueberries, blackberries and gooseberries.
Rum pot will be ready about 6 weeks after last fruit has been added.

Note: Is used to top various desserts or ice cream, one or two tablespoons at a time. Can be used as a dessert only, but in small portions. Not suitable for children of any age. Ingredients can be used in smaller portions and not all of the fruit listed has to be used. Beware of ants;. they love the rum pot. Therefore, place the rum pot on a higher shelf, away from the outer walls of the home.

BLAUBEERENKOMPOTT
(Blueberry Compote)

Ingredients:

1	quart	blueberries, washed
½	cup	sugar
1	cup	water

Directions:

Combine all ingredients and bring to boil.
Simmer just long enough for blueberries to soften.
Cool and serve.

Serves 4.

Note: Blueberry compote is very good with dampfnudeln (steamnoodles) and vanilla sauce. Blueberry compote can also be frozen for later use.

ERDBEERKOMPOTT
Strawberry Compote)

Ingredients:

1	quart	strawberries, cleaned
½	cup	sugar
½	cup	water
1	teaspoon	rum or brandy, optional

Directions:

Clean strawberries and rinse thoroughly.
Add sugar and water, and bring to boil.
Simmer just long enough for strawberries to soften.
Cool, add rum or brandy, optional, and serve.

Serves 4.

Note: Prepare compote during the Spring and Summer, freeze in small portions, and use during the winter months for dessert. Serve over sliced pound cake and top with whipping cream or serve with ice cream. Use other fruit to make compote, such as rhubarb, apples, apricots, cherries, raspberries or mixed fruit.

FRUCHT MIT SAHNE
(Fruit 'N' Cream)

Ingredients:

4		peaches, peeled, pitted and sliced
1	cup	Cool Whip

or

4	cups	strawberries, cleaned
1	cup	Cool Whip

or

4	cups	mixed fruit
1	cup	Cool Whip

Directions:

Combine prepared fruit with Cool Whip and serve.

Serves 4 - 6.

Note: These desserts are ideal from the Spring through the Fall season when fruit is plentiful and cheap, and "oh", so good when fresh. One may use whipping cream instead of Cool Whip.

FRUCHTSALAT
(Fruit Salad)

Ingredients:

1		apple, peeled, cored and sliced
2		pears, peeled, cored and sliced
2		bananas, peeled and sliced
3		peaches, peeled and sliced
1	cup	strawberries, cleaned
10		Maraschino cherries
¼	cup	raisins
¼	cup	pecans or walnuts, chopped
½	cup	marmalade or jelly
¼	cup	pear or peach schnapps
		whipping cream or Cool Whip

Directions:

Mix marmalade or jelly with pear or peach schnapps.
Prepare all fruit, raisins and nuts.
Add fruit to marmalade or jelly mixture, and blend well.
Refrigerate for 20-30 minutes.
Serve with whipping cream or Cool Whip.

Serves 4 - 6.

Note: Fruit salad can be made without schnapps. One may also use different fruit. Drained canned fruit may be mixed with fresh fruit.

PFIRSICHKOMPOTT
(Peach Compote)

Ingredients:

2	pounds	peaches, peeled, pitted and sliced
¼	cup	sugar
1½	cups	water
2	teaspoons	lemon juice
1	tablespoon	peach schnapps, optional

Directions:

Combine first 4 ingredients and bring to boil.
Simmer just long enough until peaches are soft and glossy.
Cool and add peach schnapps, optional, just before serving.

Serves 2 - 4.

Note: Compote may be frozen for later use.

ZWETSCHGENKOMPOTT
(Plum Compote)

Ingredients:

2	pounds	damson plums, pitted and cut in quarters
½	cup	sugar
2	cups	water
1	stick	cinnamon
1	teaspoon	rum, optional

Directions:

Combine first 4 ingredients and bring to boil.
Simmer until plums are soft but not mushy.
Remove cinnamon stick and cool.
Add rum, optional, and serve.

Serves 2 - 4.

Note: For this type of dessert, use only damson plums. Plum compote can be served warm or cold.

Fudge

And

Cookies

Maria Swaringen

MARZIPANKUGELN
(Marzipan Balls)

Ingredients:

2	cups	confectioners sugar
1¾	cups	ground blanched almonds
1	teaspoon	rum extract
½	teaspoon	oil
2	tablespoons	warm water
		cinnamon

Directions:

Use a coffee grinder to pulverize blanched almonds.
Blend together sugar and ground almonds.
Add rum extract and water mixed with oil.
Mix and knead until dough-like mixture.
Shape into small balls, about 1 inch in diameter and roll in cinnamon.
Serve along with Christmas cookies.

Makes 2½ dozen marzipan balls.

Note: To create small marzipan potatoes, use a toothpick to make "eyes".

NUTTY FUDGE

Ingredients:

½	cup	margarine
2¼	cups	sugar
1	can	evaporated milk, 5 oz.
1	package	semi-sweet chocolate chips, 12 oz.
1	ounce	semi-sweet chocolate square, coarsely grated
6	ounces	marshmallow cream
½	teaspoon	rum or vanilla extract
½	teaspoon	almond extract
1¼	cups	pecans or walnuts, coarsely chopped

Directions:

Line small baking pan or casserole dish with wax paper and set aside.
In large bowl, combine chocolate chips, coarsely grated chocolate square, marshmallow cream, rum or vanilla extract, almond extract and chopped nuts.
Set aside.
In 3 quart sauce pan, combine margarine, sugar and milk.
Bring to boil and cook slowly, stirring constantly for exactly 10 minutes.
Remove from stove and poor over ingredients in large bowl.
Mix until well blended and all chocolate has melted.
Spread evenly into lined baking pan or casserole dish.
Chill 12-24 hours before cutting.

Makes about 2½ pounds of fudge.

Note: For almond fudge omit rum or vanilla extract, and use 1 teaspoon of almond extract. Use 1¼ cups of ground or chopped slivered almonds instead of pecans or walnuts.

For mocha fudge omit rum and almond extract. Use ½ teaspoon vanilla extract, 2 tablespoons instant coffee and ½ cup of chopped walnuts, instead of 1¼ cups of chopped nuts. Spread into lined baking pan or casserole dish and refrigerate for 1 hour. Cut into squares, then form into small balls. Roll in chocolate flavored decors. Cool for 24 hours before storing.

Makes about 5 dozen mocha fudge balls.

GEFUELLTE SCHNITTEN
(Filled Cookie Slices)

Ingredients:

5½	ounces	semi-sweet chocolate squares
⅔	cup	butter
⅔	cup	sugar
4		eggs
1	tablespoon	Gingerbread Spice, pg. 259
7	tablespoons	corn starch
1	cup	flour
2	teaspoons	baking powder

Filling:

1	cup	marmalade or jelly

Glaze:

1¼	cups	confectionery sugar
1	tablespoon	rum
1½-2	tablespoons	hot water

Directions:

Preheat oven to 325 degrees.
Melt semi-sweet chocolate squares, and set aside.
Cream butter.
Add sugar, eggs, (one at a time) spices, melted semi-sweet chocolate squares, and mix well.
Sift together dry ingredients and stir into batter.
Spread batter onto greased cookie sheet.
Bake at 325 degrees for 25-30 minutes.
Cut cookie cake in half while still warm.

Maria Swaringen

Spread first half with marmalade or jelly.
Place second half on top of first half.
Prepare sugar glaze, and spread on top of second half.
Cut into 1½ inch squares when sugar glaze is dry.

Makes about 4 dozen cookies.

HASELNUSS BROETCHEN
(Hazelnut Cookies)

Ingredients:

2	cups	ground almonds
2	cups	ground hazelnuts
1	pound	confectioners sugar
6		egg whites (x-large eggs)
1	tablespoon	lemon extract
6	ounces	shelled, whole hazelnuts
		wafers 1½ to 2 inches in diameter

Directions:

Preheat oven to 300 degrees.
Beat egg whites until very stiff.
Gradually add confectioners sugar and mix well.
Set aside ¾ cup of egg white mixture to use as glaze for cookies.
Stir into remaining egg white mixture ground almonds, hazelnuts and lemon extract.
Place 1½-2 inches in diameter round wafers on cookie sheet.
Drop small amount of cookie batter on top of each wafer.
Top with small amount of glaze (set aside) and place one whole hazelnut in the middle of each cookie.
Bake at 300 degrees for 30-35 minutes.

Makes 4 dozen cookies.

Note: Wafers used for baking are the same as Churches use for communion, only a little larger. Check at foreign food stores. The are called "Oblaten." If not available, grease cookie sheet lightly and dust with flour.

HASELNUSS HALBMONDE
(Hazelnut Halfmoons)

Ingredients:

¾	cup	butter
⅔	cup	sugar
1	large	egg
2¼	cups	flour
1	cup	ground hazelnuts
1	teaspoon	vanilla extract
½	teaspoon	rum extract
		vanilla flavored confectioners sugar

Directions:

Preheat oven to 325 degrees.
Cream butter and sugar together.
Stir in egg, vanilla and rum extract.
Add flour, ground hazelnuts and knead quickly.
Roll out dough about ⅛ inch thick on generously floured surface.
Cut out half moons with cookie cutter or water glass.
Place onto ungreased cookie sheet.
Bake at 325 degrees for 8-10 minutes.
Remove from cookie sheet while still warm and roll in vanilla flavored confectioners sugar.

Makes 7 - 8 dozen cookies.

Note: To make vanilla flavored confectioners sugar use 4 tablespoons of homemade Vanilla Sugar, (pg. 262), and blend with 1cup of confectioners sugar.

Use same recipe for "Mandel Halbmonde" (Almond Halfmoons) by using ground almonds instead of hazelnuts and almond extract in place of rum extract.

HEIDESAND
(Butter Cookies)

Ingredients:

14	tablespoons	butter, room temperature
⅔	cup	confectioners sugar
2	ounces	raw marzipan
1	teaspoon	vanilla extract
½	teaspoon	lemon extract
2⅛	cups	flour
1		egg yolk and sugar for sugar crust

Directions:

Preheat oven to 350 degrees.
Combine butter, confectioners sugar and raw marzipan and mix well.
Add flour, vanilla and lemon extract, and knead all ingredients together.
Divide dough in half, and make 2 rolls, about 2 inches in diameter.
Cover and refrigerate overnight.
The next day brush rolls with beaten egg yolk mixed with sugar.
Cut rolls into ¼ inch thick slices.
Place onto ungreased cookie sheet and bake at 350 degrees for 12-15 minutes.

Makes 4 dozen cookies.

ISCHLER PLAETZCHEN
(Ischler Cookies)

Ingredients:

10	tablespoons	butter
1¼	cups	flour
⅔	cup	ground slivered almonds
½	cup	sugar
1	dash	salt
¼	teaspoon	lemon extract
		Chocolate Glaze, pgs. 256 and 257
		warm marmalade
		almond halves, peeled

Directions:

Preheat oven to 350 degrees.
Combine and knead first 6 ingredients together.
Refrigerate to cool dough.
Roll out dough on floured surface, about ⅛ inch thick.
Cut out cookies with a star-shaped cookie cutter.
Place on greased cookie sheet and bake at 350 degrees for 8-10 minutes.
Spread warm marmalade between two cookies.
Brush cookies with chocolate glaze and top with a peeled almond half.

Makes 2 dozen cookies.

KOKOS - RINGE
(Coconut Rings)

Ingredients:

1⅓	cups	flour
⅔	cup	butter
1¼	cups	confectioners sugar
1		egg
5½	ounces	shredded coconut
2	teaspoons	Vanilla Sugar, pg. 262
		lemon flavored Sugar Glaze, pg. 257

Directions:

Preheat oven to 350 degrees.
Sift flour, confectioners sugar and vanilla sugar together onto pastry board.
Add egg, sliced butter and shredded coconut.
Mix and knead dough well, then refrigerate to cool.
On floured surface, roll out dough about ⅛ inch thick.
Use a doughnut shape cookie cutter to cut out circles.
Place on cookie sheet and bake at 350 degrees for 8-10 minutes.
Brush cookies with lemon flavored sugar glaze.

Makes 5½ dozen cookies.

KOKOSWUERFELN
(Coconut Squares)

Ingredients:

2¼	cups	butter
7		eggs
1¾	cups	sugar
4¼	cups	flour
1	teaspoon	baking powder
3	tablespoons	cocoa

Sugar Glaze:

6	tablespoons	shortening
9	tablespoons	hot water
4¼	cups	confectioners sugar
1	teaspoon	rum extract
12	ounces	shredded coconut (see Note)

Directions:

Preheat oven to 350 degrees.
Cream together butter, sugar and eggs.
Add dry ingredients and mix well.
Spread batter into greased 10 x 15 inch baking pan and bake at 350 degrees for 20-25 minutes.
Cut cake into 1 inch squares when completely cool.
Dip squares into sugar glaze, then roll in shredded coconut.
Let coconut squares dry completely before storing.

To make glaze for coconut squares:

Melt shortening in hot water.
Stir into confectioners sugar and rum extract.

Makes about 12 dozens cookies.

Note: While regular shredded coconut is OK to use, one should really get a finer texture; perhaps use an electric coffee grinder to do so. If regular shredded coconut is used, be prepared to use a lot more and coconut squares will not look as nice. I have tried both and favor a finer texture of coconut.

Almond Rings, pg. 288

KOSUTHKIPFERL
(Kosuth Cookies)

Ingredients:

2½	cups	sugar
1⅛	cups	margarine
8		eggs
2½	cups	flour
½	teaspoon	baking powder
5	ounces	ground nuts, almonds or hazelnuts

Directions:

Preheat oven to 325 degrees.
Cream together margarine and 1½ cups of sugar.
Add four whole eggs, one at a time, and beat well.
Add four egg yolks, one at a time (setting aside egg whites), and beat well.
Combine flour and baking powder and stir into cookie batter.
Spread cookie batter onto greased and floured cookie sheet.
Bake at 325 degrees for 25-30 minutes or until done.
Meanwhile, beat egg whites until stiff.
Slowly blend ground nuts and remaining sugar into stiffly beaten egg whites.
Spread on top of warm sheet cake.
Place sheet cake on top oven shelf, and bake at 325 degrees for 8-10 minutes.
Use a round cookie cutter or wine glass to cut out narrow half moon shape cookies called "Kipferl".

Makes 3 - 4 dozen cookies.

LEBKUCHEN PLAETZCHEN
(Gingerbread Cookies)

Ingredients:

3	tablespoons	butter, softened
¾	cup	sugar
2		eggs
4	teaspoons	Gingerbread Spice, pg. 259
½	teaspoon	grated lemon rind
1	cup	candied fruit, chopped
1⅔	cups	ground hazelnuts
¾	cup	milk
2	cups	flour
1	teaspoon	baking powder
1	teaspoon	baking soda
		Sugar Glaze, pg. 257 (rum or lemon)

Directions:

Preheat oven to 350 degrees.
Combine butter, sugar and eggs, and beat until creamy.
Stir in gingerbread spice, lemon rind, candied fruit and hazelnuts.
Combine flour, baking powder and baking soda, and stir into batter, alternating with milk.
Drop dough from spoon onto greased and generously floured cookie sheet.
Use floured spoon or fork to flatten each cookie dough to about ½ inch or less thickness.
Bake at 350 degrees for 15 minutes or until done.
Brush lebkuchen cookies with lemon, or rum flavored sugar glaze while still warm.

Makes about 4 dozen cookies.

Note: Lebkuchen dough can be spooned onto 2½ inch diameter wafers, available in foreign food stores called "Oblaten". Do not grease cookie sheet if "Oblaten" are used.

MANDELRINGE
(Almond Rings)

Ingredients:

1	cup	butter
2	cups	flour
1¾	cups	ground blanched almonds
1	cup	sugar
6		egg yolks
½	teaspoon	almond extract
1		egg yolk, beaten to brush unbaked cookies
⅓	cup	blanched almonds, ground or chopped fine
1	cup	peach jam, mixed with 2 teaspoons of rum extract to use as marmalade spread.

Directions:

Preheat oven to 350 degrees.
Combine flour, ground almonds and sugar, and make a small well in the middle.
Add 6 egg yolks and almond extract to the well.
Slice butter on top, then knead together quickly.
Roll out dough about ⅛ inch thick on generously floured surface.
With doughnut shaped cookie cutter, cut out circles and place onto greased and floured cookie sheet.
Brush top of unbaked cookies with beaten egg yolk and sprinkle with ground or chopped almonds.
Bake at 350 degrees for 10-12 minutes or until done.
While cookies are still warm, spread bottom of each cookie with marmalade, then press two cookies together.

Makes 3 dozen cookies.

Note: Add a small amount of water to beaten egg yolk; it will be easier to brush unbaked cookies with. Cookies can be frozen for later use. See recipes, pgs. 294, 296 and 306 to use up egg whites.

MANDELPLAETZCHEN
(Almond Cookies)

Ingredients:

1	cup	butter
⅞	cup	sugar
8	ounces	ground blanched almonds
1	teaspoon	vanilla extract
1	large	egg
4	cups	flour
		Sugar Glaze, pg. 257 optional

Directions:

Preheat oven to 350 degrees. (next day)
Cream butter and sugar until fluffy.
Add egg, vanilla extract, ground blanched almonds, and mix well.
Add flour, one cup at a time and knead cookie dough on floured surface.
Divide in half and make 2 rolls, about 2 inches thick in diameter.
Cover and refrigerate overnight.
The next day, cut rolls into ¼ inch thick slices.
Place on greased cookie sheet.
Bake at 350 degrees for 12-15 minutes or until done.
Brush with sugar glaze, optional.

Makes 4½ dozen cookies.

Note: Cookies can be baked long before the holidays and frozen. Hard cookies can be softened by adding a slice of bread to cookies in air-tight container a few days before using cookies.

Maria Swaringen

MOKKA - NUSSKUGELN
(Mocha - Nut Balls)

Ingredients:

1	cup	soft butter
¾	cup	sugar
2	teaspoons	vanilla extract
2	teaspoons	instant coffee
⅓	cup	cocoa
1¾	cups	flour
1	dash	salt
2	cups	finely chopped nuts (pecans or almonds)
		confectioners sugar

Directions:

Preheat oven to 325 degrees.
Combine and mix first 8 ingredients.
Knead into a soft dough.
Form 1 inch balls.
Bake at 325 degrees for 15 minutes.
Roll in confectioners sugar.

Makes 4 ½ dozen mocha-nut balls.

ORANGENZUNGEN
(Orange Strips)

Ingredients:

14	tablespoons	butter
½	cup	sugar
4		egg yolks
4	ounces	raw marzipan
		juice of ½ orange
2⅓	cups	flour
		marmalade
		Chocolate Glaze, pgs. 256 and 257

Directions:

Preheat oven to 325 degrees.
Thoroughly cream butter, sugar and egg yolks together.
Stir raw marzipan and orange juice together and add to creamy batter.
Add flour and mix well.
With a cookie press, place 2 inch strips onto greased and floured cookie sheet.
Bake at 325 degrees for 8-10 minutes.
Spread marmalade between two cookies, then dip half of cookie into chocolate glaze and let dry before storing.

Makes 3 - 4 dozen cookies.

PFEFFERNUESSE
(Spicy Christmas Cookies)

Ingredients:

2		eggs
1	cup	sugar
2	cups	flour
2	teaspoons	baking powder
1	tablespoon	rum extract
⅓	cup	candied fruit, chopped very fine
		grated rind of ½ lemon
1½	teaspoons	cinnamon
½	teaspoon	fresh ground ginger
⅛	teaspoon	cardamom
⅛	teaspoon	nutmeg
⅛	teaspoon	ground cloves
¼	teaspoon	allspice
3	tablespoons	milk
		Sugar Glaze, pg. 257

Directions:

Preheat oven to 325 degrees.
Beat eggs until lemon colored.
Gradually add sugar and beat thoroughly until thick and creamy.
Add rum extract, grated lemon rind, fresh ginger and candied fruit.
Sift together flour, baking powder and dry spices.
Stir dry ingredients and milk into batter, then knead well.
If dough is sticky add a small amount of flour.
Chill for 1 hour.
Roll out about ½ inch thick on floured surface.
Cut out cookies with a small round cookie cutter, about 1 inch in diameter.
Place on greased cookie sheet, and bake at 325 degrees for 8-10 minutes.
Prepare sugar glaze and glaze pfeffernuesse while still hot.

Makes about 7 - 8 dozen cookies

Note: A narrow glass or bottle top can be used for a cookie cutter. Cool cookies completely before storing in air-tight container. These cookies need to be stored about 2-3 weeks to bring out the flavor and to soften. To soften cookies faster, add a slice of bread to air-tight container about 48 hours prior serving cookies.

RUMKUGELN
(Rum Balls)

Ingredients:

2½	cups	ground Sunshine Chocolate Grahams
2	teaspoons	cocoa
2¼	cups	ground almonds
3	tablespoons	light syrup
½	cup	rum
1	cup	confectioners sugar

Directions:

Combine first 5 ingredients and mix well.
Form into 1 inch balls.
Roll balls in confectioners sugar.

Makes 4 dozen rum balls.

Note: One may use diluted pancake syrup instead of light syrup.

SCHOKOLADEN BAISER
(Chocolate Chip Meringue Cookies)

Ingredients:

6		egg whites
1½	cups	sugar
¾	cup	chocolate chips
1	teaspoon	rum extract

Directions:

Preheat oven to 200 degrees.
Beat egg whites until very stiff.
Add rum extract.
Slowly blend sugar into stiff egg whites.
Stir in chocolate chips.
Using a teaspoon, drop cookie batter (about 1½-2 inches in diameter) onto greased and floured cookie sheet.
Bake at 200 degrees for 90-120 minutes.

Makes 4 - 5 dozen meringue cookies.

Note: For holiday cookies, add a little color such as red or green to cookie batter or sprinkle with mixed decors, chocolate shavings, etc.

SCHOKOLADEN - NUESSE
(Chocolate Nuts)

Ingredients:

7	tablespoons	shortening
1	cup	confectioners sugar
4½	ounces	unsweetened Baker's chocolate squares
1¾	cups	ground slivered almonds

Directions:

Preheat oven to 275 degrees.
Melt shortening and unsweetened Baker's chocolate together.
Add confectioners sugar, ground almonds, and mix well.
Refrigerate overnight.
Form 1 inch balls and place on cookie sheet.
Bake in pre-heated oven at 275 degrees for 30-35 minutes.

Makes 2 dozen chocolate nuts.

Note: Chocolate nuts will still be wet on top when done. Use a spatula to carefully transfer cookies onto a plate. Refrigerate for a few hours before storing. It is the chocolate and shortening that keeps the cookies wet while hot.

Maria Swaringen

SCHOKOLADEN - NUSS BAISER
(Chocolate Nut Meringue Cookies)

Ingredients:

3		egg whites
1	cup	sugar
½	teaspoon	vanilla extract
½	teaspoon	rum extract
½	cup	grated semi sweet chocolate
1	cup	chopped nuts

Directions:

Preheat oven to 250 degrees.
Beat egg whites until very stiff.
Slowly add sugar, vanilla and rum extract.
Fold in grated semi sweet chocolate and chopped almonds.
Using a teaspoon, drop cookie batter (about 2 ½ inches in diameter) onto greased and floured cookie sheet.
Bake at 250 degrees for 25-35 minutes.

Makes 2 - 3 dozen chocolate nut meringue cookies.

Note: If available, use vanilla sugar instead of vanilla extract.

SPITZBUBEN
(Marmalade Rascals)

Ingredients:

6	cups	flour
1⅓	cups	margarine
¾	cup	butter
1¾	cups	sugar
2	teaspoons	vanilla extract
2	teaspoons	baking powder
2		eggs
1		egg yolk
1¼	cups	ground hazelnuts
12	ounces	marmalade (plum, peach or raspberry)

Directions:

Preheat oven to 300 degrees.

Sift flour and baking powder together onto pastry board.

Form a small well in the center and add sugar, vanilla extract, eggs and egg yolk.

Stir ingredients in well, and mix in half of flour.

Add cold butter and margarine (cut into small pieces) and ground hazelnuts.

Cover with remaining flour and knead together well.

If dough is sticky chill for a little while.

Roll out dough onto floured surface about ⅛ inch thick.

Use either 2 or 3 round cookie cutters (1, 1½ and 2 inch in diameter), or use a 2 inch round cookie cutter and a 2 inch doughnut cutter to cut out cookies.

Place on ungreased cookie sheet, and bake at 300 degrees for 10-12 minutes.

While still warm spread cookies with marmalade and press 2 or 3 cookies together.

Makes 4½ - 5 dozen cookies.

SPRINGERLE
(Anise Cookies)

Ingredients:

2		eggs
2	cups	confectioners sugar
½	teaspoon	anise extract
2	cups	flour
¼	teaspoon	vanilla extract
½	teaspoon	baking powder
		ground anise seeds

Directions:

Preheat oven to 300 degrees.
Beat eggs until light and lemon colored.
Gradually add confectioners sugar, anise extract and vanilla extract.
Continue beating until batter is thick and creamy.
Sift together flour and baking powder, and fold into batter.
If dough is sticky add a little more flour.
Roll out about ¼ inch thick on floured surface.
Dust springerle rolling pin or mold with flour.
Press firmly to make clear design.
Cut cookies apart along imprint line.
Place cookies on greased and sprinkled with ground anise seeds cookie sheet.
Let stand overnight or at least 12 hours at room temperature to dry.
Bake at 300 degrees for 20-25 minutes, or until done.

Makes 3 - 4 dozen cookies.

Note: Cookies should have a light straw color when done. Should be kept in air tight container for 1-2 weeks for best flavor. To soften cookies place a slice of bread in air tight container for 1-2 days before serving.

SPRITZGEBAECK
(Spritz Cookies)

Ingredients:

1	cup	butter
1	cup	sugar
2		eggs
1	teaspoon	vanilla extract
½	teaspoon	rum extract
4	cups	flour
1	dash	salt
1	teaspoon	baking powder
		colored sugar

Directions:

Preheat oven to 375 degrees.
Thoroughly cream butter and sugar.
Add eggs, vanilla and rum extract, and beat well.
Sift together flour, salt and baking powder.
Gradually add flour to batter and mix until dough is smooth.
Press dough through cookie press onto ungreased cookie sheet.
Sprinkle with colored sugar.
Bake at 375 degrees for 8-10 minutes.

Makes 4 dozen cookies.

Note: Instead of colored sugar, brush or dip cookies with chocolate glaze, pgs. 256 and 257 after baking.

VANILLE - MONDE
(Vanilla Moons)

Ingredients:

1¾	cups	flour
⅔	cup	butter
¼	cup	sugar
¾	cup	ground slivered almonds
4	tablespoons	Vanilla Sugar, pg. 262
		confectioners sugar

Directions:

Preheat oven to 350 degrees.
Combine first 4 ingredients, mix and knead together.
Cool dough in refrigerator.
Roll out dough about ⅛ inch thick on floured surface and using a water glass or round cookie cutter, cut out half moons.
Place on greased cookie sheet and bake at 350 degrees for 8-10 minutes.
Blend together vanilla sugar and confectioners sugar.
Roll vanilla moons in sugar while still warm.

Makes 4 dozen cookies.

Note: Cookies should look light yellow when done. Roll with care, for cookies break easy. In Germany, one can buy vanilla sugar in small paper pouches which is used for all the baking. One paper pouch of vanilla sugar is equivalent to one teaspoon of vanilla extract. In the United States some major grocery stores carry vanilla sugar in their foreign food section. However, one can make their own vanilla sugar; see recipe on page. Use 2 pouches, or 4 teaspoons of homemade vanilla sugar and mix with 1 cup of confectioners sugar, to achieve vanilla flavored confectioners sugar.

WALNUSSPLAETZCHEN
(Walnut Cookies)

Ingredients:

14	tablespoons	butter, room temperature
¾	cup	sugar
2	tablespoons	rum
1	cup	ground walnuts
2¼	cups	flour
1	dash	salt
		warm marmalade
		Sugar Glaze, pg. 257 (rum flavored)
		walnut halves

Directions:

Preheat oven to 350 degrees.
Combine flour, sugar and salt.
Add butter, rum and walnuts, and knead well.
Place in refrigerator to chill.
Remove small amounts of dough at a time to roll out about ⅛ inch thick on floured surface.
Use cookie cutters to cut out cookies.
Place onto greased cookie sheet and bake at 350 degrees for 8-10 minutes.
Spread marmalade between two cookies while still warm.
Glaze cookies with rum flavored sugar glaze and top with walnut halves.

Makes 2½ dozen cookies.

WEIHNACHTSPLAETZCHEN
(Christmas Cookies)

Ingredients:

4	cups	flour
1¼	cups	sugar
1½	teaspoons	vanilla extract
1	teaspoon	baking powder
2		eggs
½	cup	margarine
½	cup	butter
3		egg yolks to brush cookies
1½	teaspoons	water or honey
		colored sugar

Directions:

Preheat oven to 325 degrees.
Sift flour and baking powder together onto pastry board.
Add margarine and butter and mix together using a pastry dough-cutter.
Add sugar, vanilla extract and eggs.
Mix and knead dough together well.
Chill for 30 minutes.
Roll out dough about ⅛ inch thick and cut out cookies with holiday cookie cutters.
Place cookies onto ungreased cookie sheet.
Beat egg yolks with water or honey.
Brush unbaked cookies with beaten egg yolks and sprinkle with colored sugar.
Bake at 325 degrees for 8-10 minutes.

Makes 8 dozen cookies.

* Even though I grew up in Germany during World War II and did not have much, the Christmas month or Advent season was always a happy season for all of us children. That was the time when Mother would bake cookies, and we children would be the big helpers. However, my father never cared to see us children baking with Mother; in fact, he always thought it was a waste of time, too much money, and that we didn't need it.

Mother always packed the cookies in a large box, stored it under her bed and out of the way, for not any of us children were allowed in our parents bedroom.

Well one night before Christmas, Mother woke up in the middle of the night and noticed my father was not in bed. So she got up, went to the kitchen and bathroom to look for him. But to no avail and puzzled, she came back to the bedroom when she thought she heard some noise. As Mother was listening for a moment, she realized the noise came from under the bed. Looked under the bed, Mother found my father with the cookie box open, eating the Christmas cookies. Looking back on it all now one might say that my father was "The Grinch who ate the Christmas Cookies".

Christmas Cookies, pgs. 275 to 306

WIENER KIPFERL
(Vienna Cookies)

Ingredients:

2⅛	cups	lour
¾	cup	butter
½	cup	sugar
½	cup	ground slivered almonds
½	cup	confectioners sugar
3	tablespoons	Vanilla Sugar, pg. 262

Directions:

Preheat oven to 350 degrees.
Cream butter and sugar together.
Add flour and ground almonds, and knead all ingredients together.
If dough is sticky, refrigerate for a few hours.
Using a small amount of dough at a time, form small balls, then roll and form little horns.
Place onto greased cookie sheet.
Bake at 350 degrees for 10-12 minutes, or until cookies are light yellow.
Mix confectioners sugar with vanilla sugar.
Roll cookies in sugar while still warm.

Makes 4 - 5 dozen cookies.

ZUCKERBAELLE
(Sugar Balls)

Ingredients:

1	cup	butter, softened
⅔	cup	sugar
2	teaspoons	vanilla extract
½	teaspoon	almond extract
1	tablespoon	water
2	cups	flour
	dash	salt
1	cup	chopped pecans or walnuts
		colored sugar

Directions:

Preheat oven to 300 degrees.
Cream butter, sugar, vanilla and almond extract.
Add water flour, salt and chopped nuts, and mix well.
Shape dough into 1 inch balls and roll in colored sugar.
Place on ungreased cookie sheet.
Bake at 300 degrees for 20-25 minutes, or until done.
Cool before removing from cookie sheet.

Makes 2½ dozen cookies.

ZUCKER - BUSSERL
(Sugar Kisses)

Ingredients:

2		egg whites
⅔	cup	sugar
		juice of ½ lemon
7	ounces	walnut halves

Directions:

Preheat oven to 200 degrees.
Beat egg whites until very stiff.
Gradually add sugar.
Fold in lemon juice and walnut halves.
With 2 teaspoons drop small amount of batter onto greased and floured cookie sheet.
Bake at 200 degrees for 60-90 minutes.

Makes 2 dozen sugar kisses.

Note: Do not let cookies get brown. Low heat should only dry cookies instead of baking. If cookies take longer, depending on the size, use lower heat after 90 minutes.

Some

Canning

BLAUBEEREN
(Blueberries)

Ingredients:

Blueberries

For medium syrup:

3	cups	sugar
4	cups	water

Directions:

Wash blueberries, drain and pack into clean and sterilized jars.
Combine sugar and water in stainless steel pot, and boil for 5 minutes.
Pour hot syrup over blueberries in jars leaving 1 inch headspace.
Adjust hot lids and process in water bath.

Note: Blueberries are very tender and overcook easy. Process in water bath for only 5 minutes. Save leftover syrup, if any in the refrigerator and use up within one week.

HOLUNDERBEERENSAFT
(Elderberry Juice)

See Page 182

FICHTENNADELSAFT
(Spruce Needle Juice)

See Page 181

PAPRIKASCHOTENSOSSE
(Green Pepper Sauce)

See Page 38

PFIRSICHE
(Peaches)

Ingredients:

fresh peaches

For medium syrup:

6	cups	sugar
8	cups	water
4	tablespoons	Fruit-Fresh fruit protector

Directions:

Prepare medium syrup first.
In large 6 quart stainless steel pot combine sugar with water, and boil for 5 minutes.
Add Fruit-Fresh fruit protector and set aside.
Meanwhile, wash, peel, pit and slice peaches.
Reheat syrup to boiling point, then add peaches.
Boil for 8-10 minutes in syrup or until sliced peaches look glossy.
Pack into hot sterilized jars leaving ½ inch headspace and adjust boiling hot lids.
Will seal without processing.

Note: In the past 20 years of canning peaches, I have never had an unsealed jar or bad peaches, doing it this way. I sterilize my jars in the dishwasher, and make sure my countertops, sinks and utensils are very clean. I boil my lids before using. By using this method of canning peaches, one will have a whole jar full of peaches instead of only a half jar after processing. Do not discard leftover syrup. By using more liquid as directed on Sure Jell box, one can make pancake syrup and can for later use.

RHABARBERSAFT
(Rhubarb Juice)

See Page 185

SALSA

See Page 35

SPAGHETTISOSSE
(Spaghetti Sauce)

See Page 39

TOMATEN
(Tomatoes)

Ingredients:

30-40	medium	tomatoes
7	teaspoons	fresh lemon juice
3½	teaspoons	salt

Directions:

Wash tomatoes and cut out spoiled areas, if any.
Dip tomatoes shortly into boiling hot water, then place in cold water.
Peel and cut out stem ends and cores, if present.
Quarter and/or slice peeled tomatoes into large stainless steel pot.
Bring to a boil, then simmer for about 8-10 minutes, stirring often.
Pack tomatoes and liquid into hot sterilized quart jars.
Add to each quart 1 teaspoon of lemon juice and ½ teaspoon of salt.
Adjust hot lids and process in water bath about 5 minutes.

Makes 6 - 7 quarts.

Note: Always use a stainless steel pot when canning. I cook tomatoes completely before packing in jars. Quarter small tomatoes and slice large tomatoes. This method has never failed me in 20 years. Needless to say, jars, lids and utensils are sterilized before using.

TOMATENSAFT
(Tomato Juice)

Ingredients:

30	medium	tomatoes
2	tablespoons	fresh lemon juice
		salt

Directions:

Wash tomatoes and cut out spoiled areas, if any.
Cut out stem ends and cores, if present and quarter tomatoes.
Press uncooked tomatoes through Squeezo Press.
Heat tomato juice to boiling point in large stainless steel pot.
Add lemon juice.
Pour boiling hot tomato juice into hot sterilized quart jars and add a
½ teaspoon of salt to each quart.
Adjust hot lids and process in water bath for 5 minutes.

Makes about 5 quarts.

Note: If Squeezo Press is not available, tomatoes should be cooked first and then pressed through a sieve to extract the juice.

Maria Swaringen

Plus:

KITCHEN IDEAS.

MUNICH OCTOBERFEST.

FASCHING (MARDI GRAS).

LITTLE KNOWN FACTS OF GERMANY.

GROWING UP IN GERMANY DURING AND RIGHT AFTER
WORLD WAR II.

KITCHEN IDEAS

* Add a little oil when cooking pasta, so it won't stick.

* To remove bitterness from endive lettuce, soak chopped lettuce in warm water for a few minutes, then soak in cold water to restore crispness.

* To make easy beef broth or stock, cook meat scraps and/or bones with seasoning. Add onion and onion skin for color, parsley, celery and carrot. Cook for one hour, drain and store in refrigerator.

* Save vegetable water to make soup or broth or add to recipe instead of plain water.

* Freeze broth or vegetable water in ice trays and use as needed.

* Chill cheese to grate it more easily.

* Camembert cheese spread can also be used as a dip.

* The eggs and flour in dumplings will bind. If dumpling dough is too thick, add an extra egg. If the dough is too soft, add a little extra flour.

* Use wet hands when forming dumplings to prevent dough from being sticky.

* Use only use a well known brand of butter for butter cream. Try using whipped sweet butter, available in most supermarkets.

* A leaf of lettuce dropped into the pot absorbs the grease from the top of the soup. Remove the lettuce as soon as it has served its purpose.

* To prevent splashing when frying meat, sprinkle a little salt into the pan before adding the oil or shortening.

* Rinse a pan with cold water before scalding milk to prevent sticking.

* A cake is done when it shrinks slightly from the sides of the pan or if it springs back when touched lightly with finger.

* To make American dumplings in a hurry, try using a roll of biscuits; cut each biscuit into quarters and cook to your desire.

* Potatoes soaked in salt water for 20 minutes before baking will bake faster.

* Add a little milk to water in which cauliflower is cooked, and cauliflower will remain attractively white.

* To keep egg yolks from crumbling when slicing hard-boiled eggs, wet knife before each cut.

* If the juice from apples ran over in the oven, shake some salt on it. It will cause the juice to burn to a crisp so it can be removed.

* A large roast can be carved much more easily after it stands for about thirty minutes.

* Keep a toothbrush around the sink; one will find it useful in cleaning rotary beaters, grates, choppers and other kitchen utensils.

* Baking powder will remove tea or coffee stains from china pots or cups.

* Canned cream soups make excellent sauces and/or gravies for vegetables, fish, meats, etc., such as: celery with lobster, onion with cauliflower, mushroom, chicken, and/or celery with pork, beef and poultry.

*   Hard boiled eggs will peel easily when cracked and placed in cold water immediately after removing from hot water.

*   To keep icings moist and to prevent cracking, add a pinch of baking soda to the icing.

THE MUNICH OCTOBERFEST

Munich, the capital of Bavaria, perhaps best known throughout the world for it's Octoberfest.

One might ask, what does the Octoberfest has to do with Munich? Well, the location of the Octoberfest is at the Theresienwiese, a meadow named after Princess Therese of Sachsen-Hildburghausen. Back in October 1810, Crown-Prince Ludwig, later King Ludwig I of Bavaria, married Princess Therese, and the celebration was held at the meadow. The celebration in the presence of the Royal Family ended with a horse race for all of Bavaria called the "Fest", and from then on became an annual festival called the "Octoberfest".

Each year the Octoberfest starts on the third Saturday of September at 12:00 P.M. and lasts for sixteen days. It begins with a parade at 11:00 A.M. marching to the Octoberfest led by the "Munich Kindl" riding a horse, followed by the Mayor riding in a carriage. A dozen or so brass bands, the various brewers with their beautiful horses pulling the beer wagons along with the waitresses, and the landlords with their families in decorated carriages, waving to the crowds.

Upon arriving at the Theresienwiese, the Mayor of Munich broaches the first barrel of beer, meaning "O'zapft is", which is the beginning of the festival.

The Octoberfest, celebrated on 64 acres of the 103 acres of the Theresienwiese is the largest festival in the world and known throughout the world. For sixteen days, the roller-coasters and Ferris wheel are spinning along with so many other rides for young and old. The souvenir and game booths are plenty, not to mention the aroma of roasted nuts and so many different kinds of foods, plus the chocolate and gingerbread hearts for every sweetheart one knows.

Millions of people, German and foreigners alike, visit the Octoberfest every year with it's main attraction, the large and most beautifully decorated beer tents. It is believed that within more than a dozen or so massive beer tents the total seating is estimated to over 95,000, the largest tent of all, being the Hofbraeuhaus with 10,000 seats. During my last visit in 1998, I learned that the cost of setting up one large beer tent at that time was estimated at 1.7 million DM or about $900,000.00.

Everyone who walks the fairground will eventually end up in the beer tents, if not for drinking and eating so much, but to see and enjoy the brass bands as well as watching the drinking, singing and merriment of the people. The Bavarians as well as foreigners relish their beer, and millions of liters of beer are downed at the Octoberfest, or so-called Wies'n as the citizen's call it. The amount of food eaten, such as chicken, duck, sausages, roast beef, salt fish, sauerkraut, cheese and pretzel's is enormous, and may just match the intake of beer. One of the main attractions is the bull roast, located in the "Spatenbraeu" beer tent. There, the serving of roast beef is almost like a conveyor belt atmosphere, with waitresses standing in line for their orders to be filled.

Another attraction during the Octoberfest consists of a second parade on the first Sunday, lasting about 2½ hours. People in festive and historic peasant costumes and rifle clubs from various parts of Germany and European countries, such as Belgium, France, Switzerland, Austria, Spain and Italy, to name just a few, participate in the 4.5 mile procession through Munich to the Octoberfest with over a 1000 musicians and dozens of decorated floats and wagons pulled by beautiful horses. The first Sunday ends with a beautiful fireworks display.

On the second Sunday, all the musicians from the beer tents (about 400) meet on the steps at the foot of the Bavaria (bronze statue), presenting a concert during the late morning hours.

Finally, the Octoberfest ends with the firing of small cannons called "Boellerschiessen", from the steps of the Bavaria (bronze statue), saluting once more the visitors of the Octoberfest.

Every year thousands of beer steins are lost to the breweries as visitors take them home for souvenirs, and an estimated 150,000 plus beer steins are apprehended from visitors by Octoberfest grounds police. Prior records indicate that over 6 million people visit the Octoberfest every year. Well over 5 million liters of beer are downed. An average of 85 to 90 bulls are roasted and consumed at the Spatenbraeu beer tent. Over 650,000 roasted chickens, and over 200,000 pairs of bratwurst (pork sausage) are consumed, not to mention wine, champagne, coffee and tea, water, lemonade, fish, pork knuckles, duck, etc.

The Octoberfest has its own Post Office on the fairground for millions of people to mail funny and crazy postcards, purchased at the fairground souvenir booths, and beer tents.

As of 2002, the Octoberfest will be celebrated for the 169th time since the beginning of the year 1810. Missing are the 24 years due to war's and the years right after, and widespread epidemics.

Needless to say, every time I go home to Germany during the Fall season, I visit the Octoberfest; not for the drinking, but for the fun and atmosphere. You too need to see and enjoy the Octoberfest, should you take your vacation in Germany during that time.

Maria Swaringen

FASCHING
(Mardi Gras)

Fasching or so-called Mardi Gras in the U.S.(New Orleans) is a great opportunity for merriment throughout Germany. It is known and celebrated also in other European Countries. It dates back as far as to the years of 1500. I believe it originated during the middle ages with the confession of sins before Ash Wednesday as a preparation for Lent and the upcoming fasting during the event. It was a merrymaking event before Lent with special food such as pancakes. The popularity of this dish on Shrove Tuesday (fetter Dienstag) was originally intended for a practical reason. It served to use up eggs and fat, which were prohibited foods during Lent.

The planning of Fasching begins every year on the 11th month of the year, the 11th day, hour, minute and second preceding the onset of the event. During the time of planning, a Carnival Prince and Princess is elected to take part in the various festivities and duties during this crazy merrymaking event.

Every region throughout Germany celebrates Fasching somewhat different. A new song is added every year to the collection of wonderful carnival songs and music mostly heard throughout the weeks and months of this merrymaking event. Fasching is also known for a lot of comedy, especially in the Rheinland region. People dressed up in costumes, stand before a large audience and tell wild and funny stories and/or jokes about other people, whether they are politicians, business people or anyone else. These comedies are called "Buettenreden" and can last all evening for hours and hours.

In Munich the celebration begins on January the 7th and continues on until midnight on Shrove Tuesday, the day before Ash Wednesday. During that time there are many Costume Balls (Masken Baelle) and in some of them one cannot participate in the festivity unless one wears some type of costume. The parties often extend to the early morning hours. During my time living in Germany it was not unusual for me to meet someone in the morning going home from a party while on my way to work. It was also not unusual to miss a night of sleep during Fasching. Those were the times of dancing away the nights with waltzes and polkas, along with swaying back and fourth amidst the confetti and streamers.

In the larger Costume Balls the Carnival Prince and Princess would honor the festivities with their subjects. A brass band and the Court Jester leading the group would march to the dance floor to dance away the night.

The main sights and festivities start to take place on the Sunday before Lent with big parades and parties everywhere. Rose Monday Rosenmontag) is a big party day too, and Shrove Tuesday (Fasching Dienstag), the last day of this crazy and merrymaking time, is celebrated with parties everywhere. Children and many adults alike wear costumes all day. Confetti and streamers are everywhere on the streets. During my younger days, I remember it was not uncommon for these crazy people to move and hide a car from any main street in Munich or to fill up a car with confetti if a window was conveniently open. Fasching is full of fun, craziness and pranks.

And so, Fasching ends on Shrove Tuesday at midnight with a make-believe burial of the Prince (in some places), empty wallets, good and funny memories, and pranks people will talk about for months to come.

LITTLE KNOWN FACTS OF GERMANY

Bavaria, a free State, called "Frei Staat Bayern", is known for the great hospitality it shows to all people regardless from which corner of the earth one comes. It is a region with beautiful lakes and mountains, and let's not forget the splendor of castles and churches dating back hundreds of years.

While the colors of the Bavarian flag are blue and white, the colors of the German flag consist of three horizontal equal size stripes. Black represents sorrow of the past, wars, plagues, etc.; red represents blood shed for the freedom of the country; and gold serves as a reminder of the good times of the past, present and future. It also stands for hope, anticipation, yearning, desire, etc.

Bavarians are known for showing an atmosphere of warmth and fellowship, called "Gemuetlichkeit". But they are also known to say what they think and it is sometimes misunderstood. The dialect is quite different from the written German. One learns the written German in School, then goes home and speaks the dialect. It is not uncommon to travel 5 miles and find a completely different dialect. Some words in the various dialects throughout Germany have different meanings and can be misunderstood, to say the least.

While Germany has three meals a day like the United States, it is a little different. Breakfast is usually like a continental breakfast. The main meal (dinner) is at noon, while a lighter meal is served in the evening. However, one may receive a dinner in the evening at any restaurant. Workers have two breaks during the day called "Brotzeit". Men working outdoors usually drink beer with their sandwich and so do many women, for the southern part of Germany is beer country. German people take great pride serving coffee with delicious pastry, and/or cake to their family, friends and guest's, etc., usually Sunday afternoon and/or on holidays. Pastry shops are open all day on Sunday for anyone to purchase the needed dessert for the afternoon coffee. It is not uncommon to visit a Cafe on a Sunday afternoon for coffee and cake. It is a rather nice treat, and not too expensive.

A restaurant in Germany can be called a "Restaurant," but one can also find the name "Gasthof", "Gaststaette", "Gasthaus" or "Wirtschaft". Sometimes a name or title is added, such as "Gasthaus Weber"(name) or "Gasthof zum Goldenen Krug" (title), meaning "Restaurant to the golden Pitcher" It also stands for "Public House" or "Tavern".

Bavarian beer, dating back to the 1400's is protected by law since 1516. Only the purest grains such as barley and/or wheat, yeast and hops (depending upon for which beer it will be used) is to be utilized as its ingredients.

One type of popular beer is called "Weizenbier" or "Weissbier", (wheat beer). The largest and completely computerized brewery called "Erdinger Weissbraeu" is in my hometown. This brewery provides tours every day to walk through the large fascinating complex with a small complimentary luncheon afterwards. People from all over the world visit this brewery. However, reservations have to be made about two months prior to a visit.

Among other beer's are regular "dark beer" and "light beer". Then there is the "Malzbier", a dark malt beer with a lower alcohol content. This beer is actually served to some patients in hospitals. Higher alcohol content beer's are "Maerzenbier" and the "Maibock". Maerzenbier comes in light and dark, and is brewed for Spring consumption. The "Maibock" is available only in the month of May.

All the hops are grown in the southern part of Bavaria for beer-making, while in the somewhat northwestern region of Germany, all grapes are grown and it is known as the wine country.

Summer School vacations are only six weeks and are at intervals with various regions. This is due to travel on the already overcrowded autobahn. By having summer school vacation at intervals, not all families travel at the same time and therefore have a safer and more enjoyable vacation.

The climate in Germany is very similar to some parts of the United States. The leaves will turn color sooner in the alpine regions and the cold weather will set in earlier due to the earlier snow on the mountain tops.

As for driving in Germany, there is a speed limit in cities, towns and surrounding roads, but not on the autobahn. The speed on the autobahn can be very frightening, yet they say the autobahn is the safest road in Germany. Trucks are not allowed to pass cars when climbing a steep hill on the autobahn and must stay in the right lane. Car inspections are much stricter than in the United States. The cost of gasoline is much higher in Germany then in the United States. While visiting my home in Germany in the Fall of 1998, the cost of one gallon of gas was $6.50, but to drive a car in Germany is really not as expensive as it sounds. German cars use a lot less gas then ours do. When traveling on the autobahn and then stopping for gas and something to eat, one may find a few other pleasant surprises. While there are usually large parking areas, one may find a few parking spaces close to the restaurant with a sign "for women only". This is for the protection of women. Outside a restaurant, one may find two small bowls with food and water for pets.

Germany is small compared to the United States with not much land left for building upon. The cost of land and/or homes are almost unbelievable. It is not uncommon to pay for a Townhouse with a small grass area, a quarter million dollars or more. Most people pay that much just for a quarter acre or less of land. All prices are very high in Germany. I used to buy my clothes in Germany during visits for they are of better quality, but now my purchasing of clothes is made only in the United States.

Even though one may have a most memorable vacation in Germany with all its splendor of the countryside, the atmosphere, the people, and the delicious food, one will find that the United States is still the BEST COUNTRY in the world to live in.

Maria Swaringen

GROWING UP IN GERMANY DURING AND RIGHT AFTER WORLD WAR II

What was it like and how did we live through that time? I was ten years old when the war was over. I lived through a terrible time, afraid of everyone and anything, from bombs, airplanes, and Nazis, to people in general, for one could not trust anybody in those days.

My home town, although small at that time, had a big German Air Base. My father was not in the "Party", and hated Adolf Hitler, and the Nazis, but he needed the job at the Air Base to support the family. I remember one day Dad came home from work, went out to the vegetable garden and dug up his World War I rifle. Mother was crying and begging dad to leave, as he was cleaning the rifle in the kitchen. Nobody knew what was going on until after the end of the War. It seems my father's boss, a Major at the Air Base, asked my father to join the Party. Well, knowing my father, he told the Major where he could go with his "Loosing War". So my father basically was waiting at home for the Nazis to come and take him to the Concentration Camp. I remember dad saying to mother, "I'll kill a few before they get me". Needless to say, the Major never made the report, the war was over, the Major was stripped of his rank, had no job, and my father was feeding him for some time after the war.

Towards the end of the war, there were air raids every night. All of us children would stand outside in the middle of the night watching the city of Munich burning. Twenty miles away, it looked to us like a giant half moon on fire.

One day my home town was bombed, and it was devastated. To horrible to go into details. The air raid came at the end of the "all clear alarm" so most people already left their basement and were caught in the middle. It took my father almost two hours to circle around our then small town with his bicycle to see if we were still alive. My oldest brother was at the town park with a Horticulture School group when the bombs fell. He too was very fortunate, for the tree he was previously standing by was hit with a big bomb splinter. I remember my brother coming home, his face as white as snow.

My home town is not too far from the Dachau Concentration Camp. During the war, we children did not know that there was such a thing. However, I do remember that for days I saw a caravan of people marching along the dirt road we lived near by. Not a word was spoken. Most of the people wore only rags and their footwear looked terrible. The military men walking beside them here and there had a skull insignia on their helmets. I was wondering why no one came out of their homes and offered a cup of tea to these people on those cold days. I even asked my mother about those people and was told they were going to a new home. It wasn't until much later that I learned about the Dachau Concentration Camp through an American family living in my hometown. Years later, after I had moved to the United States, I became a member of a German Book Club. I ordered the book called "Der gelbe Stern", the Yellow Star, for I wanted to find out more about the Jewish people and why there were Concentration Camps during World War II. At my first glance of the book, I saw a caravan of people marching to the Concentration Camp. It looked like the same people I watched for days marching this silent march back in my hometown. I had realized then what I had witnessed so long ago. Needless to say, I never read that book, the pictures alone were too horrible to look at.

I will never forget the day before the war was over. The white flag was flying from the Church steeple, meaning the town had surrendered. But we found out later, that this was not the case. A French man tied himself inside the steeple and whenever the S.S. shot the flag down on one side, he would fasten another flag on the other side. The S.S. finally had to give up in town, went to the Suburb and found children in the meadows waving white flags. As the S.S. came closer, they saw the flag my parents fastened to one of the windows. The S.S. rushed into our home at gunpoint ready to shoot my parents. My father begged the man not to do it, for he had six children. The S.S. then asked for matches and then said he would burn down the house. My father gave him a matchbox, not knowing it had only one match in the box. The S.S. threw it in the corner and promised my parents he would be back that night and would burn down the entire community. Well, the Lord works in mysterious ways. That night the American tanks rolled in and the S.S. were on the run for good.

Even though there were eight in our family, we pretty well had enough food. We always had a very large vegetable garden, plus lots of fruit, for fruit trees were one of my fathers hobbies. Every year, my father would receive above first prize called "Ehrenpreis" for the fruit he was growing. It was not unusual for a pear to weigh a pound or more. We also had gooseberries and lots of red current bushes for jams and jellies, plus elderberries to make desserts and juice. For extra jelly and marmalades we picked wild blueberries and raspberries in the woods. We also gathered mushrooms every year in the woods and cow pastures. Then there were the apples we picked along the roadside after a bad storm; we took them to the juice factory, so we could get free apple juice. I might say there were a lot of chores that all of us children had to do. We had to help with the weeding in the garden, and with all the picking and gathering. Then there was a lot of watering to do, even for the fruit trees during a dry spell. We would pump water for hours, taking turns after each hundred pumps.

In late summer we would help farmers with their potato harvest and our pay was extra potatoes for the family. Then after the farmers were finished, we all would go to the fields with a hoe, to still retrieve the few potatoes left behind by the farmers. We also helped farmers to harvest the Fall cabbage. The pay was a delicious meat sandwich and lemonade every afternoon during break-time, something we didn't have too often at home. We also would get paid a few pennies, plus get a few heads of cabbage so dad could make some sauerkraut.

Mother would also make syrup out of sugar beets. After putting the sugar beets through a press, the juice had to be boiled for a long time for syrup. There was a place in town one could go, to rent their big pot over an open fire, to make this syrup. It was outside and we children had to stir for hours to make syrup. We used this syrup mainly as a sandwich spread. I never knew or heard about molasses until I came to the United States, and after I had a taste of it, I thought I was back in Germany making syrup.

Our cooking stove at home was a wood and coal stove. There was not much coal to be found, so we all went to the woods, picking up pine cones and every dry stick we could find. By late Fall, we had a whole basement room full of pine cones and dry wood stick for the stove.

My father also had bees and tobacco. He would trade fruit, honey and some tobacco for other goods. Honey was in great demand during and right after the war. Besides having no sugar, there was not much medicine and people would use honey for all sorts of things. One day my father changed a bee hive around. Three of us children were out in the garden between the potato rows. Not knowing at the time what dad was doing, the bees reached us with a fury. My oldest brother dived under the potato rows, while my sister and I screamed and yelled for help in the midst of an angry swarm of bees stinging us to no end. When my mother finally got to us we were almost out of our minds. We were stung about fifty times each and were in bed for two days. Our faces were so swollen that we could not see out of our eyes.

Since we had a few acres of land, my parents raised two pigs every year, a few goats, chickens, turkeys, geese, ducks, rabbits, etc.; in short, all but a horse, ox and cow to survive. Dad still had a full-time job and Mother often helped out at the neighborhood farms so all of us children had lots of chores to do after school. We didn't have any free time and sure did not like all of the work. We also did not get paid for all of the work we had to do, for there was no allowance, only respect. Looking back now, it really was not that bad and we learned how to survive.

My mother knew every surrounding farmer. She was good with animals, and even though she was not a Veterinarian, farmers would sometimes call in the middle of the night asking Mother to help with one of their sick animals. The farmers would thank my mother with butter, bacon or whatever she needed for the family.

There were two bakeries we used to get bread from every day. While both always gave us a little more than what we were allowed to have, one bakery was exceptionally generous. We always received two extra pounds of bread per day. This baker had lost everything during an air raid in Munich, moved to my hometown and opened a new bakery. During those days, many people were hungry and were begging for food daily, but this new bakery never turned a beggar away. All those poor, displaced people and foreigners alike one day remembered those good deeds of the baker. For, a few days after the war was over, the Americans ordered all the stores to be open for one day; for foreigners, Jew's and displaced people to take what they liked. But this new bakery was "Off Limits" to all, due to the kindness this bakery showed to so many hungry people every day.

There are many more stories to tell, but allow me to just say, no one knows what war is like unless one lives through it. It took me ten years before I could see a "War Movie" without shaking all over. I pray to God that it will never happen to this Country.

Maria Swaringen

INDEX

Page:

SOUPS: Page 1

335

APPETIZERS And SAUCES: Page 31

Appetizers:

Sauces:

SALAD DRESSINGS AND SALADS: Page 41

Salad Dressings:

Salads:

Meats From The Land And Sea: Page 69

Beef:

Veal:

Pork:

Poultry:

Seafood:

MEATLESS DISHES: Page 123

VEGETABLES: Page 135

DUMPLINGS AND OTHER SIDE DISHES: Page 151

Dumplings:

Other Side Dishes:

BEVERAGES, Hot and Cold: Page 167

Hot:

Cold:

BAKING WITH YEAST, BAKING POWDER AND SOME - DEEP FRIED: Page 187

Baking with Yeast:

With Yeast, but Deep Fried:

Without Yeast, but Deep Fried:

Baking with Baking Powder:

Cheese Cakes:

CREAMS, GARNISH, GLAZES AND ICING
PLUS MARZIPAN, SPICES AND STREUSEL: Page 249

Creams:

Garnish:

Glazes:

Icing:

SOME CANNING: Page 307

PLUS: Page 315

ABOUT THE AUTHOR

Maria M. Swaringen

Born and raised in southern Bavaria, Germany, Mrs. Swaringen grew up in Germany during and after World War II. She received most of her education in Germany and graduated in eleven years. Married in 1959 and moving to the United States the same year, she became a citizen of the United States in 1963. Through the years, Mrs. Swaringen raised her two children and took care of her family during her husband's military career. She traveled extensively in the United States and abroad. Her main hobbies are crafts, traveling, cooking and writing. She has just finished writing her second book *Travel & Vacation in Germany on Your Own.*

Printed in the United States
1466600003B/115-138